SM★RT PRACTICE
WORKBOOK

Fifth Grade

READING • GRAMMAR • VOCABULARY • WRITING • MATH

P9-DDP-879

■SCHOLASTIC

New York ○ Toronto ○ London ○ Auckland ○ Sydney
New Delhi ○ Mexico City ○ Hong Kong ○ Buenos Aires

Text Credits: pages 106, 107, 109–113, 115–120, 128–132, and 153–155 taken from *Quick Practice Writing Skills (Grades 4–5)* by Marcia Miller and Martin Lee © 2003 by Marcia Miller and Martin Lee; pages 108, 114, and 134–140 taken from *40 Elaboration Activities That Take Writing From Bland to Brilliant! (Grades 5–8)* by Martin Lee and Marcia Miller © 2007 by Martin Lee and Marcia Miller; pages 121–127 taken from *Professor Grammar's Punctuation Packets* by Marvin Terban © 2011 by Marvin Terban; pages 156–166 taken from *Standardized Test Practice: Writing (Grades 5–6)* by Michael Priestley © 2008 by Michael Priestley; pages 168–215 taken from *240 Vocabulary Words Kids Need to Know (Grade 5)* by Linda Ward Beech © 2012 by Linda Ward Beech; page 253 taken from *25 Common Core Math Lessons for the Interactive Whiteboard (Grade 4)* by Steve Wyborney © 2014 by Steve Wyborney; pages 276–281 and 289–291 taken from *25 Common Core Math Lessons for the Interactive Whiteboard (Grade 5)* by Steve Wyborney © 2014 by Steve Wyborney.

Other pages from this workbook were previously published in: *Hi-Lo Nonfiction Passages for Struggling Readers (Grades 6–8)*, *25 Complex Text Passages to Meet the Common Core: Literature and Informational Texts (Grade 5)*, *Quick Cloze Passages for Boosting Comprehension (Grades 4–6)*, *Morning Jumpstarts: Reading (Grade 5)*, *Building Essential Writing Skills (Grade 5)*, *Morning Jumpstarts: Math (Grade 5)*, and *The Great Big Book of Funtastic Math*

Editor: Maria L. Chang
Cover design by Michelle H. Kim
Cover art by Mike Moran
Interior design by Adrienne Downey
Illustrations by Teresa Anderko, Delana Bettoli, Steve Cox, Jack Desroscher,
Michelle Dorenkamp, Mike Gordon, Margeaux Lucas, and Mike Moran

Photos ©: 11: Antagain/iStockphoto; 12: Azure-Dragon/iStockphoto; 14 left: Byelikova Oksana/Shutterstock, Inc.; 14 right: Chris Schmidt/iStockphoto; 16: Krzysztof Gawor/iStockphoto; 18: Frank Wa.erführer/iStockphoto; 20: Science Source/ Getty Images; 22: topten22photo/iStockphoto; 24: kwanchaichaiudom/iStockphoto; 26: wierdeau/iStockphoto; 28: wynnter/iStockphoto; 36: Gallo Images/Getty Images; 42: Jorge Saenz/AP Images.

ISBN: 978-0-545-86255-4

6 7 8 9 10   68   24 23 22 21

Dear Parent,

The fact that you're holding this book in your hands strongly indicates that you care very much about your child's learning and want him or her to succeed in school. Well, you've made the right choice in picking this workbook. The Scholastic brand is well known for high-quality educational materials for use in schools and at home. Inside you'll find hundreds of engaging practice pages designed to boost your child's skills in reading, writing, math, and more.

Smart Practice Workbook: Fifth Grade is divided into six sections: Reading Comprehension, Language Arts, Grammar, Writing, Vocabulary, and Math. The table of contents lists the specific skills your child will be practicing on each page. Feel free to move through the pages in any order you wish. An answer key is provided in the back so you can check your child's progress.

To help your child get the most out of the learning experience offered in this book, try these quick tips:

- Provide a comfortable and quiet place for your child to work.

- Make sure your child has all the supplies he or she needs, such as pencils, crayons, or markers.

- Keep work sessions short, but frequent. For a child in fifth grade, 30 minutes each day is sufficient.

- Encourage your child's efforts, praising his or her successes and offering positive help when your child makes a mistake.

All set? Then let's get started on this journey to helping your child become a successful, lifelong learner.

-The Editors

Grade-Appropriate Skills Covered in
Smart Practice Workbook: Fifth Grade

LANGUAGE ARTS

- Quote accurately from a text when explaining what the text says explicitly and when drawing inferences from the text.

- Determine a theme of a story from details in the text, including how characters in a story respond to challenges; summarize the text.

- Determine two or more main ideas of a text and explain how they are supported by key details; summarize the text.

- Determine the meaning of general academic and domain-specific words and phrases in a text.

- Read with sufficient accuracy and fluency to support comprehension.

- Read grade-level text with purpose and understanding.

- Produce clear and coherent writing in which the development and organization are appropriate to task, purpose, and audience.

- Develop and strengthen writing as needed by planning, revising, editing, or rewriting.

- Demonstrate command of the conventions of standard English capitalization, punctuation, spelling, grammar, and usage when writing.

- Use common, grade-appropriate Greek and Latin affixes and roots as clues to the meaning of a word.

- Interpret figurative language, including similes and metaphors, in context.

- Recognize and explain the meaning of common idioms, adages, and proverbs.

- Use the relationship between particular words (e.g., synonyms, antonyms, homographs) to better understand each of the words.

MATH

- Evaluate numerical expressions with parentheses.

- Generate two numerical patterns using given rules, form ordered pairs, and graph the ordered pairs on a coordinate plane.

- Use whole number exponents to denote powers of 10 and calculate with powers of 10.

- Fluently add, subtract, multiply, and divide multi-digit whole numbers using the standard algorithm.

- Add and subtract fractions and mixed numbers with unlike denominators.

- Multiply a fraction or a whole number by a fraction.

- Divide fractions by whole numbers and whole numbers by fractions.

- Read, write, and compare decimals to thousandths.

- Add, subtract, multiply, and divide decimals.

- Calculate a shape's perimeter and area; measure volume by counting unit cubes.

- Represent and interpret data; read and answer questions about bar graphs, circle graphs, line plots, and more.

Table of Contents

Reading Comprehension

Language Arts

Grammar

Writing

Vocabulary

Math

Using the Flash Cards

At the back of this book are ready-to-use flash cards featuring selected words from the Vocabulary section of this workbook. Some of these are words that we use every day in conversation, while others may be related to specific content areas. Learning these words and their meanings will help increase your child's reading comprehension as well as his or her oral communication and writing skills. Here are a few tips to make the most of these vocabulary flash cards:

- Introduce up to ten new words at a time. Choose a word card and have your child read the word aloud. Alternatively, you could read the word then have your child repeat it after you. Next, ask your child if he or she knows the meaning of the word. Encourage your child to explain what he or she thinks the word means. Then turn the card over and read the definition together. Is the definition close to what your child thought the word means? Invite your child to use the word in a sentence. You might also ask your child to think of another word that reminds him or her of the vocabulary

word, because it either means the same thing or the opposite, or because the words are related somehow. Repeat with the remaining word cards.

- Once you have reviewed all the word cards, test your child's knowledge by reading the definition side and saying "blank" in place of the boldfaced word. For example, "A *blank* is a beginner." Ask your child to name the missing word (*novice*). For an added challenge, you might ask your child to spell the missing word.

- Invite your child to sort the word cards into different categories; for example, poetry words or opposite words. Here are some other ways your child could sort the words:
  - alphabetical order
  - number of syllables
  - words with and without double letters
  - parts of speech (noun, verb, or adjective)

  You could also invite your child to come up with his or her own categories for sorting the cards.

- Use the vocabulary cards to play charades or quick draw. Place the word cards in a paper bag. Take turns picking a word card and either draw it on a large sheet of paper or act it out for the other person to guess. Give a bonus point if the guesser can also spell the word correctly.

A **plateau** is a large area of high, flat land.

plateau

Fill in the letter with the best answer for each question.

1. What is the main idea of the first paragraph?
   - Ⓐ Theodore had a natural history museum in his bedroom when he was a boy.
   - Ⓑ The museum had 12 specimens.
   - Ⓒ Theodore had two cousins.
   - Ⓓ Theodore was a brave man.

2. Which sentence best tells the main idea of the second paragraph?
   - Ⓐ Theodore loved the outdoors.
   - Ⓑ Asthma makes it hard to run around and have fun.
   - Ⓒ Theodore did not like to play.
   - Ⓓ Theodore was a sickly child.

3. Which detail does not tell about Theodore Roosevelt as a boy?
   - Ⓐ He opened his own natural history museum.
   - Ⓑ He became President in 1901.
   - Ⓒ He had asthma and often found it difficult to breathe.
   - Ⓓ He once left a collection of dead mice in the icebox.

4. From the selection, you can draw the conclusion that
   - Ⓐ Theodore's mother liked mice.
   - Ⓑ Theodore respected his father's advice.
   - Ⓒ everyone with asthma is small and frail.
   - Ⓓ working out in a gym is a waste of time.

5. In which book might you find this selection?
   - Ⓐ *Small Nature Museums*
   - Ⓑ *Living With Asthma*
   - Ⓒ *The Childhoods of America's Presidents*
   - Ⓓ *How the Teddy Bear Got Its Name*

Say No to Child Labor

The tags on your clothing say where your clothes were made. What they don't say is who made them. Many people believe they should. These people are concerned that the clothing was made by child laborers.

Lots of kids work. Many work delivering newspapers, baby-sitting, or walking dogs. They go to school all day and work only part-time—a few hours a week. Working is a good way to become more responsible. Other children, however, work full-time.

For more than 160 million children worldwide, work isn't something done for school or after school. It's something done instead of school. They work between 12 and 14 hours a day. Most are only 5 to 14 years old. They are very young, but they work very hard.

Some work in coal mines. Others work on construction sites. Still others harvest crops.

Thousands work to make clothing and things like soccer balls.

These children don't work this hard by choice but because they must. Many work to help their families earn enough money to pay for food, clothing, and shelter. Most child laborers do not go to school.

There are laws against child labor. Unfortunately, it still happens. There are child laborers all over the world, including the United States. There are many reasons why some companies hire children to work. But it is still against the law.

There are groups that are trying to help child laborers. Organizations like the United Nations Children's Fund (UNICEF) and the International Labor Organization (ILO) work to increase public awareness of the problem. Now many people and major companies won't do business with factories that employ children.

Fill in the letter with the best answer for each question.

1. **Most children are forced to work because**

   Ⓐ there aren't any schools for them to attend.

   Ⓑ other kids will make fun of them if they don't.

   Ⓒ their families need the money they earn.

   Ⓓ their brothers and sisters say they must.

2. **One effect of the work done by UNICEF and the ILO is that**

   Ⓐ many companies won't do business with factories using child labor.

   Ⓑ factory owners have started paying children more.

   Ⓒ conditions for child laborers have gotten worse.

   Ⓓ more people are buying things made by child laborers.

3. **What information would many people like to see added to clothing tags?**

   Ⓐ where it was made   Ⓒ the size

   Ⓑ who made the clothes   Ⓓ the cost

4. **Besides working very hard, what's another disadvantage faced by child laborers?**

   Ⓐ They have to wear ugly uniforms.

   Ⓑ The factory owners don't feed them.

   Ⓒ Their families spend all of their money.

   Ⓓ Because they can't go to school, they can't learn how to improve their lives.

5. **Putting a description of who made a product on the tag might help stop child labor because**

   Ⓐ factory owners don't want to spend extra money on the labels.

   Ⓑ people might not buy a product if they knew it was made with child labor, and the factory might lose money.

   Ⓒ children might quit if they were described on the labels.

   Ⓓ adult workers would quit because their names weren't being used, too.

Algae Energy

Imagine running a car with gas made from pond algae (AL-jee)! That's what Tasios Melis hopes to do. Melis is a plant biologist. He is trying to make a better fuel for cars. He believes that algae may be the answer.

Green algae are very tiny plants that have a special ability. They can convert water and sunlight into hydrogen. The green algae could churn out endless supplies of hydrogen gas. When burned as fuel, hydrogen doesn't produce any pollution. Its only by-product is water.

Hydrogen gas can be manufactured. But the process is difficult and costly. Usually, hydrogen is extracted from natural gas. This process generates pollution. It also depletes our natural gas supply. Melis is searching for a better way to produce hydrogen gas. In his quest, he has turned his lab into an algae station.

In his lab, Melis grows green algae in a container. He gives the plants sunlight, water, and nutrients. Millions of new algae cells form. Then, he covers the container

with an airtight lid to cut off the supply of sulfur. This forces the green algae to produce hydrogen gas bubbles. Melis then collects those bubbles and stores the hydrogen.

How much hydrogen can green algae produce? Imagine an algae-filled pond the size of an average swimming pool. That much algae could probably fuel ten cars for a week. But don't get too excited just yet! You won't see an algae station anytime soon. More research and development is needed before we'll see cars running on algae fuel.

Did You Know?

Some scientists think algae could help solve the world hunger problem. They are trying to make food from the plants, too.

Fill in the letter with the best answer for each question.

1. **What problem is Tasios Melis trying to solve?**

   Ⓐ the difficulty of removing algae from ponds

   Ⓑ the high cost of fast cars

   Ⓒ the need for non-polluting fuel

   Ⓓ the lack of recognition of plant biologists

2. **Why does Melis think that pond algae is the solution to the problem?**

   Ⓐ Algae can make hydrogen from water and sunlight.

   Ⓑ Algae can make sunlight from hydrogen.

   Ⓒ Algae can make gasoline from water.

   Ⓓ Algae is found everywhere in the world.

3. **Hydrogen gas is not used for fuel in cars because**

   Ⓐ it can be found only in outer space.

   Ⓑ people refuse to buy hydrogen gas.

   Ⓒ there is a shortage of water and sunlight on Earth.

   Ⓓ extracting it from natural gas is difficult and costly.

4. **Which is the last step in Melis's process?**

   Ⓐ Millions of new algae cells form.

   Ⓑ Melis collects and stores the hydrogen.

   Ⓒ The algae's sulfur supply is cut off.

   Ⓓ The algae produce hydrogen bubbles.

5. **The author wrote "Algae Energy" to**

   Ⓐ persuade people to use less gas.

   Ⓑ make fun of Tasios Melis's idea.

   Ⓒ compare hydrogen and natural gas.

   Ⓓ explain how algae may one day be useful.

The Galápagos: Can They Survive?

More than three million years ago, volcanoes erupted deep in the Pacific Ocean. The lava from these volcanoes cooled and piled up, forming the Galápagos Islands. Over time, soil covered the bare volcanic rock. Then, across the water and through the air, life arrived. The islands' native animals and plants all come from species that swam, drifted, flew, or were blown here.

A Natural Wonderland

The Galápagos lie about 620 miles (1,000 km) off the coast of South America. They are a natural wonderland. Cactus plants dot the dry lowlands. Moist, dense forests grow higher up. Higher still, treeless areas are covered with ferns and grasses.

Unique animals, plants, and insects abound. Most of the reptiles here are found nowhere else in the world! For instance, huge iguanas that look like colorful dragons bask on sunny rocks. Giant tortoises slowly amble along. These slow-moving reptiles can live for more than 150 years. Birds waddle by on bright blue, webbed feet. Their name is (of course) the blue-footed booby!

Rare creatures like these attract thousands of tourists each year. And that is part of the islands' problem.

Fighting for Survival

The Galápagos Islands have a fragile ecology. The balance of this unique environment can be destroyed easily. Today, the islands are in deep trouble for many reasons.

First, the islands have become a favorite among tourists. Some tourists trample plants and disturb the wildlife. The cruise ships that brought them dump garbage into the water.

Also, when more people came to settle in the islands, they arrived with their goats, pigs, cattle, cats, and dogs. These animals from other places disrupt the lives of native species. They compete for food, destroy habitat, and prey on the eggs and young of reptiles and birds. Dogs, in fact, have killed off most of the land iguanas on one island.

Finally, there are poachers who kill giant tortoises for their meat and fishers who overharvest the waters. Many species of sea creatures are caught illegally.

Preservation Efforts

Efforts to save the islands go back to 1930. Some islands were set aside then as wildlife sanctuaries. In 1959, most of the land—97 percent of it—became a national park. In 1986, the ocean in and around the island group became a marine reserve.

Today, environmental groups are working with the government of Ecuador. Their goal is to protect and preserve the islands. It may not be too late to save this special part of the world.

Fill in the letter with the best answer for each question.

1. This selection is an example of

   Ⓐ short fiction.

   Ⓑ a poem.

   Ⓒ an informational article.

   Ⓓ a biography.

2. Into which category do tortoises and iguanas fall?

   Ⓐ mammals

   Ⓑ birds

   Ⓒ insects

   Ⓓ reptiles

3. Which animals are causing problems for native species on the island?

   Ⓐ fish and frogs

   Ⓑ all kinds of birds

   Ⓒ tortoises and iguanas

   Ⓓ pigs, cats, and dogs

4. Tourists are drawn to the Galápagos Islands because the islands

   Ⓐ are so far from anywhere.

   Ⓑ are unlike any place in the world.

   Ⓒ have a good climate.

   Ⓓ don't have a national park.

5. Which of the following would <u>not</u> help protect the islands?

   Ⓐ limiting tourism

   Ⓑ stopping poaching

   Ⓒ prohibiting cruise ships from dumping garbage

   Ⓓ bringing in nonnative animals

Marie Curie: A Woman Ahead of Her Time

A story is told of Marie Curie. It is said that her sisters once built a pyramid of chairs around her. Marie was busy reading. She did not even notice until she stood up and knocked them all over!

It would not be surprising if this story were true. As a child, Marie loved books and experiments. Nothing could distract her from her studies. She did not lose this love of learning as she got older. In the 1880s, very few women went to college, and even fewer women became scientists. Marie did both.

After she met and married another scientist, Pierre Curie, the two of them began working together. Their studies focused on the element *radium*. They had discovered it during their research. An *element* is one of about 100 basic substances that make up everything in the world. Radium is found in some rocks. It is a white metallic element with a blue glow. The glow lasts for a thousand years.

The radium glows because it emits energy. That is one reason the Curies were so intrigued by it. But studying radium is not like opening a book. Radium must be isolated from the rock around it. That is like trying to take just the chocolate out of chocolate milk.

The couple spent their life savings on eight tons of rock called *ore*. An old shack became their workplace. They heated the rock to remove the bits of radium from it. Days of work turned into months. Ultimately, they spent four years in that shack studying the mysterious element with the blue glow.

During their research, the Curies found that radium could help treat cancer. That is when Marie and her husband became big news. They were written about often. This got the public interested in radium. Soon, the Curies' work earned them the Nobel Prize in Physics. This award is one of the highest honors in the world. Marie had come a long way from the days of chair pyramids.

◆ Marie Curie 1867–1934 ◆ Born in Poland ◆ Nobel Prize in 1903 ◆ 2nd Nobel Prize in 1911

Fill in the letter with the best answer for each question.

1. Marie Curie's love of learning

   Ⓐ began as a child.   Ⓒ ended after she met Pierre.

   Ⓑ began in college.   Ⓓ ended before she met Pierre.

2. The Curies began working in the shack

   Ⓐ before they discovered radium.

   Ⓑ before they bought their ore.

   Ⓒ while attending college.

   Ⓓ after their discovery of radium.

3. Newspapers began writing about the Curies

   Ⓐ shortly after the two met and married.

   Ⓑ when they bought eight tons of rock.

   Ⓒ when it was discovered that radium might treat cancer.

   Ⓓ after they died.

4. Which sentence supports the idea that Marie Curie
   was different from most women in the 1880s?

   Ⓐ She met and married a scientist.

   Ⓑ She went to college and became a scientist.

   Ⓒ She loved books and experiments.

   Ⓓ Nothing could distract her from her studies.

5. Which sentence states a fact about the Curies?

   Ⓐ Their work earned them the Nobel Prize in Physics.

   Ⓑ They were foolish to spend their life savings on eight tons of rock.

   Ⓒ It took them too long to find a cure for cancer.

   Ⓓ They deserved to get the highest honor in the world.

The Water Festival

Up go 50 oars! Down come 50 oars! Fifty rowers give a powerful thrust. The boat surges forward as the race begins! Thousands of people cheer their favorite boats.

It is November. More than 1,000 competitors from all over Cambodia have gathered at the nation's capital, Phnom Penh (puh-NOM-pen). Today is the first day of the annual Water Festival! For three days, hundreds of colorful boats will race along the Tonle Sap River.

Backward-Flowing River

The Water Festival celebrates an amazing natural event. Normally, the Tonle Sap River flows from Tonle Sap Lake into the Mekong River. Each summer, though, the monsoon rains come. For months, rain pours down almost every day. The Mekong River fills with raging waters. The Mekong's powerful floodwaters push the Tonle Sap River backward! Instead of flowing into the Mekong, it flows into the lake! Then, this lake—the largest in Southeast Asia—becomes even larger. The floodwaters expand the lake to many times its normal size.

In the fall, the rains lessen. The dry season begins. The water level goes down. Then the Tonle Sap River reverses its direction. Once again, it flows from the lake into the Mekong River. Tonle Sap Lake shrinks to its normal size.

Time to Celebrate

The Water Festival celebrates the reversal of the river's life-giving waters. Exciting boat races are the main events of this unusual festival. The boats are named after different farming groups and temples. On the last night, fireworks light up the skies over Phnom Penh. This signals the festival's end. Then boats hung with lighted lanterns float down the river. To watchers on the shore, the river looks like a moving stream of light.

Life-Giving Waters

Each fall, the receding floodwaters leave behind mineral-rich soil. Farmers depend on this soil to nourish their crops. Where the flooded lake's waters once spread, rice and vegetables will grow. This is also the time when the fishing season begins.

Every year, the entire cycle repeats. In the summer, the rains fall and the Tonle Sap Lake floods. In the fall, the water recedes and the Tonle Sap River reverses its direction. And once again, the Water Festival celebrates the event with boat races.

Fill in the letter with the best answer for each question.

1. **How is the Tonle Sap River different during the rainy season?**

   Ⓐ It flows directly into the ocean.

   Ⓑ It flows backward into the Tonle Sap Lake.

   Ⓒ It flows into the Mekong River.

   Ⓓ It flows much more slowly.

2. **How is Tonle Sap Lake the same during both the rainy and the dry seasons?**

   Ⓐ It increases in size many times.

   Ⓑ It is the largest lake in Southeast Asia.

   Ⓒ It shrinks in size.

   Ⓓ It provides mineral-rich soil.

3. **How is the Tonle Sap River like other rivers?**

   Ⓐ It flows in different directions in different seasons.

   Ⓑ Boat races are held on it in the fall.

   Ⓒ It flows into another body of water, such as an ocean, lake, or another river.

   Ⓓ It is the longest river in Southeast Asia.

4. **The river's backward flow during summer is caused by the**

   Ⓐ need for water at the Mekong River.

   Ⓑ increased size of Tonle Sap Lake.

   Ⓒ start of the dry season.

   Ⓓ change in the amount of rainfall.

5. **What does the Water Festival celebrate?**

   Ⓐ the growing of rice and vegetables

   Ⓑ the beginning of the tourist season

   Ⓒ the Tonle Sap River's change of direction

   Ⓓ boat races and fireworks

Crunchy Critters

It's time for lunch in Tokyo, Japan. Your friend Hiroshi is eating weird-smelling grilled octopus. "Want a bite?" he asks. "No way!" you reply. You watch the squiggly octopus legs disappear into Hiroshi's mouth. Gross!

But is it really? Octopus is good for you and very nutritious. Why not eat it?

On the other hand, Hiroshi is like people in many parts of the world. He grew up drinking very little milk or eating cheese. To him, cheese is just spoiled cow's milk, and that's disgusting! Hiroshi would rather eat a bug than your grilled-cheese sandwich.

Bugs on the Menu

Speaking of bugs, did you know there are millions of people who think insects are delectable? In parts of South America, fried grasshoppers are a snack food.

In Madagascar, an island off Africa, people eat fried crickets. In Asia, they like their crickets grilled. People in the U.S. used to eat crickets, too. Food fashions change.

If you don't want your bugs plain, how about candied? Chocolate-covered termites (bugs that eat wood) were served as part of a program about insects at a zoo in South Africa. Chocolate-covered ants have been around for years. You can find them in some fancy food stores.

Good Grub!

The word *grub* is slang for "food," but most of your friends would probably run for home if you served them grubs or worms. Yet in Australia, the aborigines, who lived there before European people came, think highly of witchetty grubs. Witchetty grubs are an Australian moth larva. When cooked in ashes, they have an almond flavor.

Then there are the mammals. In Peru, South America, guinea pigs can turn up on your dinner plate. And in Thailand, people smack their lips over roasted rat.

What you want to eat depends on where you live. You like the foods you grew up with. So do kids in other countries. And that's food for thought!

Fill in the letter with the best answer for each question.

1. **What is the best summary of the selection?**

   Ⓐ People from other parts of the world have weird taste in food.

   Ⓑ People from different parts of the world enjoy different kinds of food.

   Ⓒ Asians have better taste in food than Americans.

   Ⓓ Eating insects will make you sick.

2. **What is the best summary of the section "Bugs on the Menu"?**

   Ⓐ If you try a different food, you may like it.

   Ⓑ Some people eat roasted rats.

   Ⓒ Chocolate-covered ants are treats.

   Ⓓ People in many parts of the world eat insects.

3. **What is the best summary of the section "Good Grub!"?**

   Ⓐ *Grub* is a slang term for "food."

   Ⓑ What you like to eat depends on where you live.

   Ⓒ People in Peru eat guinea pigs.

   Ⓓ People in the United States eat cows.

4. **What is a witchetty grub?**

   Ⓐ a slang term for a great meal

   Ⓑ a moth larva that is sometimes eaten in Australia

   Ⓒ a worm that is sometimes eaten in Asia

   Ⓓ a type of toasted almond

5. **What is one probable reason why the Japanese like to eat octopus?**

   Ⓐ Japan is an island, and it is easy to get seafood.

   Ⓑ Japan is a place where they can't get hamburgers.

   Ⓒ In Japan, they serve octopus at restaurants.

   Ⓓ The Japanese enjoy watching the faces of the Americans when someone eats octopus.

Coral Crisis

If you want to see a lot of fish, then go to a coral reef. Thousands of species of ocean fish and animals, like lobsters and squid, stick close to coral reefs. These are stony structures full of dark hideaways where fish can lay their eggs and escape from predators. Without these underwater "apartment houses," there would be fewer fish in the ocean. Some species might even become endangered or disappear completely.

What some people don't realize is that reefs are living beings, too. They are made of thousands of tiny animals called *polyps*. These polyps soak seawater into their squishy bodies. They use the nutrients in the seawater to make stony tubes that fit around their bodies. These tubes protect the polyps and grow to make coral.

There are thousands of reefs in the world. Sadly, though, they are now in serious danger. According to WWF, an independent conservation organization, about a quarter of the coral reefs worldwide are damaged beyond repair, and another two-thirds are under serious threat.

Scientists are working hard to find out how to help stop this destruction. There is a lot to learn, but there are some things we do know.

Pollution

Pollution on land runs into rivers and streams, which carry the poisons into the ocean. Chemicals from pollution kill coral. They may also make polyps weak, so they have less resistance to diseases. Also, fertilizer from farms causes seaweed to grow wildly, choking polyps.

Climate Change

Many scientists believe climate change is one of the greatest threats to corals. An overall increase in Earth's temperature has led to high water temperatures, which kill the greenish-gold algae, or tiny water plants, that live on coral. Coral gets food from the algae. Without it, the coral loses its color and eventually dies. This process, known as "coral bleaching," is becoming more frequent.

People

People sometimes ram into reefs with their boats or drop anchors on them, breaking off large chunks of coral. Divers who walk on reefs can also do major damage. Since coral is so colorful and pretty, some people even break it off to collect for souvenirs.

A Solution

How can we help the reefs? We can learn more about them! We need to find out what humans do that damages reefs so we can change those activities. We can work together to make sure that coral reefs will be healthy and beautiful in the future.

Fill in the letter with the best answer for each question.

1. **Which sentence does <u>not</u> support the conclusion that reefs are important to ocean life?**

   Ⓐ Fish lay their eggs on reefs.

   Ⓑ Fish hide in the reefs to escape their predators.

   Ⓒ Coral reefs can be seen from the air in very clear water.

   Ⓓ Without coral reefs, there would be fewer fish in the ocean.

2. **Based on the information in the article, which of the following conclusions can be drawn?**

   Ⓐ Farms are the coral reefs' worst enemies.

   Ⓑ There is no solution to the coral-reef problem.

   Ⓒ Some people collect pieces of coral for souvenirs.

   Ⓓ People need to understand what endangers the coral reefs if they are to be saved.

3. **Scientists believe the coral reefs are in danger from**

   Ⓐ ocean animals like lobster and squid.

   Ⓑ greenish-gold algae.

   Ⓒ too many fish eggs hatching in them.

   Ⓓ higher water temperatures caused by global warming.

4. **When a coral reef loses its color**

   Ⓐ it eventually dies.   Ⓒ it is eaten by lobsters.

   Ⓑ it is thrown away.   Ⓓ it can't eat algae.

5. **How does land pollution get into the ocean?**

   Ⓐ Beach sand gets into the ocean.

   Ⓑ Seaweed grows wildly.

   Ⓒ Algae contains pollution from the land.

   Ⓓ Streams and rivers carry pollution from the land into the ocean.

Searching for the "Real" King Arthur

A boy sprints into the clearing, searching for a sword to help his stepbrother. There! Jutting out from a boulder, the sword gleams like a beacon. Without pausing, the boy pulls the sword from the stone.

On the stone is the inscription: *Only the rightful king shall be able to pull this sword from this stone.* The sword was called Excalibur (eks KAL uh ber). The boy was Arthur, who became England's heroic king. The story of Arthur goes back to the sixth century.

Many authors have written about King Arthur, Merlin, and the Knights of the Round Table. Some stories explained that Merlin was a magician who helped raise and educate young Arthur. Some legends tell that only the bravest of knights were honored with a seat at the Round Table. This famous table was said to have been chosen intentionally by Arthur. A round table ensured that each knight was considered an equal to all the others seated around him. There was no "head" of the table.

Not everyone thinks that Arthur stories are credible. Some say he never lived. Tales about Arthur's exploits didn't begin until 300 years after he would have ruled. As time passed, the tales were embellished with details about magic and wizards.

Still, the stories may be based on real people and places. In 1191, monks at Glastonbury Abbey were said to have dug

up two bodies and an ancient cross. The cross bore the names Arthur and Guinevere, Arthur's wife. Although there is an early burial site at the abbey, the cross and the bodies have been lost.

Arthur is said to have had many different residences. Camelot, considered his favorite place to live, was a castle in Southern England. In more recent times, findings have led some to believe that Camelot was actually Cadbury Castle. There, a slab of rock was found that dates back to the sixth century. A name similar to Arthur was carved into it.

We may never know the truth about the legendary Arthur. True or made up, the stories will continue to be enjoyed by people for years to come.

Fill in the letter with the best answer for each question.

1. **Which statement is a fact?**

   (A) Many authors have written about the legend of King Arthur.

   (B) Arthur was a very strong boy.

   (C) You can't believe stories about events that took place so long ago.

   (D) Most kings are heroes to their people.

2. **Which statement is an opinion?**

   (A) Monks found an ancient cross bearing Arthur and Guinevere's names.

   (B) Some people believe that part of the King Arthur story is true.

   (C) The whole King Arthur story is silly.

   (D) The slab at Cadbury Castle dates back to the sixth century.

3. **Some people doubt that Arthur lived because**

   (A) his story is still so popular today.

   (B) the story could not possibly be true.

   (C) there is very little real proof that Arthur ever existed.

   (D) no one has found Arthur's sword.

4. **Which event happened first in the story of King Arthur?**

   (A) Arthur pulls a sword from a stone.

   (B) Arthur becomes King of England.

   (C) Arthur marries Guinevere.

   (D) Arthur learns about magic and wizards.

5. **Arthur might have been real because**

   (A) the stories about him sound real.

   (B) a slab of rock dating to the sixth century with a name similar to Arthur carved into it has been found.

   (C) the first tales about Arthur were written 300 years after he would have ruled.

   (D) the stories were embellished over time.

Belling the Cat

Fable by Aesop

What makes it so difficult for the mice to solve their problem?

1　Mice and cats have been the bitterest of enemies for as long as anyone can
2　recall. So how is it that the swift and clever mice never found a way to control
3　their opponent? This age-old tale may guide you to understand the depth of
4　the problem.

5　Long ago, a cat in one town was especially successful at attacking the local
6　mice. Fearing for their future, the anxious mice decided to gather for a crucial
7　meeting. Their goal was to devise a strategy to outsmart their feline enemy. Every
8　mouse willingly attended, and hopes were high.

9　Many mice addressed the crowd, each with a different idea for their protection
10　and safety. But no idea seemed to satisfy the group. At last a young mouse arose
11　to speak to the crowd. "My friends, I wish to offer a new proposal. As I see it,
12　our biggest problem is the sly manner in which the cat advances toward us. If
13　we could receive a signal of its sneaky approach, we would likely escape. So I
14　recommend that we obtain a small bell that makes a clear ring. We simply hang
15　the bell from a strong cord and then tie that cord around the cat's neck. From that
16　moment onward, any movement the cat makes will cause the bell to ring. Thanks
17　to our good ears, the bell will warn us when our enemy nears. It should provide
18　ample warning to keep us safe and out of sight."

19　This new idea drew loud cheers until an elderly gray mouse slowly stood up.
20　"We must commend our young friend for a highly original idea. But before we
21　charge ahead, I must pose one simple question: Who among us volunteers to be
22　the one to bell the cat?"

23　The mice looked embarrassed and uneasy. Complete silence overtook
24　the group.

26　**MORAL:** *It is one thing to say that something should be done,*
27　*but quite a different matter to do it.*

▶ **Answer each question. Give evidence from the fable.**

1. Which of the following animals is a *feline* (line 7)?

    Ⓐ rat   Ⓑ hawk   Ⓒ leopard   Ⓓ old mouse

How did you determine your response? _____

_____

_____

2. Which is another way to state the lesson that this fable teaches?

    Ⓐ Trouble comes from the direction we least expect it.   Ⓒ Necessity is the mother of invention.

    Ⓑ It is easy to suggest impossible remedies.   Ⓓ Slow and steady wins the race.

What evidence in the text helped you answer? _____

_____

_____

_____

3. According to the young mouse, what characteristic behavior of the mouse-eating cat makes it so especially dangerous?

_____

_____

_____

4. Explain in your own words the problem with the young mouse's idea.

_____

_____

_____

5. Why did "complete silence" overtake the group after the old mouse's question (line 23)?

_____

_____

_____

The Talking Dog

What is funny about the dog owner's explanation?

1   Kerry was driving through a rural part of Montana when she came upon an
2   undistinguished diner in a small town that the Interstate bypassed. A sign out front
3   announcing "Talking Dog for Sale" caught her eye. She parked in the lot, entered
4   the woebegone eatery, and took a seat at the empty counter.
5   "I see that you have a talking dog for sale," she said to the man who approached
6   her from behind the counter.
7   "I do indeed," he replied and then whistled in the direction of some booths
8   hugging a far wall. "Over here, Max!" he called. A medium-sized hound
9   immediately lifted its head up from one of them, jumped down, scampered over
10 to where Kerry was sitting, and perched himself on an adjacent stool.
11   "You can talk?" she asked.
12   "Can I ever!" Max answered. "I speak so well that I've made quite a handsome
13 living from it. Why, I've worked the world over—Europe, Asia, Africa, mountains,
14 deserts, under water—you name it. In fact, I'm so extraordinarily verbal
15 that I've been in the employ of the FBI and the CIA in a number of critical
16 covert operations."
17   "The FBI? The CIA? Really?"
18   "You'd better believe it, sister. I can proudly assert that I've infiltrated a host of
19 hostile groups, listened quietly and intently to their conversations while reclining
20 under tables or curled up in corners pretending to be snoozing. *Psst; they all thought*
21 *I was some dumb dog.* When I was back at the office, I communicated precisely what
22 I'd learned to generals and State Department higher-ups." With that, Max took a
23 long slurp from a bowl of water his owner had placed before him, jumped down
24 from his stool, and trotted back to the comfort of his booth.
25   "Wow!" Kerry exclaimed. She stared,
26 completely taken aback, at the man behind
27 the counter. "Max is amazing! How much do
28 you want for him?"
29   "Ten dollars," came the casual reply.
30   "Ten dollars? Why so cheap?" inquired a
31 puzzled Kerry.
32   "Why? Because he's one darned liar, that's
33 why," the man answered. "He's never been
34 anywhere, ever. Spends all his time sprawled
35 out in the yard or snoring in one of my
36 booths!"

▶ **Answer each question. Give evidence from the story.**

1. Which is mostly likely to be *adjacent* (line 10) to a couch?

   Ⓐ a laundry basket   Ⓑ a bed   © a carpet   Ⓓ an end table

How did you determine your response? _____

_____

_____

2. A *woebegone* (line 4) dog house would probably benefit most from a _____.

   Ⓐ paint job   Ⓑ bigger dog © welcome mat   Ⓓ shady location

What evidence in the text helped you answer?

_____

_____

_____

3. Why did Kerry stop at the diner? _____

_____

_____

_____

4. Describe elements of this story that are like elements of a tall tale.

_____

_____

_____

_____

5. What makes the last paragraph of the story so funny? Explain.

_____

_____

_____

Dark and Stormy Night
Cape Cod Legend

What details of this story develop its mystery and scary atmosphere?

1 Mr. and Mrs. Grant were driving past the dunes late one turbulent night in 1923,
2 trying to make it home safely through a raging storm. When their car suddenly
3 broke down, they found themselves stranded near a rickety shack. They wrapped
4 their coats tightly around themselves, hurried to the shack, banged on its door,
5 but got no answer. They peeked through a cracked window whose broken shutters
6 clattered in the gusty wind. Straining their eyes, all they could see was one shabby
7 room with three lopsided chairs and a sagging bed. Everything lay covered under a
8 thick blanket of dust.

9 Realizing the dangers of struggling by foot through the fierce winds and rain, the
10 couple decided to take shelter for the night in that sorry shack. They figured they
11 would deal with the car the next day. Carrying in blankets from the car, they left
12 footprints in the dust as they settled in. Soon they were fast asleep.

13 At midnight, the Grants both sat bolt upright in bed. A thin young sailor,
14 dripping wet, stood by the stone-cold fireplace as if drying himself. His skin had a
15 green glow in the darkness. Mrs. Grant nervously called, "Who's there?" The sailor
16 coughed and vanished.

17 Thinking they were dreaming, the Grants went back to sleep. Next morning,
18 they found a salty puddle near the fireplace. Yet they saw no other footprints in the
19 dust but their own.

20 The weather was calm, so they
21 walked to the nearest town for help.
22 A mechanic towed their car to his shop
23 and set to work on it while the Grants
24 waited in the local diner. They struck
25 up conversation with Mrs. Whaley,
26 the owner who had lived in the area
27 her whole life. Upon asking after the
28 shack, the Grants learned that it had
29 been empty for almost 40 years. Mrs.
30 Whaley recalled that, after losing their
31 only son at sea, the heartbroken owners
32 moved to Iowa, never to return.

▶ **Answer each question. Give evidence from the legend.**

1. Which of the following words is an antonym for the word *turbulent* (line 1)?

Ⓐ agitated   Ⓑ parched   Ⓒ serene   Ⓓ somber

How did you determine your response? _____

_____

_____

2. Why did Mr. and Mrs. Grant spend the night in the old shack?

Ⓐ They were on vacation.   Ⓒ They planned to meet their son there.

Ⓑ They needed shelter in the bad storm.   Ⓓ They parked their car in its driveway.

What evidence in the text helped you answer? _____

_____

_____

3. What clue do the Grants' footprints in the dust reveal about the shack?

_____

_____

4. Why did the author include the character of Mrs. Whaley?

_____

_____

_____

5. What elements of this story help you know that it is a legend?

_____

_____

_____

_____

"Just Like Her"

What do the dancer's memories reveal about her character?

1 Michaela DePrince (b. 1995) is a
2 professional performer with the Dutch
3 National Ballet. She began life as Mabinty
4 Bangura in the war-torn West African
5 nation of Sierra Leone. Orphaned by
6 age three, she lived for some months in a
7 harsh orphanage. Fortunately, at the age of
8 four, she was unexpectedly adopted by an
9 American family. From that day forward,
10 her life improved dramatically.
11 Michaela shares some recollections
12 about experiences that shaped her.

13 **Earliest Memories** *I don't remember*
14 *much, but it was just terrible. I do remember*
15 *that I lost a lot of people that I cared about.*
16 *In the orphanage, I got the least amount of*
17 *food, the worst clothes, and the last choice*
18 *of toys. I had really bad malnutrition, and*
19 *I was really sick all the time—I would've*
20 *probably died if my parents didn't adopt me.*

21 **Drawn to Dance** *I found a magazine by the orphanage gate. In it I noticed a*
22 *picture of a ballerina wearing a tutu and pointe shoes. She just looked so happy, and*
23 *I was in such a terrible place that I thought, if I ever got adopted, maybe I could be*
24 *just like her.*
25 *I'd never seen anything like that before, so I took the cover off and put it in my*
26 *underwear because I had nowhere else to put it. I kept the picture with me every day*
27 *until I got adopted. It kept me believing and looking forward to something.*

28 **Challenges** *I've had my bad patches where I wanted to quit ballet, but I would*
29 *say to myself, this is what I've been dreaming of for so long, I really need to keep trying.*
30 *Nothing else has ever made me feel like that. Dance is a part of who I am, and I can't*
31 *see myself doing anything else.*

▶ **Answer each question. Give evidence from the memoir.**

1. Who was Mabinty Bangura (lines 3–4)?
   Ⓐ She was the person who adopted Michaela.
   Ⓑ She was Michaela before she was adopted.
   Ⓒ She was the director of the orphanage in Sierra Leone.
   Ⓓ She was the dancer pictured in the magazine Michaela found.

   What evidence in the text helped you answer?

   _____

   _____

2. Someone who suffers from *malnutrition* (line 18) _____.

   Ⓐ has no parents   Ⓒ will never be able to succeed in life

   Ⓑ was born in another country   Ⓓ has not been getting enough healthy food

   What evidence in the text helped you answer?

   _____

   _____

3. What beliefs helped Michaela overcome challenges as a dancer?

   _____

   _____

4. Michaela recalls being in "such a terrible place" (line 23). How can this comment have
   two meanings?

   _____

   _____

5. What can you infer from this piece about the impact the DePrinces had on Michaela's life?
   Explain.

   _____

   _____

   _____

Thank an Author

What features of the author's work does the writer most appreciate?

1   Dear Jack London,

2   I know that you're not alive to read this letter, and
3   that your most famous books were written a century
4   or so ago. But you are one of my new favorite
5   authors. Most of my friends enjoy reading fantasy
6   and science fiction, maybe some sports stories or a
7   biography now and then. But I like books that tell
8   realistic stories with challenging and unexpected
9   turns. This may seem strange since I've never been
10   anywhere dangerous, and most things in my life are
11   pretty safe and routine.
12   Maybe that's just it. I read *Call of the Wild* while
13   I was recovering from a broken arm. I didn't do
14   anything wild or heroic to break my arm; I just
15   slipped down the stairs and landed badly. But
16   reading your book took me to a distant place, and
17   I couldn't put the book down.

18   The story of Buck's wilderness life was shocking, sad, thrilling, and inspiring at the
19   same time. You made me feel sorry for him, root for him, even dislike him at times.
20   But Buck always felt so real to me, struggling with obstacles in his life. It made my
21   broken arm seem so minor—and that felt good!
22   I read that you never finished high school and traveled around the United States
23   trying to figure out what you wanted to do. You went to Alaska during the great
24   Klondike Gold Rush and experienced hard times there yourself. Maybe that's why
25   Buck comes across as so realistic.
26   Some people argue that an animal has no business being the hero of a realistic
27   story, but I disagree. We don't know for sure what animals think—if they even do.
28   But to me it's a great idea to use an animal to introduce curious readers to bigger
29   ideas, such as loyalty or survival, and using instinct and overcoming hardships.
30   Thank you, Jack London, for a great read. I plan to read *White Fang* next. My
31   mom promises to read me one of your famous short stories, called "To Build a
32   Fire," which is also set in the far north and has a dog in it.

33   Your 21st-century fan,
34   Tyler Hicks

▶ **Answer each question. Give evidence from the letter.**

1. Which word is most nearly opposite of the word *routine* (line 11)?

   Ⓐ normal   Ⓑ expected   Ⓒ unscheduled   Ⓓ challenging

How did you determine your response?

_____

_____

2. Which best explains Jack London's skill and success at writing adventure stories?

   Ⓐ He had little schooling.   Ⓒ He lived over a hundred years ago.

   Ⓑ He was no stranger to hard times.   Ⓓ He experienced adventures of his own.

What evidence in the text helped you answer?

_____

_____

3. What draws Tyler Hicks to Jack London's work?

_____

_____

_____

4. What could Tyler mean by saying that reading about Buck "made my broken arm seem

so minor" (lines 20–21)?

_____

_____

_____

5. Explain why Tyler might write a fan letter to someone who will never be able to read it.

_____

_____

_____

To Buckle Up or Not?

Why are school buses not required to install seat belts for children?

1 **The Issue**   In America, all car passengers must wear seat belts, and all cars
2 come with them installed. Yet, although 23 million children ride school buses
3 every weekday, the great majority of the buses transporting them do not have
4 seat belts. They aren't legally required to. Indeed, those in favor of changing
5 the law to make seat belts compulsory face a tough sell. Why is this so?
6   It's not just because kids squirm too much and wouldn't use them correctly.
7 It comes down to two things: design and cost.

8 **Design**   Our nation's large, yellow school buses have been designed to be
9 remarkably safe, the safest form of ground transportation we have. For one
10 thing, they are really heavy. In addition, the kids sit high up, above
11 where most collisions take place. Furthermore, all bus seats have
12 high, heavily cushioned backs. Their four inches of thick foam
13 padding absorb impact; they act like air bags. So, in their tightly
14 packed seats, kids are, in effect, sitting in protective bubbles. It
15 should surprise no one that according to statistics compiled by the
16 National Highway Traffic Safety Administration, riding in a large
17 school bus is 40 times safer than riding in a car.

Forty times safer!

18 **Cost**   Design issues aside, cost issues must be
19 considered, as well. Installing seat belts is very
20 expensive. Doing so would add thousands to the
21 cost of producing each bus, *with minimal, if any,*
22 *impact on safety*. Plus, putting in seat belts would
23 take up space and cause manufacturers to take out
24 seats. With fewer seats in a bus, more buses would be needed.

More buses = more money!

25 **Conclusion**   Frankly, although the bus driver should (and does) use
26 one, kids riding a school bus have no need for seat belts. The risk they take
27 in riding them is nowhere near the risk they take each time they approach
28 or leave one. So I agree with what many organizations dedicated to school
29 transportation safety say. I oppose making it mandatory that all school buses
30 be equipped with seat belts.

▶ **Answer each question. Give evidence from the essay.**

1. Which is *not* a reason the writer gives for why school buses are so safe?

Ⓐ The buses weigh a great deal.   Ⓒ The seat backs are heavily padded.

Ⓑ The seats are high above the road.   Ⓓ The buses move slowly and stop often.

What evidence in the text helped you answer?

_____

_____

2. Which other word in this essay is a synonym for *mandatory* (line 29)?

Ⓐ compulsory   Ⓑ expensive   Ⓒ majority   Ⓓ protective

What evidence in the text helped you answer?

_____

_____

3. According to the writer, how does the safety of riding in a school bus compare with the safety of riding in a car?

_____

_____

4. What techniques does the writer use to emphasize key points?

_____

_____

_____

5. List three examples of facts and three examples of opinions in this essay.

_____

_____

_____

_____

Transforming Trash

In what ways does the writer explain the idiom about trash and treasure?

1   **Los Reciclados**   *One person's trash is another person's treasure.* So says an old idiom.
2   A project that started in a desperately poor slum in Cateura, Paraguay, proves the
3   truth of these words. The musicians of the Paraguay Youth Orchestra have gained
4   hope for the future through the power and joy of making music together. But
5   something rare distinguishes them from other ensembles. All their instruments began
6   as garbage found in the local landfill. This explains their nickname, "The Recycled
7   Orchestra" (*Los Reciclados*).

8   **Favio Chávez**   Music teacher and environmentalist Favio Chávez learned to play
9   clarinet and guitar as a child. He was working at a small music school in Paraguay
10   when he got a new job to teach the trash-pickers of Cateura to protect themselves
11   from injury and disease.

12   **Clever Cola**   When Chávez observed the terrible living
13   conditions of the local families, he knew he had to help
14   them. So he opened a music school. He had no money,
15   just five old instruments to share among the eager students,
16   and little idea where it all might lead. He soon asked one
17   of the trash-pickers, Cola, to make instruments from found
18   objects. Cola first repaired a broken drum. Then he built a
19   guitar from spare pieces of wood and a flute from tin cans.
20   Favio Chávez always says, "The world sends us garbage.
21   We send back music." The musicians display their
22   instruments with honest pride: a guitar fashioned from two
23   large cans, drums with skins made from old x-rays, a violin
24   whose body was a dented metal bowl.

25   **Landfill Harmonic**   As of this writing, Los Reciclados
26   has played in Brazil, Panama, Colombia, and hopes to visit
27   the United States to perform at the Musical Instrument
28   Museum in Arizona. The curator of that museum marvels
29   at "the ingenuity of humans around the world using what
30   they have at their disposal to create music." In 2014,
31   the documentary film *Landfill Harmonic* brought this
32   remarkable story to audiences all over the world.

Noelia Rios, 12, tuning her guitar made of recycled materials

▶ **Answer each question. Give evidence from the article.**

1. Which of the following statements is the most unique fact about *Los Reciclados*?

   Ⓐ They plan to visit the United States one day.   Ⓒ They are poor children.

   Ⓑ Their instruments are made from trash.   Ⓓ They live in Paraguay.

What evidence in the text helped you answer?

_____

_____

2. Which of the following is an example of *ingenuity* (line 29)?

   Ⓐ living in Cateura, Paraguay   Ⓒ creating a flute from tin cans

   Ⓑ learning to play the clarinet   Ⓓ conducting a youth orchestra

What evidence in the text helped you answer?

_____

_____

3. What made Favio and Cola such a successful team?

_____

_____

4. How does the idiom that begins the article apply to the story of the Paraguay Youth Orchestra? Refer to the title, photo, and text.

_____

_____

_____

5. Write a brief character sketch of Favio Chávez. Use details from this article.

_____

_____

_____

Smokejumpers

What do smokejumpers do? Fill in the blanks to find out.

A wildfire is spreading in the Montana wilderness. A fire management officer has to decide—and quickly: Should she put the fire out or let it burn? Since the forest is so

_____, she doesn't want to take any chances that it will spread too far. Time to call in the smokejumpers.

The smokejumpers _____ down from airplanes to try to control wildfires. Their routine begins with digging a fire line to clear a wide path around the fire. If that doesn't work, they change plans. They try to _____ the fire to the forest floor by clearing away low-hanging branches. Flames can climb these branches and speed along _____.

Next, smokejumpers dig through the burned area with special axes and hoes. They dig up cool dirt, trying to _____ the fire.

Their final task is to crawl through the area and feel the ground to make sure it isn't hot. Fires that _____ to be out can sometimes start again.

> **Word List**
>
> **arid**
> **appear**
> **confine**
> **overhead**
> **parachute**
> **smother**

Think About It!

What sequence do smokejumpers follow to contain a wildfire?

The Perfect Pet

Do snakes scare you? Fill in the blanks in this story to read about one girl who loves them.

"Why not a cat or a dog…or even a hamster?" Carolyn's mom asked.

"Because they aren't as magnificent as snakes," Carolyn replied. Her mother sighed. Carolyn always had to be different! But Carolyn had

_____ her mother relentlessly for months…

so off to Perfect Pets they went. Carolyn made a beeline to the reptile

_____, where she'd already scoped out some

_____.

"I'd like to see this Royal Python," Carolyn requested, indicating a spectacular cinnamon-colored specimen.

Carolyn's mom _____ as the clerk reached into the

aquarium. "It's not poisonous, is it?"

"No," the man reassured her. "This python is a real sweetheart…but you do want

to handle him carefully." He _____, and then offered to let

Carolyn hold the python. She grasped the snake gently but firmly below the head and

above the tail. "Do you want a turn?" she offered her mom.

"Absolutely not! Are you sure you wouldn't prefer a gerbil?"

"Positive," said Carolyn. "Cinnamon will make the perfect pet!"

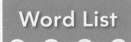

Word List

- **badgered**
- **candidates**
- **demonstrated**
- **department**
- **winced**

Think About It! Find one fact about pythons in the story. Then find an opinion.

The Bear Facts

You probably know at least two things about bears: They're big, and they can be scary. Fill in the blanks to learn more about two different kinds of bears.

Although black bears and polar bears are different in many

ways, they also have a lot in common. Their body shape is

_____, and they both have thick coats

of fur. _____ bear cubs of all kinds

are very tiny and stay with their mother for a year or more.

A major difference between black bears and polar bears

is their size. A full-grown black bear can be five to six feet long

and weigh up to 600 pounds. The huge polar bear, at six to eight feet long,

can weigh up to 1,700 pounds! Black bears eat mostly green plants, berries,

nuts, ants, and small animals, such as _____.

The _____ food of polar bears is seals, although

they also eat birds' eggs and berries.

Black bears have black or dark brown fur. Polar bears have fur that

is yellowish-white. What's another way the two types of bears differ?

Black bears _____ during the winter, while

polar bears remain active.

Word List

- chief
- hibernate
- newborn
- rodents
- similar

Think About It!

How are the black bear and the polar bear alike and different?

Knuckle Cracking

Some people cringe when they hear the "crack!" of others popping their knuckles. Fill in the blanks to find out what really goes on inside those cracking joints.

_____ to popular belief, cracking your knuckles doesn't _____ your joints, _____ to Dr. Thomas Trumble. He's a professor and surgeon at the University of Washington's _____ of hand and microvascular surgery in Seattle, Washington.

Dr. Trumble _____ cracking your knuckles to "pulling a suction cup off a window." You don't harm the window or the suction cup at all. But you do hear a loud pop. The same is true for knuckles.

"All joints have a normal _____ that helps them move smoothly," Dr. Trumble says. "When you crack your knuckles, you're just breaking that seal, so it doesn't do any harm at all. In fact, it feels good."

Word List

- **according**
- **contrary**
- **damage**
- **division**
- **likens**
- **vacuum**

Think About It!

Which of these statements is a fact, and which is an opinion?
Cracking your knuckles does no harm to them.
Cracking your knuckles feels good.

We All Scream for Ice Cream!

Do most of your friends like ice cream? Chances are they do—Americans are big ice cream lovers. Fill in the blanks to find some interesting facts and figures about just how much we love ice cream.

People in the United States love their ice cream. The average American eats about 48 pints each year. That's almost two hundred scoops of the frozen stuff! There's no _____ about it: We're the second biggest ice-cream eaters in the world! Who's number one? Believe it or not, New Zealand. New Zealanders _____ about 60 pints a year. Australians are in third place at about 38 pints each.

You might _____ that Canadians would be big ice-cream eaters. After all, Canada is right next to the United States. The average Canadian, however, eats only about 27 pints. Maybe it's just too cold in Canada to eat that much ice cream.

The top-selling flavor is _____. Some call it boring, but people seem to eat it up. Other _____ flavors include chocolate (of course), strawberry, butter pecan, neapolitan, and mint chocolate chip. What's your favorite?

Word List

- **consume**
- **doubt**
- **expect**
- **popular**
- **vanilla**

Think About It!

The article implies that it's too cold to eat ice cream in Canada. Is that a fact or an opinion?

Leonardo da Vinci

Read this article to learn about some of the amazing things created by Leonardo da Vinci. Use the word list to fill in the missing words.

Leonardo da Vinci was born in Italy more than 500 years ago. He had many talents and ideas. He was a true _____.

Leonardo was an _____. He drew a picture of a bicycle. At the time, that was a new idea. The first bicycle was built 300 years later. He also drew a picture of an airplane, another new idea. The first airplane was built 400 years later. Leonardo never ran out of ideas.

Leonardo was also a great painter. He painted the *Mona Lisa.* The woman in the painting has a _____ look on her face. What is she thinking? Why is she smiling? As you walk in front of the painting, her eyes seem to follow you.

Leonardo _____ nature and asked questions: Why do waves form in water? Why does the moon shine? He wrote his ideas in a notebook . . . backwards! Today, people use a _____ to read his notes!

Word List

genius

inventor

mirror

studied

puzzled

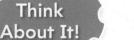

Think About It!

What were some of Leonardo da Vinci's accomplishments?

Helpful Houseplants

They sit on a desk or table and look pretty. You need to remember to water them. But what are houseplants actually good for? Fill in the blanks to find out.

Scientists say houseplants do more than _____ homes and offices. They can also improve the _____ of the air we breathe. Buildings today are often airtight and have plenty of _____. This makes them energy-efficient, but it also makes it hard for fresh air to enter.

Many houseplants can "clean" the stale air trapped inside buildings. Plant leaves take in the carbon dioxide gas from the air. In return, they give out clean _____.

Plants also take other dangerous gases from the air. For instance, the peace lily takes in benzene, a _____ found in paint and gasoline. Spider plants take in carbon monoxide. So why not keep a lot of houseplants around? They just might help you breathe easier.

Word List

chemical
decorate
insulation
oxygen
quality

Think About It!

What are some benefits of houseplants?

Faithfully Ours

Fill in the blanks to learn about the world's most famous geyser.

Whoosh! A stream of water shoots into the sky, spraying visitors with mist. The _____ continues for a few seconds more and then is gone. Cheers burst from the crowd. Old Faithful did it again, right on _____.

As geysers go, Old Faithful in Wyoming's Yellowstone National Park is probably the world's most famous. Geysers are hot springs that shoot water into the air.

The trouble with most geysers is that no one knows when they will decide to spout off. They're an _____ lot. One geyser in New Zealand hasn't been active since 1917. Another geyser, called Giant, sometimes spouts once a week, and other times waits for months.

Old Faithful, however, lives up to its name. It hasn't skipped a single _____ in the last few decades. About every 90 minutes or so, it shoots its water stream around 150 feet into the air. That kind of _____ draws millions of people to see it every year.

Word List

performance
reliability
schedule
spectacle
unpredictable

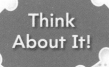

Think About It!   How has the geyser called Old Faithful earned its name?

Who Says Ball Games Are for the Birds?

What do ball games and birds have in common? More than you think! Fill in the blanks to find out.

The Trinity College Bantams were proud of their name. Bantams are a type of rooster, which suited the

_____ spirit of this basketball team.

One day in 1954, the Trinity Bantams were set to battle Yale's team. The Trinity fans hatched a "fowl" plan to support their players. When the Bantams scored their first basket, their fans gently

_____ a dozen live chickens onto the court! The chickens raced wildly around the floor. The game had to be

_____ until all the birds were collected.

Another bird-brained _____ involved Casey Stengel. He played baseball with the Brooklyn Dodgers until 1918. Then he was traded to the Pittsburgh Pirates. Casey loved playing jokes, and the fans loved his

_____. When Casey returned to his old stadium for the first time as a Pirate, he planned a special prank for his former fans. When it was his turn to bat, Casey jogged onto the field and tipped his cap to the booing crowd. As he did, a sparrow hidden in his cap flew out. The crowd's boos turned into loud

_____, welcoming Casey back.

Word List

- antics
- applause
- released
- scheme
- spunky
- suspended

Think About It!   **What does the article suggest about Casey Stengel?**

Presidential Pets

The White House is a stately place, but it has been home to many pets—who don't always follow presidential etiquette! Fill in the blanks to find out more about pets in the White House.

The White House is usually a serious place. Leaders of other countries bring important _____ to the President. Senators give and receive advice. The President signs bills into law.

However, some presidential pets have turned the White House into a wild and crazy place! President Obama got his family a new pet, Bo, as part of a _____ he made during his election _____.

Bo _____ chewed up the President's gym shoes!

Other presidents have had more unusual pets. John Quincy Adams once kept an alligator. Calvin Coolidge had two _____, a donkey, and a bobcat.

Teddy Roosevelt loved animals and proved it when he moved into the White House in 1901. His six children, plus snakes, rats, and a badger joined him. William Henry Harrison kept a goat and a cow. Woodrow Wilson had a flock of sheep. Thomas Jefferson owned a pair of grizzly bear cubs!

Word List

- business
- campaign
- promise
- promptly
- raccoons

Think About It!

Why do pets make the White House a more interesting place?

Why Penguins Wear Tuxedos

Have you ever noticed that penguins look like funny little men in tuxedos? Fill in the blanks to find out how their distinctive look may help keep them safe.

Walking around on two legs with their arms flapping around, penguins are a _____ and adorable sight. But how did they get their special look?

Most _____ of penguin developed a similar color pattern. They have black or dark blue feathers on their backs and white feathers on their chests and _____.

Scientists think that this basic pattern _____ because it protected penguins so well from their enemies, such as sharks and seals, in the water. From below, its white chest and stomach hide a penguin in the glare of _____. From above, its dark back makes a penguin hard to see against the darkness of the water.

Word List

- comical
- evolved
- species
- stomachs
- sunlight

Think About It!

Why do scientists think that penguin species developed a similar color pattern?

Language Arts

Sentence Mender

Rewrite the sentence to make it correct.

I one furst prize kerry said with pride

_____

Cursive Quote

Copy the quotation in cursive writing.

Words are the voice of the heart.

—Confucius

_____

_____

_____

What do you think the philosopher meant?
Write your answer in cursive on another sheet of paper.

Analogy of the Day

Complete the analogy.

Bear is to **den** as _____ is to **web**.

ⓐ house   ⓑ cub   ⓒ search engine   ⓓ spider

Explain how the analogy works: _____

_____

Sentence Mender

Rewrite the sentence to make it correct.

Jasons brews on he leg caused him to lemp.

_____

Cursive Quote

Copy the quotation in cursive writing.

A sense of curiosity is nature's original school of education.

—Dr. Smiley Blanton

_____
_____
_____
_____

What did Dr. Blanton mean?
Write your answer in cursive on another sheet of paper.

Analogy of the Day

Complete the analogy.

Big is to **small** as _____ is to **wet**.

Ⓐ drenched   Ⓑ dry   Ⓒ soaked   Ⓓ hot

Explain how the analogy works: _____
_____

Sentence Mender

Rewrite the sentence to make it correct.

The new glass Building on Spring street sparkels like a dimind.

_____

Cursive Quote

Copy the quotation in cursive writing.

Many argue; not many converse.

—Louisa May Alcott

_____
_____
_____
_____

What does *converse* mean?
Write your answer in cursive on another sheet of paper.

Analogy of the Day

Complete the analogy.

Sad is to **frown** as _____ is to **smile**.

Ⓐ worried   Ⓑ annoyed   Ⓒ happy   Ⓓ awkward

Explain how the analogy works: _____

_____

Sentence Mender

Rewrite the sentence to make it correct.

We should ask he to seize playing him's drums so late at knight.

_____

Cursive Quote

Copy the quotation in cursive writing.

Delay is preferable to error.

—Thomas Jefferson

_____

_____

_____

Is this good advice? Explain.
Write your answer in cursive on another sheet of paper.

Analogy of the Day

Complete the analogy.

Lunch is to **dinner** as _____ is to **evening**.

Ⓐ afternoon   Ⓑ darkness   Ⓒ breakfast   Ⓓ television

Explain how the analogy works: _____

_____

Sentence Mender

Rewrite the sentence to make it correct.

The Detroit tigers played a Double Header on labor day.

_____

Cursive Quote

Copy the quotation in cursive writing.

Those who lose dreaming are lost.

—Australian proverb

_____
_____
_____
_____

What is the meaning of this proverb?
Write your answer in cursive on another sheet of paper.

Analogy of the Day

Complete the analogy.

Instrument is to **trombone** as _____ is to **oak**.

Ⓐ acorn   Ⓑ trumpet   Ⓒ oatmeal   Ⓓ tree

Explain how the analogy works: _____

_____

Sentence Mender

Rewrite the sentence to make it correct.

What is the hieght, in feat, of that ate-story building.

_____

Cursive Quote

Copy the quotation in cursive writing.

Wonder is the beginning of wisdom.

—Anonymous

_ _ _ _ _ _ _ _ _ _ _ _ _ _ _ _ _ _ _ _

_ _ _ _ _ _ _ _ _ _ _ _ _ _ _ _ _ _ _ _

_ _ _ _ _ _ _ _ _ _ _ _ _ _ _ _ _ _ _ _

Do you agree? Explain.
Write your answer in cursive on another sheet of paper.

Analogy of the Day

Complete the analogy.

Grass is to **green** as _____ is to **jagged**.

Ⓐ park   Ⓑ knife   Ⓒ jar   Ⓓ jogged

Explain how the analogy works: _____

_____

Sentence Mender

Rewrite the sentence to make it correct.

The determinned inventer would not conceed defeet.

_____

Cursive Quote

Copy the quotation in cursive writing.

Excellence is not an act, it is a habit.

—Aristotle

_____

What else do you think should be a habit rather than an act?
Write your answer in cursive on another sheet of paper.

Analogy of the Day

Complete the analogy.

Toe is to **foot** as _____ is to **house**.

    Ⓐ tree   Ⓑ room   Ⓒ yard   Ⓓ apartment

Explain how the analogy works: _____

_____

Sentence Mender

Rewrite the sentence to make it correct.

H'es the older and bigger of the three brother.

_____

Cursive Quote

Copy the quotation in cursive writing.

Nothing is so burdensome as a secret.

—French proverb

Do you think this is true? Explain.
Write your answer in cursive on another sheet of paper.

Analogy of the Day

Complete the analogy.

Sailor is to **navy** as _____ is to **class**.

Ⓐ soldier   Ⓑ room   Ⓒ school   Ⓓ student

Explain how the analogy works: _____

_____

Sentence Mender

Rewrite the sentence to make it correct.

The Park Ranjer lead us on the dissent trom the mountin.

_____

Cursive Quote

Copy the quotation in cursive writing.

Bad is never good until worse happens.

—Danish proverb

_____

_____

_____

_____

Share an experience that proved this proverb to be true.
Write it in cursive on another sheet of paper.

Analogy of the Day

Complete the analogy.

Clean is to **spotless** as _____ is to **gigantic**.

Ⓐ nature   Ⓑ vacuum   Ⓒ large   Ⓓ small

Explain how the analogy works: _____

_____

Sentence Mender

Rewrite the sentence to make it correct.

Dan and iris went to paris to take a french cookin Class.

_____

Cursive Quote

Copy the quotation in cursive writing.

What is reading but silent conversation?

—Walter Savage Landon

_____
_____
_____
_____

What do you think Landon meant by this?
Write your answer in cursive on another sheet of paper.

Analogy of the Day

Complete the analogy.

Cry is to **laugh** as _____ is to **down**.

   Ⓐ whimper   Ⓑ up   Ⓒ floor   Ⓓ high

Explain how the analogy works: _____

_____

Sentence Mender

Rewrite the sentence to make it correct.

Us visited south Carolinas first light house.

_____

Cursive Quote

Copy the quotation in cursive writing.

The wastebasket is a writer's best friend.

—Isaac Bashevis Singer

_____

_____

_____

_____

What did Singer mean by this?
Write your answer in cursive on another sheet of paper.

Analogy of the Day

Complete the analogy.

Clock is to **tick** as _____ is to **buzz**.

Ⓐ bee   Ⓑ wing   Ⓒ swatter   Ⓓ paper

Explain how the analogy works: _____

_____

Sentence Mender

Rewrite the sentence to make it correct.

This mourning, I had breckfist in my pajomas and split orange juice on it.

_____

Cursive Quote

Copy the quotation in cursive writing.

Quarrels end, but words once spoken never die.

—African proverb

_____

Do you agree? Explain.
Write your answer in cursive on another sheet of paper.

Analogy of the Day

Complete the analogy.

Apple is to **fruit** as _____ is to **clothing**.

Ⓐ shirt   Ⓑ store   Ⓒ shopper   Ⓓ peach

Explain how the analogy works: _____

_____

Sentence Mender

Rewrite the sentence to make it correct.

Waht should we doe about the worrysome leek in the kichen?

_____

Cursive Quote

Copy the quotation in cursive writing.

Kindness, like a boomerang, always returns.

—Author unknown

- -

- -

What do you think the author meant by this?
Write your answer in cursive on another sheet of paper.

Analogy of the Day

Complete the analogy.

Dessert is to **tasty** as _____ is to **sticky**.

Ⓐ soup   Ⓑ tack   Ⓒ cookie   Ⓓ glue

Explain how the analogy works: _____

_____

Sentence Mender

Rewrite the sentence to make it correct.

The number has too sixs and three fores.

_____

Cursive Quote

Copy the quotation in cursive writing.

The quieter you become, the more you can hear.

—Ram Dass

Is this good advice? Explain.
Write your answer in cursive on another sheet of paper.

Analogy of the Day

Complete the analogy.

Car is to **garage** as _____ is to **hangar**.

Ⓐ clothing   Ⓑ airplane   Ⓒ closet   Ⓓ parking

Explain how the analogy works: _____

_____

Sentence Mender

Rewrite the sentence to make it correct.

Megs teacher and her mom agrees that Meg handwrite is eligible

_____

Cursive Quote

Copy the quotation in cursive writing.

Goals are the fuel in the furnace of achievement.

—Brian Tracy

- -

- -

- -

Explain what this means in your own words.
Write your explanation in cursive on another sheet of paper.

Analogy of the Day

Complete the analogy.

Tornado is to **destruction** as _____ is to **flooding.**

Ⓐ rain   Ⓑ wind   Ⓒ drought   Ⓓ fire

Explain how the analogy works: _____

_____

Sentence Mender

Rewrite the sentence to make it correct.

It is easiest to put an bridal on a horse then on a mewl?

_____

Cursive Quote

Copy the quotation in cursive writing.

Comedy is simply a funny way of being serious.

—Peter Ustinov

What did Ustinov mean by this?
Write your answer in cursive on another sheet of paper.

Analogy of the Day

Complete the analogy.

Drawer is to **dresser** as _____ is to **mug**.

Ⓐ closet   Ⓑ pug   Ⓒ cup   Ⓓ handle

Explain how the analogy works: _____

_____

Sentence Mender

Rewrite the sentence to make it correct.

The track teems captian can run like a dear.

_____

Cursive Quote

Copy the quotation in cursive writing.

Children have more need of models than critics.

—Carolyn Coats

What did Coats advise about how best to guide children?
Write your answer in cursive on another sheet of paper.

Analogy of the Day

Complete the analogy.

Athlete is to **team** as _____ is to **crew**.

   Ⓐ owner   Ⓑ boat   Ⓒ stadium   Ⓓ co-pilot

Explain how the analogy works: _____

_____

Sentence Mender

Rewrite the sentence to make it correct.

That wonderfull dog gracie is the apple of her owner's i.

_____

Cursive Quote

Copy the quotation in cursive writing.

A writer only begins a book. A reader finishes it.

—Samuel Johnson

What did Johnson mean by this? Do you agree?
Write your answer in cursive on another sheet of paper.

Analogy of the Day

Complete the analogy.

Cow is to **moo** as _____ is to **ring**.

    Ⓐ circus   Ⓑ bell   Ⓒ bull   Ⓓ finger

Explain how the analogy works: _____

_____

Sentence Mender

Rewrite the sentence to make it correct.

Many cabel customers have finded the new servic to be worser than it were before.

_____

Cursive Quote

Copy the quotation in cursive writing.

The best way to predict your future is to create it.

—Unknown

What did the author mean by this advice?
Write your answer in cursive on another sheet of paper.

Analogy of the Day

Complete the analogy.

Airplane is to **travel** as _____ is to **drink**.

Ⓐ water   Ⓑ car   Ⓒ straw   Ⓓ eat

Explain how the analogy works: _____

_____

Sentence Mender

Rewrite the sentence to make it correct.

Erin was upsit when she had been learning that she could'nt go with her friends.

_____

Cursive Quote

Copy the quotation in cursive writing.

To ease another's heartache is to forget one's own.

—Abraham Lincoln

Do you think this is true? Tell why.
Write your answer in cursive on another sheet of paper.

Analogy of the Day

Complete the analogy.

Ice is to **cold** as _____ is to **blue**.

Ⓐ show   Ⓑ sky   Ⓒ steam   Ⓓ green

Explain how the analogy works: _____

_____

Sentence Mender

Rewrite the sentence to make it correct.

She were born in troy new York on January 9 2,012.

_____

Cursive Quote

Copy the quotation in cursive writing.

If you judge people, you have no time to love them.

—Mother Teresa of Calcutta

_____

_____

_____

_____

Do you think this is true or not? Why?
Write your answer in cursive on another sheet of paper.

Analogy of the Day

Complete the analogy.

Purple is to **color** as _____ is to **music**.

    Ⓐ jazz   Ⓑ red   Ⓒ loud   Ⓓ fantasy

Explain how the analogy works: _____

_____

Sentence Mender

Rewrite the sentence to make it correct.

Either Jack and andrew will enter a muffin resippy in the context.

_____

Cursive Quote

Copy the quotation in cursive writing.

Don't wait for people to be friendly. Show them how.

—Author unknown

Is this good advice? Explain why or why not.
Write your answer in cursive on another sheet of paper.

Analogy of the Day

Complete the analogy.

Flame is to **bright** as _____ is to **waxy**.

Ⓐ candle   Ⓑ water   Ⓒ heat   Ⓓ lamp

Explain how the analogy works: _____

_____

Sentence Mender

Rewrite the sentence to make it correct.

Hay where are you going with my sell phone.

_____

Cursive Quote

Copy the quotation in cursive writing.

Time is a circus, always packing up and moving away.

—Ben Hecht

What else might time be like?
Write your answer in cursive on another sheet of paper.

Analogy of the Day

Complete the analogy.

Peril is to **danger** as _____ is to **stream**.

Ⓐ shore   Ⓑ drown   Ⓒ water   Ⓓ river

Explain how the analogy works: _____

_____

Sentence Mender

Rewrite the sentence to make it correct.

The shef realize that she needs more pepper salt and onion in the Stu.

_____

Cursive Quote

Copy the quotation in cursive writing.

It is far easier to start something than it is to finish it.

—Amelia Earhart

_____

_____

_____

What have you started, but not finished?
Write your answer in cursive on another sheet of paper.

Analogy of the Day

Complete the analogy.

Star is to **constellation** as _____ is to **faculty**.

    Ⓐ planet   Ⓑ school   Ⓒ teacher   Ⓓ student

Explain how the analogy works: _____

_____

Sentence Mender

Rewrite the sentence to make it correct.

I finely got to play for the maestro, but him was'nt impressed with my etterts.

_____

Cursive Quote

Copy the quotation in cursive writing.

Do what you can, with what you have, where you are.

—Theodore Roosevelt

_____

_____

_____

What do you think Roosevelt thought about complainers or people who always made excuses? Write your answer in cursive on another sheet of paper.

Analogy of the Day

Complete the analogy.

Ladder is to **reach** as _____ is to **cook**.

 Ⓐ restaurant Ⓑ stove Ⓒ fork Ⓓ table

Explain how the analogy works: _____

_____

Sentence Mender

Rewrite the sentence to make it correct.

After triping on a gopher whole in the pastor, she couldn't hardly walk.

_____

Cursive Quote

Copy the quotation in cursive writing.

Laughter is the shortest distance between two people.

—Victor Borge

What do you think Borge meant?
Write your answer in cursive on another sheet of paper.

Analogy of the Day

Complete the analogy.

Enemy is to **friend** as _____ is to **tense**.

Ⓐ present   Ⓑ buddy   Ⓒ bitter   Ⓓ calm

Explain how the analogy works: _____

_____

Sentence Mender

Rewrite the sentence to make it correct.

The singer now have won a oscar and a grammy award.

_____

Cursive Quote

Copy the quotation in cursive writing.

Ask advice from everyone, but act with your own mind.

—Yiddish proverb

_____
- -
_____
- -
_____

Is this good advice? Explain why or why not.
Write your answer in cursive on another sheet of paper.

Analogy of the Day

Complete the analogy.

Plant is to **harvest** as _____ is to **drink**.

Ⓐ tea   Ⓑ pour   Ⓒ apple   Ⓓ glass

Explain how the analogy works: _____

_____

Sentence Mender

Rewrite the sentence to make it correct.

Both her and nina mist the sience test.

_____

Cursive Quote

Copy the quotation in cursive writing.

Whatever creativity is, it is in part a solution to a problem.

—Brian Aldiss

How have you solved a problem creatively?
Write your answer in cursive on another sheet of paper.

Analogy of the Day

Complete the analogy.

Train is to **track** as _____ is to **sea**.

 Ⓐ caboose Ⓑ driver Ⓒ ship Ⓓ beach

Explain how the analogy works: _____

_____

Sentence Mender

Rewrite the sentence to make it correct.

Miguel told victor that he didnt need to practiss no more.

_____

Cursive Quote

Copy the quotation in cursive writing.

A bit of fragrance always clings to the hand that gives roses.

—Chinese proverb

- -

- -

- -

What do you think this proverb means?
Write your answer in cursive on another sheet of paper.

Analogy of the Day

Complete the analogy.

Screen is to **television** as _____ is to **school**.

  Ⓐ classroom   Ⓑ work   Ⓒ bus   Ⓓ neighborhood

Explain how the analogy works: _____

_____

Sentence Mender

Rewrite the sentence to make it correct.

then he poured the cereal and first he addded fruit and milk.

_____

Cursive Quote

Copy the quotation in cursive writing.

Tomorrow belongs to the people who prepare for it today.

—African proverb

- -

- -

- -

Do you agree? Explain.
Write your answer in cursive on another sheet of paper.

Analogy of the Day

Complete the analogy.

Violin is to **musician** as _____ is to **golfer**.

Ⓐ guitar   Ⓑ swing   Ⓒ course   Ⓓ club

Explain how the analogy works: _____

_____

Sentence Mender

Rewrite the sentence to make it correct.

Many peoples get sick from mosquitoe bytes.

_____

Cursive Quote

Copy the quotation in cursive writing.

The bamboo that bends is stronger than the oak that persists.

—Japanese proverb

_____

_____

What do you think this proverb means?
Write your answer in cursive on another sheet of paper.

Analogy of the Day

Complete the analogy.

Exercise is to **sweating** as _____ is to **weeping**.

   Ⓐ celebrate   Ⓑ tears   Ⓒ sadness   Ⓓ crying

Explain how the analogy works: _____

_____

Sentence Mender

Rewrite the sentence to make it correct.

Before labor day, we was happy and everything seamed perfict.

_____

Cursive Quote

Copy the quotation in cursive writing.

The good we do today becomes the happiness of tomorrow.

—William James

_____

_____

_____

Was James correct? Explain.
Write your answer in cursive on another sheet of paper.

Analogy of the Day

Complete the analogy.

Terrier is to **dog** as _____ is to **flower**.

    Ⓐ cat   Ⓑ rose   Ⓒ tree   Ⓓ plant

Explain how the analogy works: _____

_____

Sentence Mender

Rewrite the sentence to make it correct.

"There is bear tracks ahead on the trail, so be carful, the ranger warn."

_____

Cursive Quote

Copy the quotation in cursive writing.

You have to expect things of yourself before you can do them.

—Michael Jordan

_____
_____
_____
_____

Do you think this is true for everyone? Explain.
Write your answer in cursive on another sheet of paper.

Analogy of the Day

Complete the analogy.

Annoy is to **please** as _____ is to **hate**.

Ⓐ love   Ⓑ pester   Ⓒ thank   Ⓓ spinach

Explain how the analogy works: _____

_____

Sentence Mender

Rewrite the sentence to make it correct.

Henry wondered whom winned the world series last year?

_____

Cursive Quote

Copy the quotation in cursive writing.

Lack of patience in small matters can create havoc in great ones.

—Chinese proverb

_____
_____
_____
_____

What do you think this proverb means?
Write your answer in cursive on another sheet of paper.

Analogy of the Day

Complete the analogy.

Bright is to **brilliant** as _____ is to **exhilarated.**

Ⓐ miserable   Ⓑ delighted   Ⓒ calm   Ⓓ careful

Explain how the analogy works: _____

_____

Sentence Mender

Rewrite the sentence to make it correct.

I red an article called how to joining social Networks.

_____

Cursive Quote

Copy the quotation in cursive writing.

If you see no reason for giving thanks, the fault lies in yourself.

—Native American proverb, Minquass tribe

- -
_____
_____
- -

Do you agree? Explain.
Write your answer in cursive on another sheet of paper.

Analogy of the Day

Complete the analogy.

See is to **view** as _____ is to **sleep**.

Ⓐ awaken   Ⓑ snooze   Ⓒ tired   Ⓓ snore

Explain how the analogy works: _____

_____

Sentence Mender

Rewrite the sentence to make it correct.

The umpire state Building is more taller then the Chrysler building.

_____

Cursive Quote

Copy the quotation in cursive writing.

If you don't have confidence, you'll always find a way not to win.

—Carl Lewis

Rewrite Lewis's quote without using the negative words. Do you agree with the new statement? Write your explanation in cursive on another sheet of paper.

Analogy of the Day

Complete the analogy.

Employee is to **company** as _____ is to **mammal**.

Ⓐ zoo   Ⓑ fur   Ⓒ whale   Ⓓ reptile

Explain how the analogy works: _____

_____

Sentence Mender

Rewrite the sentence to make it correct.

Matt clark opened the door and steps out.

_____

Cursive Quote

Copy the quotation in cursive writing.

Life is like a ten-speed bike. Most of us have gears we never use.

—Charles Schultz

_____

_____

_____

Have you used all your gears? Explain.
Write your answer in cursive on another sheet of paper.

Analogy of the Day

Complete the analogy.

Hour is to **day** as _____ is to **bed**.

Ⓐ breakfast   Ⓑ night   Ⓒ sleep   Ⓓ mattress

Explain how the analogy works: _____

_____

Sentence Mender

Rewrite the sentence to make it correct.

The night show his bravery in battel and was rewarded with land and a Title.

_____

Cursive Quote

Copy the quotation in cursive writing.

What is told in the ear of one person is often heard 100 miles away.

—Chinese proverb

What do you think this proverb means?
Write your answer in cursive on another sheet of paper.

Analogy of the Day

Complete the analogy.

Silk is to **soft** as _____ is to **rough**.

Ⓐ clothing   Ⓑ flannel   Ⓒ sandpaper   Ⓓ coarse

Explain how the analogy works: _____

_____

Sentence Mender

Rewrite the sentence to make it correct.

"Were gone to the zoo when the new monkies arrive," said Maxs sister."

_____

Cursive Quote

Copy the quotation in cursive writing.

Early to bed and early to rise, makes a man healthy, wealthy, and wise.
—Benjamin Franklin

What do you think about Franklin's advice?
Write your answer in cursive on another sheet of paper.

Analogy of the Day

Complete the analogy.

Easy is to **challenging** as _____ is to **tricky**.

Ⓐ puzzle   Ⓑ hard   Ⓒ confusing   Ⓓ simple

Explain how the analogy works: _____

_____

Sentence Mender

Rewrite the sentence to make it correct.

It use to be that few College graduates lived with there parent's.

_____

Cursive Quote

Copy the quotation in cursive writing.

Kindness is the language which the deaf can hear and the blind can see.
                                                    —Mark Twain

Do you agree with Twain's idea about a common language?
Write your answer in cursive on another sheet of paper.

Analogy of the Day

Complete the analogy.

Shovel is to **dig** as _____ is to **music**.

Ⓐ guitar   Ⓑ sweater   Ⓒ thread   Ⓓ fabric

Explain how the analogy works: _____

_____

Sentence Mender

Rewrite the sentence to make it correct.

Ethan Ellis and eli is the best tenners in the church quire.

_____

Cursive Quote

Copy the quotation in cursive writing.

Reading gives us someplace to go when we have to stay
where we are.

—Mason Cooley

_ _

_____

_ _

What did Cooley mean by "someplace to go"?
Write your answer in cursive on another sheet of paper.

Analogy of the Day

Complete the analogy.

Wrench is to **mechanic** as _____ is to **painter**.

    Ⓐ painting   Ⓑ brush   Ⓒ museum   Ⓓ gallery

Explain how the analogy works: _____

_____

Sentence Mender

Rewrite the sentence to make it correct.

Marie curie was a scientist whom was a head of her time.

_____

Cursive Quote

Copy the quotation in cursive writing.

Every day do something that will inch you closer to a better tomorrow.

—Doug Firebaugh

Do you agree? Explain.
Write your answer in cursive on another sheet of paper.

Analogy of the Day

Complete the analogy.

Desk is to **office** as _____ is to **ocean**.

Ⓐ bird   Ⓑ sky   Ⓒ submarine   Ⓓ land

Explain how the analogy works: _____

_____

Sentence Mender

Rewrite the sentence to make it correct.

You and me should recieve awards for spelling and grammer grateness.

_____

Cursive Quote

Copy the quotation in cursive writing.

If you can, help others; if you cannot do that, at least do not harm them.

—Randy Rind

_____

_____

_____

_____

Do you agree that it's enough just not to do harm?
Write your answer in cursive on another sheet of paper.

Analogy of the Day

Complete the analogy.

Knife is to **cut** as _____ is to **light**.

    Ⓐ glass   Ⓑ lamp   Ⓒ darkness   Ⓓ heavy

Explain how the analogy works: _____

_____

Sentence Mender

Rewrite the sentence to make it correct.

It taked me a long time to ketch my first fowl ball.

_____

Cursive Quote

Copy the quotation in cursive writing.

Say nothing about another that you wouldn't want to hear about yourself.
— El Salvadoran proverb

_____
_____
_____
_____

What other proverb do you know that expresses the same idea?
Write your answer in cursive on another sheet of paper.

Analogy of the Day

Complete the analogy.

Abundant is to **plentiful** as _____ is to **fearful.**

Ⓐ bountiful   Ⓑ many   Ⓒ fearless   Ⓓ scared

Explain how the analogy works: _____

_____

Sentence Mender

Rewrite the sentence to make it correct.

1 of our friends Teresa lost their house keys during the buss trip.

_____

Cursive Quote

Copy the quotation in cursive writing.

The beautiful thing about learning is that no one can take it away from you.
—B. B. King

_____

_____

_____

_____

What is something else that is beautiful for the same reason?
Write your answer in cursive on another sheet of paper.

Analogy of the Day

Complete the analogy.

Leg is to **limb** as _____ is to **tool**.

　Ⓐ fix　　　Ⓑ carpenter　　　Ⓒ shed　　　Ⓓ pliers

Explain how the analogy works: _____

_____

Sentence Mender

Rewrite the sentence to make it correct.

My indian classmates' speak english and hindi.

_____

Cursive Quote

Copy the quotation in cursive writing.

Education is the ability to listen to almost anything without losing your temper.
                                                                    —Robert Frost

How do you define *education*?
Write your answer in cursive on another sheet of paper.

Analogy of the Day

Complete the analogy.

Actor is to **cast** as _____ is to **state**.

Ⓐ city   Ⓑ country   Ⓒ happiness   Ⓓ desert

Explain how the analogy works: _____

_____

Sentence Mender

Rewrite the sentence to make it correct.

my brother doe'snt swim as fast as me can

_____

Cursive Quote

Copy the quotation in cursive writing.

If you like things easy, you'll have difficulties; if you like problems, you'll succeed.

—Laotian proverb

_____
_____
_____
_____

Do you agree? Explain.
Write your answer in cursive on another sheet of paper.

Analogy of the Day

Complete the analogy.

Engine is to **truck** as _____ is to **camera**.

    Ⓐ photographer   Ⓑ photograph   Ⓒ lens   Ⓓ digital

Explain how the analogy works: _____

_____

Sentence Mender

Rewrite the sentence to make it correct.

Grady and Rob is the too host's of the partay.

_____

Cursive Quote

Copy the quotation in cursive writing.

Reading takes us away from home, but more important, it finds homes for us everywhere.   —Hazel Rochman

_____

_____

_____

What do you think this means?
Write your answer in cursive on another sheet of paper.

Analogy of the Day

Complete the analogy.

Warm is to **sizzling** as _____ is to **exhausted**.

   Ⓐ awake   Ⓑ peppy   Ⓒ weary   Ⓓ boiling

Explain how the analogy works: _____

_____

Sentence Mender

Rewrite the sentence to make it correct.

Nikos dad really nose the rope when it come to sayling.

_____

Cursive Quote

Copy the quotation in cursive writing.

Tell me and I'll forget. Show me and I may not remember. Involve me, and I'll understand.

—Native American saying

How do you learn best? Explain.
Write your answer in cursive on another sheet of paper.

Analogy of the Day

Complete the analogy.

High is to **low** as _____ is to **bored**.

Ⓐ zero   Ⓑ wood   Ⓒ board   Ⓓ interested

Explain how the analogy works: _____

_____

Grammar

Write a proper noun that is an example of each common noun.
The first one has been done for you.

1. state   Minnesota _____

2. singer _____

3. river _____

4. artist _____

5. woman _____

6. mountain _____

7. athlete _____

8. game _____

9. shampoo _____

10. song _____

11. medicine _____

12. doctor _____

Write a common noun to name the group that includes each proper noun.
The first one has been done for you.

13. Brazil   country _____

14. Harry Potter _____

15. New York Mets _____

16. Asia _____

17. Taylor Swift _____

18. Honda _____

19. Lord of the Rings _____

20. Indiana _____

21. Superior _____

22. April _____

23. Tuesday _____

Read each phrase. Decide whether the underlined word(s) is a common noun, a proper noun, a collective noun, or not a noun at all. Mark the correct letter.

A = common noun	B = proper noun	C = collective noun	D = not a noun

1. at <u>The Bead Museum</u> Ⓐ Ⓑ Ⓒ Ⓓ

2. located in the <u>center</u> of Arizona Ⓐ Ⓑ Ⓒ Ⓓ

3. started by a retired interior <u>decorator</u> Ⓐ Ⓑ Ⓒ Ⓓ

4. vast <u>collection</u> of jewelry Ⓐ Ⓑ Ⓒ Ⓓ

5. in the small town of <u>Prescott</u> Ⓐ Ⓑ Ⓒ Ⓓ

6. <u>visited</u> the research library Ⓐ Ⓑ Ⓒ Ⓓ

7. examples from nearly every <u>country</u> Ⓐ Ⓑ Ⓒ Ⓓ

8. made of wood, <u>glass</u>, bone, metal, and stone Ⓐ Ⓑ Ⓒ Ⓓ

9. can reveal important <u>information</u> Ⓐ Ⓑ Ⓒ Ⓓ

10. accepted in <u>payment</u> Ⓐ Ⓑ Ⓒ Ⓓ

11. the <u>Acoma</u> people of New Mexico Ⓐ Ⓑ Ⓒ Ⓓ

12. <u>used</u> beads for trading purposes Ⓐ Ⓑ Ⓒ Ⓓ

13. the <u>staff</u> of the museum Ⓐ Ⓑ Ⓒ Ⓓ

14. unusual <u>Chinese</u> beads Ⓐ Ⓑ Ⓒ Ⓓ

15. free <u>admission</u> to the museum Ⓐ Ⓑ Ⓒ Ⓓ

16. on a computer <u>network</u> Ⓐ Ⓑ Ⓒ Ⓓ

17. assisted by a <u>team</u> of scholars Ⓐ Ⓑ Ⓒ Ⓓ

18. a lovely wrist <u>ornament</u> Ⓐ Ⓑ Ⓒ Ⓓ

19. delicate glass beads from <u>Italy</u> Ⓐ Ⓑ Ⓒ Ⓓ

20. long <u>string</u> of stones Ⓐ Ⓑ Ⓒ Ⓓ

A **general noun** gives a broad or all-purpose name. A **specific noun** names a *certain* person, place, thing, or idea in a way that is easier to imagine. Specific nouns are more precise. Proper nouns can be the most precise.

General:	My _relative_ served in the U.S. Navy.
Specific:	My _aunt_ served in the U.S. Navy.
More Specific:	My _Aunt Janet_ served in the U.S. Navy.

Complete the chart of nouns from general to specific to more specific.

HINT: Be sure you can explain how the sample row goes from general to specific.

GENERAL	SPECIFIC	MORE SPECIFIC
1. stars	constellation	Orion
2. garment	coat	
3. fruit	apple	
4. instrument	drum	
5. vehicle	truck	
6. beverage	milkshake	
7. mammal		stallion
8. seabird		emperor penguin
9. tool		sledgehammer
10.	fantasy	*The Wizard of Oz*
11.	bread	pita
12.	turtle	leatherback

Mark the correct **antecedent** (the noun that matches the meaning) of each underlined pronoun.

1. Checkers is a very old game; <u>it</u> was played in Egypt over 4,000 years ago!

   Ⓐ old   Ⓒ checkers

   Ⓑ Egypt   Ⓓ years

2. Players then were neither children nor old folks; <u>they</u> were warriors and rulers.

   Ⓐ players   Ⓒ folks

   Ⓑ children   Ⓓ warriors

3. What proof do we have for checkers in Egypt? <u>It</u> appears in ancient paintings.

   Ⓐ ancient   Ⓒ paintings

   Ⓑ checkers   Ⓓ Egypt

4. "Enemy" pieces were "captured" by opponents <u>who</u> tried to defeat each other.

   Ⓐ enemy   Ⓒ opponents

   Ⓑ pieces   Ⓓ other

5. Another name for checkers is "draughts." <u>This</u> is pronounced *drafts*.

   Ⓐ name   Ⓒ drafts

   Ⓑ draughts   Ⓓ checkers

6. Many famous people through history loved to play checkers. One was Ulysses S. Grant—the Civil War general <u>who</u> later became president.

   Ⓐ general   Ⓒ famous person

   Ⓑ president   Ⓓ history

7. The oldest known book about checkers (draughts) was published in Spain in 1547. <u>Its</u> author was Antonio Torquemada.

   Ⓐ the book's   Ⓒ the game's

   Ⓑ the author's   Ⓓ Spain's

8. The world's largest checkerboard, <u>which</u> uses big round pillows for playing pieces, is in Petal, Mississippi.

   Ⓐ pieces   Ⓒ pillows

   Ⓑ Mississippi   Ⓓ checkerboard

Mark the letter of the verb form that best
completes the sentence.

1. Jenny and I decided to _____ members of the camera club.

   Ⓐ become   Ⓑ becoming   Ⓒ became

2. We _____ meetings twice a week—on Tuesdays and Saturdays.

   Ⓐ has   Ⓑ have   Ⓒ having

3. Our advisor _____ once a photojournalist in Chicago.

   Ⓐ were   Ⓑ will   Ⓒ was

4. Some of his pictures _____ in newspapers and magazines.

   Ⓐ appeared   Ⓑ appear   Ⓒ appearing

5. Our advisor has _____ some famous people through his work.

   Ⓐ know   Ⓑ knew   Ⓒ known

6. Each member may also _____ a digital camera to use.

   Ⓐ borrowed   Ⓑ borrowing   Ⓒ borrow

7. We _____ so lucky to be able to use such good equipment.

   Ⓐ be   Ⓑ is   Ⓒ are

8. We are _____ to capture a scene to make it interesting.

   Ⓐ learned   Ⓑ learn   Ⓒ learning

9. We _____ to mount a photo show next May to show our best work.

   Ⓐ plan   Ⓑ planned   Ⓒ plans

10. Each of us can _____ our five favorite pictures for the show.

   Ⓐ chose   Ⓑ choose   Ⓒ choice

Write the correct form of the verb in boldface to finish each sentence.
The first one has been done for you.

1. Yesterday I **fed** the cat tuna, but today I will _____ feed _____ her liver.

2. At last year's water balloon fight, Jack **broke** only two balloons.

   This year, he hopes to _____ all six of them!

3. Today Jed **draws** with pastels, but yesterday he _____
   with markers.

4. Can you **hang** this painting as high as the one we _____
   over there?

5. Peg **sleeps** on the top bunk tonight since Jill _____
   there last night.

6. Ed **spent** his allowance on candy, but I'll _____
   mine only on books.

7. Claire **leaves** for the bus early, but I don't _____
   until almost nine.

8. Greg **grew** two inches this summer, but I haven't _____
   an inch since spring!

9. I **thought** the movie was much too sad. What did you _____?

10. He has **written** a fine story—far better than the one I _____.

These sentences have plain verbs in boldface.
Rewrite each sentence using an exciting verb.

1 Karen **ran** to the bus stop.

_____

2. The thirsty athlete **drank** some cool water.

_____

3. Marco **walked** past the sleeping baby.

_____

4. The lost hikers **called** for help.

_____

5. When coyotes howl, rabbits **go** into the nearest hole.

_____

6. Aunt Clara loves to **make** fancy salads.

_____

7. After the game, Fran **sat** on a shady bench.

_____

8. "Where did I leave my backpack?" **said** Dan.

_____

These sentences have boring adjectives in boldface.
Rewrite each sentence with a more exciting adjective.

1. That cat has **nice** fur.

_____

2. The gardens were **pretty** today.

_____

3. The way they dance is so **cute**.

_____

4. That was a **bad** excuse.

_____

5. We saw a **good** play.

_____

6. The Rocky Mountains are **big**.

_____

7. They had a **fine** time at the picnic.

_____

8. We took one **interesting** tour together.

_____

9. The soup tasted **awful**.

_____

10. What a **great** vacation we had!

_____

Adverbs can help describe *how* a person speaks or acts.

Okay: *"It's my turn now," said Travis.*

Better: *"It's my turn now," said Travis <u>boastfully</u>.*

Pretend you are a movie director. Tell each actor how to say his or her line by writing an adverb after the verb. The first one has been done for you.

HINT: Imagine coaxing the most believable performance out of each actor!

1. *[At a hospital]* "What did the doctor say?" asked Gina _____anxiously_____.

2. *[In a traffic jam]* "How close are we?" said Haroun _____.

3. *[On a raft]* "I dropped the oars," Jim admitted _____.

4. *[In a tent]* "I'm sitting on rocks and roots," complained Kate _____.

5. *[While skydiving]* "Whose bright idea was this?" thought Dan _____.

6. *[In bed]* "Stop that barking, King!" yelled Marcy _____.

7. *[At a mall]* "I need a bigger allowance," stated LaNiqua _____.

8. *[In a blizzard]* "Come inside right now!" called Dad _____.

9. *[While dancing]* "Whoa! This is my favorite song!" Amy said _____.

10. *[At dinner]* "I have something important to say," announced Zane _____.

11. *[Exercising]* "I can't keep this up forever!" called Lyndee _____.

12. *[Weeping]* "Nobody warned me about this," said Eliza _____.

Mark the letter of the answer that best completes each sentence.

1. That is the _____ of the two rocks to climb.

   Ⓐ hard   Ⓑ harder   Ⓒ hardest   Ⓓ more harder

2. It has the _____ face of all the beginner's rocks in the area.

   Ⓐ smooth   Ⓑ smoother   Ⓒ smoothest   Ⓓ most smoothest

3. Rock climbing is _____ nowadays thanks to high-tech gear.

   Ⓐ safer   Ⓑ most safe   Ⓒ most safer   Ⓓ safest

4. Climbers wear special shoes that have the _____ grip and give.

   Ⓐ great   Ⓑ greatest   Ⓒ greater   Ⓓ more greater

5. Beginning climbers _____ retrace their steps to build confidence and skill.

   Ⓐ often   Ⓑ more often   Ⓒ most often   Ⓓ oftenest

6. They are told not to go _____ than their trainers tell them to go.

   Ⓐ farther   Ⓑ more far   Ⓒ farthest   Ⓓ more farthest

7. Some cities have indoor climbing walls that are _____ than actual rocks.

   Ⓐ difficult   Ⓑ more difficulter   Ⓒ difficulter   Ⓓ more difficult

8. The _____ my local indoor climbing wall opens is 6:00 a.m.

   Ⓐ early   Ⓑ earlier   Ⓒ most early   Ⓓ earliest

A **preposition** is a word that helps relate nouns in time and space. Each sentence below has a preposition shown in boldface. Finish each sentence by adding a phrase that makes sense. The first one has been done for you.

1. The monkeys ran **along**

the jungle path   .

2. These playful creatures scurried **up**

_____.

3. They were up high, but they could see **through**

_____.

4. A hungry leopard paced eagerly **below** _____.

5. The monkeys screeched **at** _____.

6. Will the monkeys be safe **from** _____?

7. The sun began to set **behind** _____.

8. The leopard lost interest and took off **toward** _____

_____.

9. With the leopard gone, the monkeys scampered down **to** _____

_____.

10. There, they chased and groomed each other **until** _____

_____.

11. At last, they curled up to sleep **near** _____

_____.

12. And who knows what the monkeys will do tomorrow **for** _____

_____!

Prepositional phrases can help to add details and description. Notice how the underlined prepositional phrase makes the following sentence better.

They left the house early <u>while the street lamps were still shining</u>.

Rewrite each sentence below to make it more descriptive. Add a prepositional phrase anywhere in the sentence that works. The first one has been done for you.

1. Figure skaters practice regularly.

   <u>Figure skaters in training practice regularly.</u>

2. Many skaters practice in the morning.

   _____

   _____

3. Renting ice time can be very expensive.

   _____

4. But it takes repetition to perfect the routines.

   _____

5. Ice skaters expect to fall.

   _____

6. They wear protective gear.

   _____

7. Many skaters practice off the ice.

   _____

8. They jump and fall.

   _____

Some words sound alike but have different spellings and different meanings.
Pick the right word for each sentence. Write it on the line.

acts or **ax** **1.** Pioneers used the _____ for many chores.

brake or **break** **2.** He warned his little brother not to _____ the toy.

ceiling or **sealing** **3.** The painter used a ladder to reach the
_____.

chili or **chilly** **4.** Add hot peppers to your _____
to spice it up.

coarse or **course** **5.** The dog's whiskers feel _____
to the touch.

fair or **fare** **6.** Students pay a reduced _____ to ride the bus.

flour or **flower** **7.** The bread recipe requires three cups of
_____.

higher or **hire** **8.** The store needs to _____ some
part-time helpers.

heard or **herd** **9.** Megan _____ an odd sound coming
from the roof.

pedal or **petal** **10.** A beetle is chewing on the _____ of that rose.

ring or **wring** **11.** Please _____ out your towel before
you hang it up.

soar or **sore** **12.** We watched the jet _____ into the clouds.

A **contraction** blends two words into one by replacing one or more letters with an apostrophe ('). For example:

it + is = ***it's***   she + would = ***she'd***

In each sentence, find the contraction. Underline it. Then write the two separate words that formed the contraction. The first one has been done for you.

1. He wonders <u>what's</u> keeping Sally.   what is

2. We're going to Canada for a vacation.   _____

3. She might've been to our old school.   _____

4. He said that it'll probably snow tonight.   _____

5. They just can't seem to untie that knot.   _____

6. You may feel cozy, but I'm freezing!   _____

7. Gee, wouldn't it be wild if cats really talked?   _____

8. Well, you needn't be so snippy about it!   _____

9. People say she'd be better off on her own.   _____

10. Eric, you'd better walk the dog before school.   _____

11. I promise I won't peek until you say so.   _____

12. Okay, let's have Granny's brownies now.   _____

Read each sentence. Notice the three underlined words. If you see an error in capitalization, mark the letter beneath the word that has the error. If all the underlined words are capitalized correctly, circle *No Error*.

1. At a <u>Museum</u> in <u>Philadelphia</u>, you can walk in a model human <u>heart</u>. *No Error*
   Ⓐ   Ⓑ   Ⓒ

2. Do you <u>know</u> what time your <u>Mother</u> is getting to <u>Kansas City</u>? *No Error*
   Ⓐ   Ⓑ   Ⓒ

3. My favorite <u>basketball</u> team used to be the <u>Chicago</u> <u>bulls</u>. *No Error*
   Ⓐ   Ⓑ   Ⓒ

4. Lake <u>Erie</u> forms part of the long border between the <u>U.S.</u> and <u>Canada</u>. *No Error*
   Ⓐ   Ⓑ   Ⓒ

5. <u>The</u> very first <u>Earth</u> Day was celebrated on <u>april</u> 22, 1970. *No Error*
   Ⓐ   Ⓑ   Ⓒ

6. More than 900 <u>million</u> people practice the <u>hindu</u> <u>faith</u>. *No Error*
   Ⓐ   Ⓑ   Ⓒ

7. Do <u>you</u> know who was <u>President</u> of IBM in the <u>year</u> you were born? *No Error*
   Ⓐ   Ⓑ   Ⓒ

8. I baby-sit for my <u>cousin</u> <u>Jake</u> every <u>thursday</u> after school. *No Error*
   Ⓐ   Ⓑ   Ⓒ

9. <u>Alaska</u> is the largest state, but <u>new</u> <u>York</u> has the largest city! *No Error*
   Ⓐ   Ⓑ Ⓒ

10. <u>North</u> <u>Carolina</u> has exactly one hundred <u>Counties</u> in it. *No Error*
    Ⓐ   Ⓑ   Ⓒ

11. Do you think there is a <u>Main</u> <u>Street</u> in every small town in <u>America</u>? *No Error*
    Ⓐ   Ⓑ   Ⓒ

12. The <u>declaration</u> of <u>Independence</u> was adopted on the 4th day of <u>July</u>. *No Error*
    Ⓐ   Ⓑ   Ⓒ

Use commas to separate three or more words and phrases (groups of words) in a series to make it easier for people to read your sentences.

Example:

I put lettuce, tomatoes, cucumbers, and cheese in my salad.

In the sentences below, put in the missing commas where they belong. Then circle the letter that comes right after each comma you have inserted. The letters you circled will spell out the answers to the animal questions.

1. Six of the longest rivers in the world are the Nile in Africa Congo in Central Africa Lena in Russia Amazon in South America Mississippi in the USA, and the Yangtze in China.

   What's a kind of shellfish?

   Answer: _____

2. Earth Jupiter Uranus Mars Pluto (a dwarf planet) Saturn, and Neptune are some of the planets in our solar system.

   What does a kangaroo do?

   Answer: He _____

3. William Shakespeare wrote many great plays like Hamlet King Lear Othello As You Like It Love's Labours Lost and Macbeth.

   What is a small Australian animal that lives in eucalyptus trees?

   Answer: _____

4. Goslings squabs hatchlings ephyrae eyases polliwogs, and fawns are the names of baby geese, pigeons, dinosaurs, jellyfish, hawks, frogs, and deer.

   What's a woolly farm animal?

   Answer: _____

5. Some of the instruments in an orchestra are violins horns oboes organs flutes saxophones, and drums.

   What are the hard coverings over the feet of horses?

   Answer: _____

6. My favorite animated movies are *Up Ratatouille Alice in Wonderland Bambi Beauty and the Beast Ice Age Toy Story Shrek*, and *Happy Feet*.

   What are bunnies?

   Answer: _____

Put commas where they belong after the mild interjections in the sentences below. (Careful! Not all the sentences have interjections.) Then circle the first letter of the word that comes right after the comma. The letters you circled will spell out the answer to the riddle at the end.

Put a comma after a mild interjection (like *oh, yes, aha, well,* and *uh-huh*) at the beginning of a sentence.

Note: An interjection is a word or short phrase that expresses a feeling like surprise, pleasure, disgust, or amazement. It usually comes at the beginning of a sentence.

1. My brother really doesn't like peanut butter and mushroom sandwiches.

2. My goodness rabbits can hop fast when they want to.

3. Gosh all my licorice melted in the sun.

4. Yuck cotton candy really sticks to your face, doesn't it?

5. My dear friend from camp is visiting this weekend.

6. Uh-oh everybody just went out the wrong door.

7. Oops Carl squirted ketchup on my new shirt.

8. Oh dear a page from my homework just blew out the window.

9. Gee whiz raccoons broke into the kitchen and ate Grandma's apple pie.

Riddle

What very fast vehicle is spelled the same backwards and forwards? (Hint: The answer can be spelled as one or two words.)

Answer: _____ _____ _____ _____ _____ _____ _____ or

_____ _____ _____ _____   _____ _____ _____

In the e-mail below, put in all the missing commas where they belong after clauses and phrases at the beginnings of sentences.

Put a comma after a clause or phrase (including a prepositional phrase) at the beginning of a sentence.

This kind of clause usually begins with a word like *before, after, although, because, in, on, over, under, unless, whether,* etc.

From: Summerv22@happycamp.org

To: Bestgrandma@kryt.com

Subject: My first week at camp

Dear Grandma,

Although I've been here for only one week I've already made a lot of new friends. Because kids come here from my school I knew some of them already. Since this camp is right on a lake we do a lot of water sports like swimming and boating. Unless it's really raining we're outside all day long. After the swim across the lake we had a picnic. Before the talent show yesterday I had to practice singing with my mouth full of pretzels. I won for funniest act! If you can come on visiting day that would be awesome. Until I see you again stay well.

Hug Fluffy for me.

Love,

Summer

Note: The e-mail addresses above are not real.

The sentences below don't make sense because some commas are missing. Put commas between some of the words to make sure the sentences are not confusing. Add just one comma to each sentence. Circle the letter after each comma you put in. The circled letters will spell out the answer to the riddle at the end.

> Use commas between certain words that might cause confusion together. The comma will separate the words, making readers pause slightly to think about what they are reading. For example:
> This sentence—without the comma—is confusing.
> *If he calls his mother will know where he is.*
> With the comma, the sentence is very clear.
> *If he calls, his mother will know where he is.*

1. When the mosquitoes came out in went the people.

2. While they were flying nine planes flew in front of them.

3. Outside the bedroom carpet the hallway.

4. Though we believe in recycling our brother doesn't.

5. After you read the book report on it to the class.

6. Please tell Paul Revere is a city in Massachusetts.

7. When he began painting everyone said he needed art lessons.

8. To make ice chill water.

9. Before they finished eating the chicken flew away.

10. To Abraham Lincoln seemed like a good capital for Nebraska.

11. Inside your grandpa's barn was noisy.

Riddle Which word is spelled incorrectly in every dictionary?

Answer: ____ ____ ____ ____ ____ ____ ____ ____ ____ ____ ____

Here are some riddles. Put commas where they belong to set off the nouns of direct address.

Use one or two commas to set off a noun of direct address at the beginning, middle, or end of a sentence. The "noun of direct address" is the word or words that name the person who is being spoken to directly.
Examples:
Ladies and gentlemen, the show is about to begin.
Thanks, Dad, for helping me with my homework.
Your new cat really meows loudly, Sue.

What is full of holes Amanda but still holds water?

A sponge Justin.

Which weighs more Steve a pound of feathers or a pound of iron?

Jane they both weigh a pound.

Why didn't the skeleton go to the dance Sophie?

Because Matt he had no body to go with.

Dennis why did Dracula's mother get him cough medicine?

Because of his coffin Lynda.

Below are groups of three sentences. One sentence asks a question; one makes a statement; one expresses strong emotions. Put an exclamation point after the sentences that express strong emotions. Add the other end punctuation, too. Then, circle the letters that come right before the exclamation points you added and write them on the lines below. At the end, when you read the letters aloud, they will sound out the answer to the riddle.

Use an exclamation point at the end of an exclamatory sentence (a sentence that expresses very strong feelings). Here are some sentences with powerful emotions.

Joy: It stopped raining, so we can have the wedding outside!

Fright: There's a weird thing under my bed!

Excitement: We're winning! We're winning!

Surprise: John, you came to my party!

What is that loud sound
Run! It's an erupting volcano
That was just my stomach rumbling

I will not dance in the ballet tonight
Why not, madam
I refuse to wear that totally terrible tutu

A boa constrictor is crawling up my leg
It's a snake from Central and South America
How is that going to help me

Here's the lion house at the zoo
How are you feeling, lion
Roar

Is there a police station around here
There's one next to the Italian pastry shop
Help, someone stole my cannoli

Do you hear that loud buzzing
It's just a bumblebee
Ow! It just stung my arm

What act are you doing for the talent show
I'm dressing up as a duck and singing opera
That's amazingly fantastic

It's nice here in the woods
Did you hear that scary noise
It's Bigfoot

Riddle   What did the surprised bank robber say when he cracked open a safe with no money in it?

Answer: ____ ____ ____ ____ ____ ____ ____ ____ !

Below are little conversations between people. The sentences are missing their punctuation marks. Some of the sentences are declarative (they make statements). Others may ask a question or express strong emotions or commands. Decide which sentences are declarative and state facts. Add periods to the end of those sentences only. Then, add up all the numbers in front of the sentences that needed periods, and you'll have the answer to the question at the end. (If you like, you can add question marks and exclamation points to the other sentences.)

> Use a period at the end of a declarative sentence (a sentence that states a fact), like this:
> *Hummingbirds can fly backwards.*

1. The dinosaur is loose

2. What should we do

3. I am going to wave when it goes by

4. Is today Wednesday

5. It is

6. Yikes, I forgot to study for the math test

7. I like turopoljes

8. What are they

9. They're spotted pigs

10. I spotted one once

11. Why did you say that

12. What did I say

13. You said you like asparagus

14. I do

15. But why did you say it

16. Help Help

17. What's the matter

18. An earthquake is shaking the house

19. That's just an elephant walking by

20. Money doesn't grow on trees

21. Then why do banks have branches

Question

What number does the Roman numeral *C* stand for?

Answer: _____

Each sentence below is missing one or more punctuation marks. Rewrite the sentences, adding end marks, commas, quotation marks, or apostrophes.

1. Do you want to set up a clubhouse Fred asked Wayne

_____

_____

2. Fred pointed to the old tool shed the one that nobody used anymore

_____

3. We could paint it add rugs and pillows and hang out there said Fred

_____

4. So the boys began to clean out the shed which took several long dusty days

_____

5. Yuck yelled Wayne as he walked through sticky cobwebs

_____

6. After a few weeks they barely recognized that old shed

_____

7. Freds aunt gave them a rug Waynes mom gave them some old pillows

_____

8. They painted the door to say F & W Club Private Stay Out

_____

9. Its amazing how those boys turned that old shed into a perfect hideaway

_____

10. Now all we need is room service joked Wayne

_____

Read each pair of short sentences. Combine both ideas into one longer sentence.
Write the combined sentence using words from the box to join ideas.

and	because	but	for	neither	or	since
although	if	until	while	so	when	such as

1. The coach blows her whistle. The game stops.

_____

_____

2. Gina loves hip-hop music. Tony prefers salsa.

_____

_____

3. Arbor Day is in June. Labor Day is in September.

_____

_____

4. I selected a purple bedspread. Purple is my favorite color.

_____

_____

5. The traffic stops. The crossing guard escorts the children.

_____

_____

6. Abby enjoys writing poetry. Limericks are poems.

_____

_____

Mark the answer that has the same meaning as the expression in boldface.

1. Don't **beat around the bush** anymore.
   - Ⓐ avoid the main point
   - Ⓑ rake the leaves
   - Ⓒ repeat yourself
   - Ⓓ get frustrated

2. Let's wait until all this **blows over**.
   - Ⓐ comes apart
   - Ⓑ gets worse
   - Ⓒ exhales
   - Ⓓ passes

3. It's an enjoyable way to **break the ice**.
   - Ⓐ climb a mountain
   - Ⓑ relax and interact
   - Ⓒ chill the room
   - Ⓓ stop the arguing

4. We must never **cut corners** on safety.
   - Ⓐ be foolish
   - Ⓑ disagree
   - Ⓒ take shortcuts
   - Ⓓ get excited

5. Dan **got cold feet** at the last minute.
   - Ⓐ became brave
   - Ⓑ wore heavy socks
   - Ⓒ lost his nerve
   - Ⓓ stepped in a puddle

6. I'm totally ready to **hit the hay**.
   - Ⓐ go to bed
   - Ⓑ be a farmer
   - Ⓒ do my exercises
   - Ⓓ take a break

7. He's sick of **playing second fiddle**.
   - Ⓐ practicing country music
   - Ⓑ counting his blessings
   - Ⓒ hurrying
   - Ⓓ being the next best

8. That attitude makes them **see red**!
   - Ⓐ feel embarrassed
   - Ⓑ get angry
   - Ⓒ want to read
   - Ⓓ blush

9. Okay, it's time to **throw in the towel**.
   - Ⓐ do the laundry
   - Ⓑ give up
   - Ⓒ calm down
   - Ⓓ ask for seconds

10. That movie was really **for the birds**.
   - Ⓐ about nature
   - Ⓑ breezy and light
   - Ⓒ terrible
   - Ⓓ scary

Each sentence has a figure of speech in boldface. Think about what the words mean. Rewrite each sentence in your own words. Keep the same meaning without using the figure of speech.

1. When my parents saw the damage, they really **flew off the handle**.

_____

_____

2. The theater usher was **pulling my leg** when he said to fasten my seat belt.

_____

_____

3. That new suit **fits like a glove**.

_____

_____

4. I'd really like to join you, but can I **take a rain check** until later?

_____

_____

5. Dad was sorry, but he said it would **cost an arm and a leg**.

_____

_____

6. She was feeling **under the weather** so she stayed home from school.

_____

_____

To link ideas together smoothly, writers use signal words and phrases.
Mark the best signal word or phrase to fit each sentence.

1. It was the annual barbecue, _____ our entire family gathers for a picnic.

   Ⓐ with   Ⓒ when

   Ⓑ although   Ⓓ then

2. We always gather for this all-day party on the third Sunday in July, _____ what the weather may bring.

   Ⓐ despite   Ⓒ likewise

   Ⓑ because of Ⓓ during

3. The kids usually play _____ the adults prepare the food and visit.

   Ⓐ like   Ⓒ while

   Ⓑ during   Ⓓ since

4. Some of the older folks entertain by playing instruments, _____ the younger ones usually bring their own music.

   Ⓐ thus   Ⓒ although

   Ⓑ since   Ⓓ already

5. My favorite thing is the family tug-of-war, _____ one team is made up of everyone under 35, and the other team is made up of everyone over 35.

   Ⓐ in which   Ⓒ unless

   Ⓑ against   Ⓓ instead of

6. We always take group photos; _____ who'd believe that we were all there?

   Ⓐ otherwise Ⓒ now

   Ⓑ and   Ⓓ while

7. I usually don't eat meat, _____ that steak looked too good to resist.

   Ⓐ like   Ⓒ therefore

   Ⓑ but   Ⓓ since

8. There were pies of all kinds—_____ apple, peach, lemon, cherry, and berry.

   Ⓐ unlike   Ⓒ likewise

   Ⓑ then   Ⓓ namely

Writing

A **simile** is a form of figurative language used to compare two things. Use similes to link things in fresh, imaginative ways. Similes usually use the word *like* or the phrase *as _____ as.*

Ordinary statement:	*The scientist focused for hours.*
Simile with *like*:	*The scientist focused like a laser beam for hours.*
Simile with *as*:	*The scientist was as focused as a microscope for hours.*

Revise each statement by adding a simile. First try *like*. Then try *as _____ as.*

HINT: Visualize the idea to help you find ways to make better comparisons.

1. Grandpa walks slowly. _____

   _____

2. We gaped at the double rainbow. _____

   _____

3. That old sofa is worn. _____

   _____

4. The foxes slip away. _____

   _____

5. She works hard every day. _____

   _____

6. It was dusty at the building site. _____

   _____

A **metaphor** compares two things that seem unrelated.
A metaphor gets readers to understand or experience
one idea in terms of another in fresh or interesting ways.

Metaphor:	*Zach is a fish all summer long.*
Objects compared:	*Zach = fish*
Meaning conveyed:	*Zach spends a lot of time swimming.*

HINT: There are no rights and wrongs to writing metaphors—be creative!

A. Read each metaphor. Identify what is being compared by completing the
equation. Then explain the meaning of the metaphor in your own words.

1. That typewriter is a dinosaur. _____ = _____

   _____

2. My brother is a total couch potato. _____ = _____

   _____

3. The meal was a rock in my stomach. _____ = _____

   _____

B. Read each "plain" sentence below. Improve it by reworking it with a metaphor.

4. Trixie sleeps all day long. _____

   _____

5. The cadets marched in the midday heat. _____

   _____

6. Her salty tears fell as she read the letter. _____

   _____

When you **exaggerate**, you s-t-r-e-t-c-h the truth. Exaggeration makes things seem much bigger or smaller than they really are. Exaggerate to add humor, zing, and emphasis to your writing.

Plain: *Kevin was very hungry.*
Exaggerated: *Kevin wanted to order ninety hot dogs and ten watermelons.*

Make each sentence better by adding some exaggeration. It's fine to be funny!

HINT: Think of how tall tales, folk songs, and jokes use exaggeration.

1. The coat was too long.

_____

2. She parked far from the store.

_____

3. Our dog snores loudly.

_____

4. Maria was thirsty.

_____

5. We waited for a moment.

_____

6. The movie was long.

_____

7. I burned our dinner.

_____

8. The ride made him sick.

_____

Use this table to help you create original sentences. Pick a word or phrase from each column. Add details to weave them together into an interesting sentence. See the example below.

HINT: Arrange the sentence parts in any order that makes sense.

When?	Who/What?	Did What?	Where?	How?
after lunch	two horses	appeared	in the tunnel	easily
before dawn	a message	came forward	behind the house	fearlessly
during art	my neighbor	exploded	below the surface	foolishly
earlier	a package	raced	on a bus	in silence
last night	a siren	shrieked	over the hill	lovingly
on Tuesday	her sister	snuck	through the gate	modestly
yesterday	that stranger	warned	under the porch	with humor

1. _On Tuesday, the two horses fearlessly raced through the gate_
   to reach shelter.

2. _____

3. _____

4. _____

5. _____

6. _____

There are four types of sentences. Good writers use all four kinds.

A **declarative** sentence *declares* or states. It ends with **.** It is the most common kind of sentence.	An **interrogative** sentence *asks.* It ends with **?**	An **exclamatory** sentence *exclaims* or *cries out.* It conveys feelings. It ends with **!**	An **imperative** sentence *commands* or *requests.* It ends with **.** The subject is *You,* even if unwritten.

HINT: Pick the type of sentence that best conveys an idea.

A. Identify each sentence by its type.

1. Maria Tallchief was a Native American dancer. _____

2. Have you ever heard of her? _____

3. How famous she was in her time! _____

4. Look her up online. _____

5. Did you know she was born in Oklahoma? _____

6. I totally adore ballet! _____

7. Read this biography of Tallchief. _____

B. Write …

1. an *interrogative* sentence about Oklahoma.

_____

2. a *declarative* sentence about dance.

_____

3. an *exclamatory* sentence about a celebrity.

_____

4. an *imperative* sentence about proper behavior at a concert.

_____

Here are three kinds of sentence structures. Good writers alternate sentence structures for variety.

A **simple** sentence has one main clause, with one subject and one verb.	A **compound** sentence has two or more main clauses, usually linked with *and*, *or*, or *but*.	A **complex** sentence has one main clause and one or more subordinate clauses.
Nola plays the harp.	*Nola plays the harp, but she wants to learn the trombone.*	*After her lesson, Nola walked home, where she had a slice of cold pizza.*

HINT: Vary sentence structures to create paragraphs that are interesting to read.

A. Identify each sentence by its structure.

1. The ptarmigan is a unique bird.   _____

2. Although it is white in winter, it changes color in spring.   _____

3. Color can be good camouflage,
   but it won't always protect an animal.   _____

4. Stick insects look like branches,
   which helps them to get food.   _____

B. Write a sentence of each type on the given topic.

1. Write a *simple* sentence about insects.

   _____

2. Write a *compound* sentence about winter.

   _____

3. Write a *complex* sentence about a meal.

   _____

A powerful paragraph focuses on only one main idea or topic. It does not include extra information. The **main idea** is the most important point that readers should know and understand after reading your paragraph.

Read the paragraph. Then answer the questions below.

The Eiffel Tower

The famous Eiffel Tower in Paris, France, was built to be the entrance to the 1889 World's Fair. For several years, the 1,000-foot-tall wrought-iron tower was the tallest manmade structure in the world. But that title was awarded to the Chrysler Building in New York City when it was finished in 1930. The Seattle Space Needle and the Tokyo Skytree are other famous towers. To reach the top of the Eiffel Tower, visitors can either walk up 1,710 steps or take the elevator. The view of Paris from the top is magnificent! Consequently, more than 250 million people have visited the Eiffel Tower since it opened. In fact, it is the most-visited paid monument in the world.

1. What is the main idea of this paragraph?

   Ⓐ the 1889 World's Fair

   Ⓑ the Eiffel Tower

   Ⓒ Paris

   Ⓓ towers around the world

2. Which sentence is off topic and does not belong in this paragraph?

   _____

3. What additional information could be included in this paragraph?

   _____

   _____

   _____

A paragraph has *unity* when all its sentences relate to its main idea. Even a sentence that may be interesting and well-written just doesn't belong if it fails to support the main idea.

HINT: Imagine a paragraph as a team with one goal.
        Take out any ideas that are off-topic.

Read each paragraph. Each has a sentence that states its main idea. Underline it. Next, cross out the sentence that does not belong.

1. Tutankhamun ruled Egypt for less than ten years starting in about 1332 B.C. He reigned in the eighteenth dynasty of the New Kingdom. Although historians don't think that King Tut was an influential monarch in his day, a rare find in 1922 made him a celebrity. That was when archaeologist Howard Carter discovered the hidden tomb of the so-called Boy King. Carter died in 1939 at home in England. His findings were so spectacular that the whole world soon learned about King Tut and eagerly sought information about the treasures of his tomb.

2. Ancient Egypt was a land of many perils. Scorching heat was a fact of life. Deadly animals, such as lions, crocodiles, snakes, and scorpions, prowled regularly. The Nile River provided water, transportation, and fertile soil. There were floods, dust storms, and earthquakes. Little was known about the invisible causes of most diseases. So Egyptian healers gathered as much knowledge as they could about treating injury and disease. They mixed science with mythology and religion to come up with effective treatments for the body.

3. Natron, a type of salt, was a primary ingredient in the process of mummification. It normally took up to three months to bury a pharaoh after his death. The delay was due to the many steps of the embalming process, which began with removal of the internal organs. Then the body was soaked for up to ten weeks in a drying solution. After that, the dried body was wrapped in a layer of linen bandages. Atop that layer, amulets were set in specific places to protect against evil. Then the body was wrapped in a second layer of wider bandages. These bandages were soaked in resin and aromatic oils.

Supporting details add information about the main idea. They make your paragraph stronger and more interesting.

Read each topic sentence below. Then write two sentences with supporting details that could be included in a paragraph about it.

1. My favorite season is fall for several reasons.

   Ⓐ _____

   Ⓑ _____

2. I think lions are fascinating animals.

   Ⓐ _____

   Ⓑ _____

3. Our town held a huge celebration on the Fourth of July.

   Ⓐ _____

   Ⓑ _____

4. Living in a big city sounds very exciting.

   Ⓐ _____

   Ⓑ _____

The **topic sentence** is usually the first sentence of a paragraph. It clearly states the main idea of the paragraph while grabbing the reader's attention.

Read the paragraph. Then answer the questions below.

On the Fast Track

Have you ever wanted to know what it's like to drive really, really fast? Danica Patrick has dreamed of driving fast ever since she was a young girl. Growing up in Roscoe, Illinois, Patrick raced go-karts. She even won the World Karting Association Grand National Championship in three different years. These early experiences led her to racing cars as an adult. Danica Patrick became one of the most influential drivers in race-car history! She has carved out a path for a whole generation of female race-car drivers.

1. How does the writer grab the reader's attention and introduce the topic?

_____

_____

2. What is the main idea of the paragraph?

_____

_____

3. Write another sentence the writer could use to grab the reader's attention.

_____

_____

The **concluding sentence** comes at the end of your paragraph. It often restates the topic sentence in a different way. New ideas should not be part of the conclusion.

Read the paragraph. Underline the topic sentence. Then finish the paragraph by writing a concluding sentence on the lines below.

Dangers of Scuba Diving

Scuba diving sounds fun and exciting, but it can be dangerous, too. Divers need to be aware of many different dangers, such as strong underwater currents. These currents can carry divers away from the group. In addition, sea life can also introduce problems. Divers may get cut on the sharp edges of coral. Or they may get nervous swimming near large fish and sharks. Even coming to the surface can be dangerous. If divers swim to the surface too quickly, they may experience muscle cramps or other more serious problems.

_____

_____

_____

_____

Your introduction should summarize the main point about the topic in the paragraph. The sentence containing the main idea is also called the **topic sentence**. The concluding sentence restates the topic sentence.

Read the paragraph. Then answer the questions below.

The Panama Canal

(1) The Panama Canal changed ocean travel for people and goods. (2) The American-built canal connected the Atlantic and Pacific Oceans. (3) Ships no longer needed to go all the way around South America. (4) Instead, they could take a shortcut through the Panama Canal. (5) Before the canal was finished in 1914, an ocean trip from California to New York took 60 days. (6) Thousands of ships cross this "seventh wonder of the modern world" every year. (7) The trip was 13,000 miles long.

(8) Passing through the Panama Canal, the trip is shortened by about 7,000 miles and 30 days.

1. Which sentence in the paragraph is the topic sentence?

_____

2. What is the main idea of the text?

_____

3. Write a sentence that could be added to the introduction to explain why the Panama Canal was built.

_____

_____

4. Which sentence is the concluding sentence and should be moved to the end of the paragraph?

_____

Transitional words and phrases help connect your ideas. Without transitions, the reader might not understand how sentences relate to each other.

Add transitional words or phrases from the box to complete the paragraph below.

To introduce an idea	To give more details	To indicate time
So	In addition	After
For that reason	Also	Before
As a result	I should also mention (that)	Later

A Bright Light

Famous inventor Thomas Edison was born in 1847. Edison wanted to create innovations

that would change the world. _____ , he designed the
                                        (1)

light bulb. _____ , people used candles to see in the dark.
                        (2)

_____ , light bulbs powered by electricity changed the way people
            (3)

lived and worked. _____ , Edison invented the phonograph and
                              (4)

kinetograph, among several other important inventions. You might know them by their other

names—the record player and movie camera.

Write a short paragraph to describe an invention that you think changed the world. Use transitional words or phrases to connect your ideas.

_____

_____

_____

Transitional words and phrases connect one idea with another. They can add emphasis, show similarities or contrasts, make comparisons, or indicate results.

Look at this chart of transitional words and phrases. Then fill in the blanks below with linking words or phrases from the chart.

Emphasis	Similarity	Contrasts	Comparisons	Results/Reasons
also	similarly	although	like	because of
in addition	specifically	instead	meanwhile	for that reason
moreover				

The Hoover Dam

The Hoover Dam lies on the border between Arizona and Nevada. It was built to control the floodwaters of the Colorado River. Construction was dangerous. Men hung from 800-foot-high canyon walls. They _____ (1) worked in 120-degree heat. More than 21,000 workers helped build the dam. _____ (2) , the government created Boulder City to house all these workers. _____ (3) , it built roads between the town and the dam. _____ (4) the Southwest is still mostly desert, many people live there. _____ (5) the Hoover Dam, there's enough water and power for everybody.

When writing a paragraph, make sure the sentences follow a logical order.

Read the sentences below. Number them in the order that makes the most sense.
The first sentence has been numbered for you.

_____ Both companies hired thousands of workers to perform the extremely
dangerous construction.

___1___ Around the mid-1800s, many trains were already operating in the eastern United States.

_____ In January 1863, the Central Pacific Railroad began laying tracks in Sacramento,
California, and worked eastward.

_____ Union Pacific workers crossed hot deserts and faced angry Native Americans,
whose lands had been taken away.

_____ Eighteen months later, the Union Pacific started in Omaha, Nebraska,
moving westward.

_____ On that day, Leland Stanford, president of the Central Pacific Railroad, hammered
in the Golden Spike that joined the rails of the Transcontinental Railroad.

_____ But more and more people were moving westward, so the country needed
a railroad that would connect the East to the West.

_____ The First Transcontinental Railroad was completed on May 10, 1869, at
Promontory Point, Utah.

_____ Officials then sent a telegraph message to the East and West Coasts,
simply saying, "Done."

_____ Central Pacific workers blasted solid rock to tunnel through mountains.

When writing a story, tell the events in **sequence**, or time order. Some words and phrases to transition from one event to the next include: *first, next, last, then, afterwards, before, at the same time, meanwhile, as soon as, during, in the meantime, later.*

Read the paragraph. Then answer the questions below.

First, Don't Panic!

(**1**) Major Stevens gave some pointers to the student astronauts. (**2**) He said, "Your tether on a spacewalk will probably never break. (**3**) But just in case, here's what you do. (**4**) First, stay calm. (**5**) Second, try to grab it. (**6**) Third, try to reach one of the handles on the spacecraft. (**7**) Fourth, throw a tool away from the spacecraft. (**8**) The force will propel you toward the craft. (**9**) Fifth, activate your manned maneuvering unit (MMU). (**10**) _____ it's working, steer back to the craft. (**11**) _____, your partner on the spacewalk will attach several tethers together. (**12**) He or she will try to reach you."

1. What other sequence word could you use in sentence 6 instead of the word *third*?

_____

2. What sequence words or phrases can you use in sentences 10 and 11?

_____

3. Imagine that the tether on an astronaut's space walk breaks and the procedure described above doesn't work. Brainstorm a plot idea for what happens next to the astronaut.

_____

_____

_____

_____

_____

Whether you're writing an opinion or an informative text, choose a topic that interests you. Make sure the topic is not too broad and that you can support it with facts and details.

Read the broad topics below. Try to narrow them down to something more specific. The first one has been done for you.

Here I go again!

Broad		Narrow		Narrower
1. sports	→	_extreme sports_	→	_rock climbing_
2. weather	→	_____	→	_____
3. holidays	→	_____	→	_____
4. news	→	_____	→	_____
5. architecture	→	_____	→	_____
6. books	→	_____	→	_____
7. space	→	_____	→	_____
8. mountains	→	_____	→	_____
9. the Internet	→	_____	→	_____
10. movies	→	_____	→	_____

Circle the topic that interests you the most. Write a topic sentence about it.

_____

_____

To help you plan your informative text, ask yourself questions about your topic. What do you know about the topic? What else do you want to know? How can you find the answers?

Use the chart to complete the activities below.

The Golden Gate Bridge	
Questions	**Answers**
What two places does the bridge connect?	The city of San Francisco and Marin County, across the Golden Gate Strait
How was the bridge designed?	

1. Which detail provides an answer to the second question in the chart?

   Ⓐ The U.S. Navy wanted to paint the bridge black with yellow stripes.

   Ⓑ About 55 people work full time to paint and repair the bridge.

   Ⓒ Two cables suspended from the steel towers support the roadway.

   Ⓓ Over 2 million cars have crossed the bridge.

2. Think of two other questions about the Golden Gate Bridge. Write them in the chart and find the answers to them.

To prepare for writing an opinion text, use an organizer to brainstorm reasons that support your opinion.

Choose a topic you have a strong opinion about. Write it in the topic box. Write your opinion in the appropriate box. Then list reasons that support your opinion.

Topic:

Opinion:

Reason 1:

Reason 2:

Reason 3:

Plan a story for each title below. Fill in the blocks with your ideas for the story's setting, as well as the beginning, middle, and end.

Lost in the Woods!

Setting:		
Beginning	**Middle**	**End**

In the Old Trunk

Setting:		
Beginning	**Middle**	**End**

Develop a character for a story. Use this character map to figure out what this character is like.

Personality

_____

_____

_____

_____

_____

Looks

_____

_____

_____

_____

_____

Character's Name:

Age:	Gender:

Habits

_____

_____

_____

_____

_____

Feelings

_____

_____

_____

_____

_____

You can use a chart to gather details before you write. Later, you can use the words to express your ideas vividly. Complete the chart for a whale watch off Cape Cod.

Watching for Whales in the Atlantic Ocean

Emotion Words	Five-Senses Words	Setting Details	People Details
curious	salty smell	choppy sea	crusty captain
	mist on glasses		

For a school project, Regina plans to write about the Navajo. She starts her planning by making these notes. Use the notes to answer the questions that follow.

The Navajo

1. The Navajo settled in the Southwest around 1000 A.D.

2. In the Navajo language, the word *Diné* means "the people."

3. Among Diné families, the closest ties are to the mother's clan.

4. Today, you can buy Navajo jewelry from tourist shops and catalogs.

5. The Navajo were mainly farmers, but they also hunted and gathered food.

6. In the 1600s, the Navajo adopted sheep, goats, and horses from Spanish settlers.

7. The women wove blankets and rugs.

1. Which of these details does not belong in Regina's notes?

   Ⓐ Among Diné families, the closest ties are to the mother's clan.
   Ⓑ In the 1600s, the Navajo adopted sheep, goats, and horses from Spanish settlers.
   Ⓒ The Navajo were mainly farmers, but they also hunted and gathered food.
   Ⓓ Today, you can buy Navajo jewelry from tourist shops and catalogs.

2. Which detail best fits with Regina's notes and could be added?

   Ⓐ The first Spanish explorer to reach the Southwest was Francisco Coronado.
   Ⓑ The Pueblo and the Hopi also lived in the Southwest.
   Ⓒ The Navajo lived in hogans made of sticks and mud or adobe.
   Ⓓ The Navajo reservation is one of many in the United States.

3. Which of these would help Regina write her paper?

   Ⓐ Looking up the Navajo in an online encyclopedia
   Ⓑ Going to a store to look for Navajo jewelry
   Ⓒ Searching the Internet for information about "Spanish settlers"
   Ⓓ Reading newspapers to check for articles about Navajo businesses

4. Based on these notes, what does Regina plan to write?

   Ⓐ A story that tells about a visit to a Navajo village
   Ⓑ A report that describes what life was like for the Navajo
   Ⓒ A newspaper story that tells about an event in a Navajo town
   Ⓓ A report that explains what Spanish explorers found in the Southwest

Claude wrote this profile of Mark Twain. Read the draft and think about ways to improve the writing. Then answer the questions that follow.

Mark Twain: Literary Giant

(1) Mark Twain was the first great literary voice in America. (2) He recorded the history and culture of America in his writing, and brings to life all sorts of characters based on people he knew and met. (3) Born in 1835 as Samuel Clemens, Twain lived through the Civil War and joined the Confederate Army. (4) His various careers included riverboat pilot, prospector, and newspaper reporter.

(5) Mark Twain achieved fame by writing humorous fiction, and his work is still enjoyed by young and old today. (6) His most famous works include *The Adventures of Tom Sawyer* and *Adventures of Huckleberry Finn*. (7) Both of these novels is modeled on his childhood in Hannibal, Missouri. (8) He also wrote *The Prince and the Pauper* and *A Connecticut Yankee in King Arthur's Court*, who criticize the way people treat the poor and disadvantaged.

1. What change, if any, should be made in sentence 2?

   Ⓐ Change *brings* to *brought*.

   Ⓑ Insert *those* before *people*.

   Ⓒ Change *knew* to *knows*.

   Ⓓ Make no change.

2. What sentence could best be added after sentence 3 to add more detail?

   Ⓐ However, he didn't like soldiering and left the army after two weeks.

   Ⓑ His father died when he was eleven years old.

   Ⓒ In Hannibal, Missouri, you can visit Mark Twain's boyhood home.

   Ⓓ He enjoyed playing pranks as a child.

3. What change, if any, should be made in sentence 7?

   Ⓐ Change *Both* to *All*.

   Ⓑ Change *these* to *them*.

   Ⓒ Change *is* to *were*.

   Ⓓ Make no change.

4. What word or words should you use to replace *who* in sentence 8?

   Ⓐ in which

   Ⓑ whereas

   Ⓒ both

   Ⓓ which

Here is the first draft of an informational paper.
Use it to answer the questions on the following page.

Hurricane Katrina and New Orleans

(1) Hurricane Katrina has been called one of the worst natural disaster in the history of the United States. (2) When the storm striked in 2005, no place was harder hit than New Orleans, Louisiana. (3) The wind tore off roofs and wooden siding like it was peeling an orange. (4) Then, the worst disaster of all happened.

(5) New Orleans is about five feet below sea level. (6) A series of levees protect the city from flood waters that might come in from lakes and the ocean. (7) But on August 29 and 30 the levees broke, and water flowed into the city. (8) Soon 80 percent of the city was covered in filthy water. (9) The water tossed cars around like toys, and homes floated from one lot to another. (10) The wind crunched up wooden homes like huge piles of pickup sticks.

(11) After the storm, there was no drinking water or electricity. (12) There was little food and no way to get around except by boat. (13) The storm snuffed out the life of the city like it was blowing out a candle.

(14) Many people left New Orleans before the storm, but others did not. (15) Some older people wanted to stay and brave the storm as they had with Hurricane Betsy forty years earlier. (16) Others were too poor to pay for transportation out of harm's way. (17) Many people watched the storm on television.

(18) People crowded together in the Superdome and the New Orleans convention center for safety. (19) Others sought high places like highway overpasses and bridges. (20) When the storm ended, everyone had to be bused or flown out of the city until it was safe to return. (21) Many people from New Orleans moved to other parts of the United States until their city could be put back together.

1. What change should be made in sentence 2?

   (A) Change *When* to *After*.

   (B) Change *striked* to *struck*.

   (C) Remove the comma after 2005.

   (D) Change *harder* to *hardly*.

2. What sentence can be added to state the main idea in paragraph 2?

   (A) The storm was violent and destructive.

   (B) People knew the storm was coming, but many did not leave.

   (C) Cars and homes were abandoned.

   (D) People were frightened by the high winds.

3. Which sentence does not belong in paragraph 4?

   (A) Sentence 14

   (B) Sentence 15

   (C) Sentence 16

   (D) Sentence 17

4. What word could replace the word *left* in sentence 14 to give the sentence more meaning?

   (A) examined

   (B) evacuated

   (C) evaded

   (D) excused

5. Which transition phrase should be added to the beginning of sentence 18 to improve the last paragraph?

   (A) In spite of the storm,

   (B) Of course,

   (C) During and after the storm,

   (D) As a matter of fact,

Here is the first draft of a personal narrative that Emilio wrote. It contains mistakes. Read the narrative to answer the questions on the following page.

The Lady Next Door

(1) That lady next door never seemed to like me very much. (2) I've been walking my dog past her yard for months, and whenever she sees me, she shoos us away. (3) "Keep off my lawn!" she yells, and then she slams the door. (4) This has been going on for a long time.

(5) I've tried to be nice to her, but I think she just doesn't like my dog. (6) The dog I had before this one was a black Labrador. (7) She might even be afraid of it.

(8) Then our relationship changed drastic yesterday. (9) When I came home from school, I saw her standing by the side of the house in the driveway trying to see inside the window. (10) She looks worried, so I put down my books and walk into her driveway.

(11) "Is anything wrong?" I asked.

(12) She said, "I'm locked out, and I have something burning on the stove. (13) I can't get through the window because it's too small."

(14) I said, "I'll climb through it for you."

(15) She looked at me in great relief and actually smiled at me for the first time. (16) She said, "Would you do that?"

(17) Instead of answering, I picked up a plastic milk crate, put it next to the window, and climbed up. (18) I hoisted myself through the opening and scrunched my body inside. (19) As I stood up in the kitchen, I saw some bacon burning on the stovetop. (20) I turned off the burner and then opened the back door.

(21) As my neighbor hurried in, she looked at me and asked, "What is your name?"

(22) "Emilio," I said.

(23) She took my hand and said, "Then thank you very much, Emilio."

(24) I left rather quickly. (25) Frankly, I still didn't trust her to be nice to me.

(26) But the next day when I walked the dog past her house, she didn't yell or slam the door. (27) She just waved a little shyly.

1. Which sentence contains a detail that is unimportant to the story?

   Ⓐ Sentence 2   Ⓒ Sentence 6

   Ⓑ Sentence 4   Ⓓ Sentence 9

2. Which is the best revision of sentence 8?

   Ⓐ Then our drastic relationship changed yesterday.

   Ⓑ Then our relationship changed drasticly yesterday.

   Ⓒ Yesterday, then our relationship changed drastical.

   Ⓓ But then yesterday, our relationship changed drastically.

3. How should the writer revise this sentence in the third paragraph?

   She looks worried, so I put down my books and walk into her driveway.

   Ⓐ She looked worried, so I put down my books and walked into her driveway.

   Ⓑ She is looking worried, so I am putting down my books and walking into her driveway.

   Ⓒ She was looking worried, so I was putting down my books and walked into her driveway.

   Ⓓ She looked worried, so I put down my books and walk into her driveway.

4. How can these two sentences best be combined?

   I left rather quickly. Frankly, I still didn't trust her to be nice to me.

   Ⓐ I left rather quickly so, frankly, I still didn't trust her to be nice to me.

   Ⓑ I left rather quickly because, frankly, I still didn't trust her to be nice to me.

   Ⓒ I left rather quickly while frankly, I still didn't trust her to be nice to me.

   Ⓓ I left rather quickly when frankly, I still didn't trust her to be nice to me.

5. Which sentence would be a good ending to this story?

   Ⓐ It's too weird.

   Ⓑ My dog likes her, too.

   Ⓒ And everyone lived happily ever after.

   Ⓓ I guess that's a good start.

Luisa wrote the letter below to her town newspaper. It contains some mistakes. Read the letter then answer the questions on the following page.

To the Editor:

(1) I am a fifth-grade student at East Bakerley Middle School. (2) I own a three-year-old Labrador named Susie, and I often exercise her on Upton's Field. (3) I was very upset to read your editorial about dogs and that well-loved piece of land ("Let's Keep Roaming Dogs Out of Upton's Field," April 8).

(4) You state that dogs have become a pest on Upton's Field. (5) You also state that Upton's Field is a park, and that people should stick to the rules. (6) You seem to think that one of those rules is that dogs should be kept on a leash.

(7) I take good care of Susie. (8) She loves Upton's Field and does not bother anyone. (9) Maybe some dogs are pests, like you say. (10) Must all dogs and dog-owners suffer because a few people can't keep control of their pets?

(11) Dogs have been running free on Upton's Field for nearly 100 years. (12) It is traditional. (13) In 1912, a farmer named Elias Upton gave the land to the people of our town. (14) In his will, he stated that the citizens of Bakerley should always be allowed to graze animals on it and use it for recreation. (15) Mr. Upton was ninety-eight when he died.

(16) Upton's Field is not a park. (17) Elias Upton did not say anything about keeping dogs on leashes, and lots of people see letting their dogs go for a run as good recreation. (18) I think Mr. Upton would have felt the same way.

Luisa Suarez
Bakerley, CA

1. Which sentence is off topic and should be taken out of the fourth paragraph?

   Ⓐ Sentence 12   Ⓒ Sentence 14

   Ⓑ Sentence 13   Ⓓ Sentence 15

2. Which transition should be added to the beginning of sentence 10 to help connect the ideas in the paragraph?

   Ⓐ Even so,   Ⓒ Whatever,

   Ⓑ On the other hand,   Ⓓ Although,

3. Which sentence below should be added to support the ideas in the fifth paragraph?

   Ⓐ Parks have fountains and flowerbeds.

   Ⓑ Dogs can't tell the difference between parks and open fields.

   Ⓒ It does not have the same rules as a park.

   Ⓓ Upton's Field is a field named after Mr. Upton.

4. The writer wants to add the following sentence to the letter:

   With respect, I disagree with you.

   Where should this detail be added to organize the ideas correctly?

   Ⓐ After sentence 3   Ⓒ After sentence 5

   Ⓑ After sentence 4   Ⓓ After sentence 6

5. The writer wants to add a new paragraph to her letter. Which topic should be added after the last paragraph to keep the letter focused on the main idea?

   Ⓐ A detailed description of Susie, the writer's dog

   Ⓑ Suggested ways to keep Upton's Field open for dogs

   Ⓒ A set of rules for city parks that everyone should follow

   Ⓓ Recommended schedules and activities for exercising dogs

Read the letter from Shannon. Choose the word or words that correctly fit in each blank.

July 30

Dear Isabel,

We finally got to Acadia National Park a couple of days ago, and it's beautiful. We are staying in a small cottage on the ocean in ____(1)____.

On Thursday we took a long hike and ____(2)____ Cadillac Mountain. It was really hot and very tiring, but the view from the top made the effort worthwhile. On Friday we rented bicycles and rode for miles along these dirt roads that ____(3)____ about a hundred years ago for horse-drawn carriages.

Last night we were sitting in a restaurant and the power ____(4)____ went off! At first it was kind of scary, but then it turned out to be fun. The waiters lit candles for us, and everybody in the restaurant talked together. We were almost sorry to see the lights come back on!

I miss you, Isabel. I wish you were here.

Love,

Shannon

---

1. Which answer goes in blank 1?

Ⓐ Bar Harbor, Maine

Ⓑ Bar harbor, Maine

Ⓒ Bar Harbor, maine

Ⓓ Bar Harbor Maine

2. Which answer goes in blank 2?

Ⓐ climed

Ⓑ climbed

Ⓒ climmed

Ⓓ clymed

3. Which answer goes in blank 3?

Ⓐ were builded

Ⓑ built

Ⓒ was built

Ⓓ were built

4. Which answer goes in blank 4?

Ⓐ sudden

Ⓑ more sudden

Ⓒ suddenly

Ⓓ suddenest

For questions 1–12, choose the best answer to each question.

1. Which is a complete sentence?

   Ⓐ Mario and his three friends.

   Ⓑ A long walk to the library.

   Ⓒ Arrived just before five o'clock.

   Ⓓ It closes early on Fridays.

2. Read the following sentence. What is the *best* way to rewrite the sentence?

   > Geckos are interesting pets, so they are active only at night.

   Ⓐ Geckos are interesting pets, or they are active only at night.

   Ⓑ Geckos are interesting pets, but they are active only at night.

   Ⓒ Geckos are interesting pets, until they are active only at night.

   Ⓓ Leave as is.

3. Which sentence below is written correctly?

   Ⓐ "Don't move!" shouted the zookeeper.

   Ⓑ "Don't move! shouted the zookeeper."

   Ⓒ "Don't move" shouted the zookeeper!

   Ⓓ Don't move! "shouted the zookeeper."

4. In the sentence below, which word is the subject?

   > On Sunday, Dad took us to the baseball game.

   Ⓐ Sunday

   Ⓑ Dad

   Ⓒ us

   Ⓓ game

5. Which word best fits in the blank in the sentence below?

   > Danny noticed that one of the twins _____ missing.

   Ⓐ were

   Ⓑ isn't

   Ⓒ was

   Ⓓ are

6. In the sentence below, which underlined word is not spelled correctly?

   > Our <u>neighbors</u> <u>invited</u> us to their house
   >   Ⓐ   Ⓑ
   > for <u>dinner</u> on <u>Saterday</u>.
   >   Ⓒ   Ⓓ

   (continued)

7. What is the best way to combine the sentences below?

> Drew picked up the books.
> He picked them up quickly.
> He put them back on the shelf.

Ⓐ Drew quickly picked up the books and put them back on the shelf.

Ⓑ Drew picked up the books and quickly put them back on the shelf.

Ⓒ Drew picked up and put back the books on the shelf quickly.

Ⓓ Quickly, Drew picked up the books on the shelf and put them back.

8. Which sentence is written correctly?

Ⓐ Nina and I changed mine clothes.

Ⓑ Nina and me changed her clothes.

Ⓒ Nina and I changed our clothes.

Ⓓ Nina and me changed our clothes.

9. Which sentence below is an imperative sentence?

Ⓐ Was that barn red?

Ⓑ Paint the walls first.

Ⓒ The door is huge.

Ⓓ What a beautiful building!

10. What is the correct way to write the following book title if you include it in a report?

Ⓐ "A Guide to North American Wildlife"

Ⓑ A Guide to North American Wildlife

Ⓒ "A Guide to North American Wildlife"

Ⓓ A Guide to North American Wildlife

11. Which word best fits in the blank in the sentence below?

> Mr. Wyman thinks that _____ the best candidate.

Ⓐ your

Ⓑ yore

Ⓒ you're

Ⓓ you'll

12. Which sentence is written correctly?

Ⓐ Sheldon is the most nice person I know.

Ⓑ Sheldon is the most nicest person I know.

Ⓒ Sheldon is the nicest person I know.

Ⓓ Sheldon is the more nicer person I know.

Vocabulary

A **synonym** is a word that means the same or almost the same thing as another word.

| veto | variable | receptacle | quiver | blunder |
| rash | novice | outstanding | generally | hazardous |

If you **veto** something, you say no to it.

When you are careless, you are **rash**.

Something that is **variable** means it is likely to change.

A **novice** is a beginner.

A **receptacle** is a container.

Something that is **outstanding** is extremely good.

If you **quiver**, you shake.

Generally means "usually."

A **blunder** is a mistake.

When something is **hazardous**, it is dangerous.

A. Read the vocabulary word.
Find and circle three other words that mean almost the same thing.

1. **quiver**	tremble	stop	shake	shiver
2. **hazardous**	hazelnut	harmful	risky	dangerous
3. **novice**	newcomer	expert	beginner	learner
4. **blunder**	error	mistake	noisy	misjudgment
5. **generally**	commonly	usually	mostly	generous
6. **outstanding**	notable	important	remarkable	outside
7. **rash**	careful	foolhardy	reckless	careless
8. **veto**	prohibit	permit	forbid	ban

B. Write a vocabulary word for each clue.

1. what the weather is from day to day _____

2. a good place for trash _____

veto	variable	receptacle	quiver	blunder
rash	novice	outstanding	generally	hazardous

Write a vocabulary word that is a synonym for each word on the list.
Then use the words to help you get through the maze.

1. foolish _____

2. ban _____

3. holder _____

4. injurious _____

5. first-timer _____

6. exceptional _____

7. customarily _____

8. blooper _____

9. shudder _____

10. unstable _____

Start   Finish

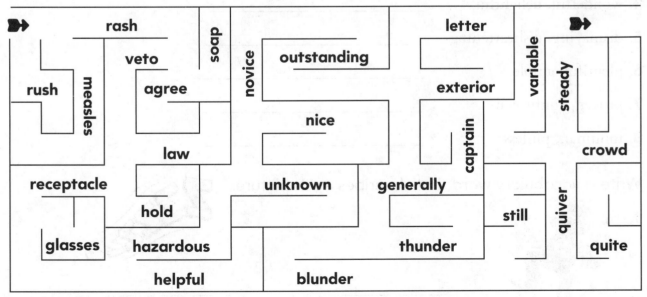

A **synonym** is a word that means the same or almost the same as another word.

brutal	daunting	treacherous	bewildered	bountiful
blissful	valid	cumbersome	dormant	ceaseless

Brutal means "cruel."

If you are very happy, you are **blissful**.

If a task is **daunting**, it is discouraging.

Something that is **valid** is true.

When someone is **treacherous**, that person cannot be trusted.

Something that is **cumbersome** is heavy and difficult to move.

A person who is **bewildered** is very confused.

When an animal is **dormant**, it is sleeping.

Bountiful means "plentiful."

Something that is **ceaseless** is unending.

A. Read the words in each row.
  Write a vocabulary word that means almost the same thing.

1. continuing, perpetual _____

2. puzzled, perplexed _____

3. deceptive, traitorous _____

4. wonderful, delightful _____

5. dismaying, disheartening _____

6. plentiful, ample _____

7. proven, confirmed _____

8. inhuman, pitiless _____

B. Write a vocabulary word that describes each picture.

1.  **2.**

_____   _____

| brutal | daunting | treacherous | bewildered | bountiful |
| blissful | valid | cumbersome | dormant | ceaseless |

Play a game of Move On. Find a word in the first box that does not have the same meaning as the other three words. Move that word to the next box by writing it on the blank line. The first one is done for you. Continue until you reach the last box. Complete the sentence in that box.

Start here.

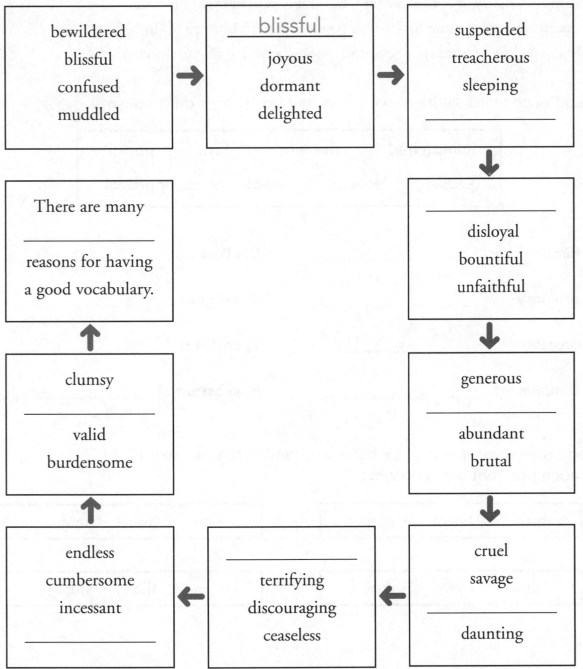

bewildered
blissful
confused
muddled

→

blissful
joyous
dormant
delighted

→

suspended
treacherous
sleeping
_____

↓

_____
disloyal
bountiful
unfaithful

↓

generous
_____
abundant
brutal

↓

There are many
_____
reasons for having
a good vocabulary.

↑

clumsy
_____
valid
burdensome

↑

endless
cumbersome
incessant
_____

←

_____
terrifying
discouraging
ceaseless

←

cruel
savage
_____
daunting

An **antonym** is a word that means the opposite of another word.

compliment	unique	flimsy	allow	fatigue
criticism	ordinary	substantial	prohibit	vigor

You give a **compliment** when you say something positive about someone or something, but offer **criticism** when you say an unfavorable remark.

If something is **unique**, it is one of a kind, but something **ordinary** is common.

If something is **flimsy**, it is weak or frail, but if it is **substantial**, it is solid.

Allow means to permit something to happen, while **prohibit** means "forbid."

Fatigue is a feeling of great tiredness, and **vigor** is a feeling of great strength.

A. Read each word. Write a word from the box that is an antonym.

unmatched	prevent	firm	permit
praise	energy	weak	disapproval

1. flimsy _____   5. allow _____

2. ordinary _____   6. fatigue _____

3. prohibit _____   7. criticism _____

4. compliment _____   8. substantial _____

B. Read the words in each box below. Underline the two words in each box that are antonyms.

1. | exhaustion   vigor   vitamin | 3. | union   usual   unique |

2. | allow   give   forbid | 4. | enemy   flimsy   sturdy |

criticism	unique	flimsy	allow	fatigue
compliment	ordinary	substantial	prohibit	vigor

A. Write the best word from the box to complete each sentence.

1. Wendy gave Jack a _____ when his project won a prize.

2. The neighbors don't _____ us to play ball on their lawn.

3. Don is always full of vim and _____ .

4. Although it was an _____ glass, Mom was sorry about breaking it.

5. After a hard workout, Noah felt a sense of _____ .

6. The owner is happy because her shop made a _____ profit this year.

7. Those signs _____ cars from driving in the park at certain hours.

8. The piano student knew she would receive _____ because she hadn't practiced.

9. Each piece of pottery is _____ because it is made by hand.

10. Everyone was annoyed when the girls gave only a _____ excuse for being late.

B. Read each question. Choose the best answer.

1. Which one is the most substantial? ☐ tent ☐ house ☐ hut

2. Which one is pleasing? ☐ complaint ☐ criticism ☐ compliment

3. What causes fatigue? ☐ jumping ☐ sleeping ☐ resting

4. Which painting is unique? ☐ copy ☐ original ☐ reproduction

An **antonym** is a word that means the opposite of another word.

frisky	permanent	tiresome	considerate	sensible
sluggish	unstable	interesting	heedless	ridiculous

Frisky means "lively," but **sluggish** means "slow."

Permanent means "lasting."

Unstable means "unsteady."

If something is **tiresome**, it's boring; if it holds your attention, it's **interesting**.

Someone who is **considerate** is thoughtful, but someone who is **heedless** is not.

If you're **sensible**, you're wise, and if you're silly, you're **ridiculous**.

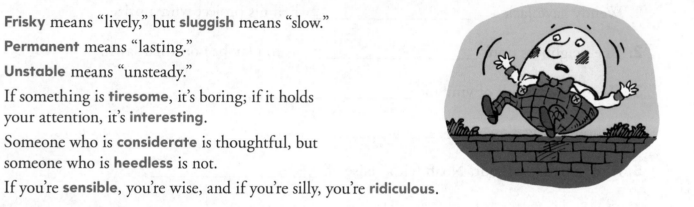

A. Read the word in the first column.
  Find and circle the word in the row that is an antonym.

1. frisky	frittering	freezing	inactive
2. unstable	unable	precarious	settled
3. ridiculous	wise	laughable	rickety
4. interesting	boring	inviting	intense
5. sensible	logical	separate	ridiculous
6. considerate	careful	continuing	thoughtless

B. Read the word in the first column. Circle the word that is an antonym,
  and underline the word that is a synonym.

1. permanent	**a.** unsettled	**b.** stable	**c.** perfect
2. sluggish	**a.** hit	**b.** lazy	**c.** playful
3. heedless	**a.** thoughtful	**b.** headless	**c.** inconsiderate
4. tiresome	**a.** dull	**b.** talkative	**c.** fascinating

frisky	permanent	tiresome	considerate	sensible
sluggish	unstable	interesting	heedless	ridiculous

Play Tic-Tac-Antonym. Read each vocabulary word. Then draw a line through three words in the box that are antonyms for that word. Your line can be vertical, horizontal, or diagonal.

1. frisky

busy	nosy	playful
slow	sluggish	idle
happy	frilly	frizzy

2. sensible

rowdy	smart	absurd
serious	neat	rash
sensitive	sorry	ridiculous

3. permanent

perfect	fearful	temporary
lasting	unstable	curly
impermanent	forever	perfume

4. interesting

intentional	delightful	exceptional
exciting	curious	investing
dull	tiresome	uninteresting

5. considerate

inattentive	careless	heedless
impressed	fragile	casual
gifted	hopeful	concerned

A **compound word** is a word made up of two smaller words put together.

earthquake	**vine**yard	**whirl**pool	**head**quarters	**guide**book
touchdown	**blue**print	**spell**bound	**master**piece	**wind**shield

An **earthquake** is a shaking of the ground caused by a movement of the plates beneath Earth's surface.

A **touchdown** is a score in a football game.

A **vineyard** is a field where grapes are grown.

A **blueprint** is a plan for a building.

A **whirlpool** is a current of water that spins around rapidly.

Spellbound means "enchanted."

A **headquarters** is a command post for a group.

A **masterpiece** is something made with great skill.

A **guidebook** is a book of information for tourists.

The front window of a car is called a **windshield**.

A. Complete each sentence with a vocabulary word.

1. A shield from the wind is a _____.

2. A book that's a guide is a _____.

3. A quake of the earth is an _____.

4. A print that is blue is a _____.

5. A yard where vines grow is a _____.

6. A pool that whirls around is a _____.

7. A piece by a master is a _____.

B. Write the two words that make up each compound word.

1. headquarters   **2. touchdown**   **3. spellbound**

_____   _____   _____

_____   _____   _____

earthquake	vineyard	whirlpool	headquarters	guidebook
touchdown	blueprint	spellbound	masterpiece	windshield

Write the vocabulary word for each clue. Then write the circled letters on the numbered lines at the bottom of the page to answer the riddle.

What goes up and down but doesn't move?

1. a natural disaster _ (○) _ _ _ _ _ _ _ _

2. found above a car hood _ _ _ (○) _ _ _ _ _

3. a great work of art _ _ (○) _ _ _ _ _ _ _

4. a kind of farm _ _ _ _ (○) _ _ _

5. dangerous water _ (○) _ _ _ _ _ _ _

6. a diagram of a place _ _ _ (○) _ _ _ _

7. between the goalposts _ _ _ (○) _ _ _ _ _

8. a kind of office _ _ _ _ (○) _ _ _ _ _ _

9. fascinated (○) _ _ _ _ _ _ _ _

10. a handy book for travelers _ _ _ (○) _ _ _ _

_ _ _ _ _ _ _ _ _ _
1   2   3   4   5   6   7   8   9   10

A **homophone** is a word that sounds like another word but has a different meaning, spelling, and origin.

lute	cruise	foul	course	bridal
loot	crews	fowl	coarse	bridle

A **lute** is a musical instrument.
Loot means "to rob or steal."
A **cruise** is a trip on a ship.
Groups of people working together are **crews**.
Something that is **foul** is unclean.
A **fowl** is a bird, such as a goose.
A **course** is a direction or movement.
Coarse is the opposite of *fine*.
Bridal means "related to a wedding."
A **bridle** is used to control a horse.

A. Complete each riddle with a vocabulary word. Use the pictures to help you.

1. I sound like **bridal**, but I am a

_____.

3. I sound like **loot**, but I am a

_____.

2. I sound like **fowl**, but I am a

_____.

4. I sound like **crews**, but I am used for a

_____.

B. Write a vocabulary word for each clue.

1. I am a path you might take. _____

2. I describe something rough. _____

lute	cruise	foul	course	bridal
loot	crews	fowl	coarse	bridle

These book titles have errors in them. Rewrite each title so it is correct.

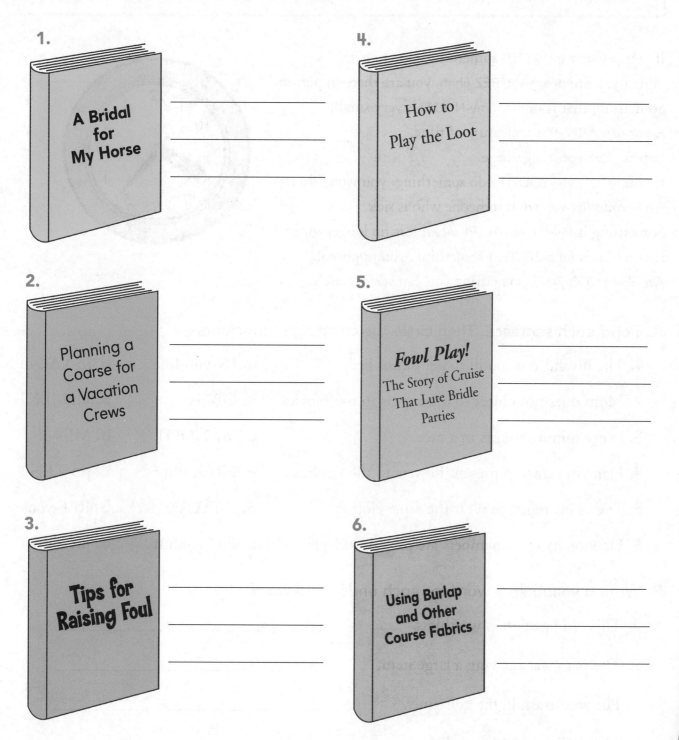

1.

A Bridal for My Horse

_____
_____
_____

4.

How to Play the Loot

_____
_____
_____

2.

Planning a Coarse for a Vacation Crews

_____
_____
_____

5.

Fowl Play!
The Story of Cruise That Lute Bridle Parties

_____
_____
_____

3.

Tips for Raising Foul

_____
_____

6.

Using Burlap and Other Course Fabrics

_____
_____
_____

A **homograph** is a word that is spelled the same as another word but has a different meaning and sometimes a different pronunciation.

present	minute	refuse	invalid	object
present	minute	refuse	invalid	object

If you **present** (pri-ZENT) something, you give it.

When you are **present** (PREZ-uhnt), you are there in person.

Something that is **minute** (my-NOOT) is very small.

A **minute** (MIN-it) is a measure of time.

Refuse (REF-yoos) is garbage.

If you **refuse** (ri-FYOOZ) to do something, you won't do it.

An **invalid** (IN-vuh-lid) is someone who is sick.

Something is **invalid** (in-VAL-id) when it is no longer in force.

If you **object** (uhb-JEKT) to something, you oppose it.

An **object** (OB-jikt) is something you can see or touch.

A. Read each sentence. Then circle the correct pronunciation.

1. The invalid was too ill to get out of bed.   **a.** IN-vuh-lid   **b.** in-VAL-id

2. Mom does not object to driving us to the movies.   **a.** OB-jikt   **b.** uhb-JEKT

3. Every minute counts in a race.   **a.** my-NOOT   **b.** MIN-it

4. Hannah wants to present flowers to the teacher.   **a.** PREZ-uhnt   **b.** pri-ZENT

5. The twins refuse to wear the same clothes.   **a.** ri-FYOOZ   **b.** REF-yoos

6. How many class members are present today?   **a.** PREZ-uhnt   **b.** pri-ZENT

B. Write a vocabulary word for each underlined word.

1. This old passport is worthless.   _____

2. The man was carrying a large item.   _____

3. Put your trash in the container.   _____

4. The dollhouse had tiny dishes.   _____

present	minute	refuse	invalid	object
present	minute	refuse	invalid	object

Read each sentence. Circle the letter beside the correct meaning for each underlined word.

1. Please plan to be <u>present</u> at the meeting tomorrow.

    a. make an appearance   **b.** give a gift

2. Peg and Sue <u>refuse</u> to sing in public because they are shy.

    a. rubbish   **b.** decline

3. Kareem was glad to recover because he didn't like being an <u>invalid</u>.

    a. sick person   **b.** null and void

4. It's a surprise party so don't be a <u>minute</u> late.

    a. something tiny   **b.** one-sixtieth of an hour

5. This document is outdated and <u>invalid</u>.

    a. in poor health   **b.** not in effect

6. My parents <u>object</u> to letting the dog in the living room.

    a. are against   **b.** a thing

7. Even though it was a <u>minute</u> scratch, the child still cried.

    a. really small   **b.** 60 seconds

8. Kathy will <u>present</u> the trophy to the winner.

    a. appear   **b.** deliver

9. The <u>refuse</u> is collected from the curb on Mondays and Thursdays.

    a. waste material   **b.** reject

10. On the shelf were some vases and a strange <u>object</u>.

    a. opposition   **b.** article

An **eponym** is a word that comes from the name of a person or place.

sardines	tuxedo	vaudeville	bikini	marathon
cologne	bologna	tarantula	tangerine	cantaloupe

Sardines are small fish often packed in cans for sale.

Cologne is a fragrant liquid.

A **tuxedo** is a kind of dress coat.

Bologna is a lunch meat.

Vaudeville is a variety show.

A **tarantula** is a large, hairy spider with a poisonous bite.

A **bikini** is a small, two-piece bathing suit.

A **tangerine** is an orange-colored citrus fruit.

A **marathon** is a running race of just over 26 miles.

A **cantaloupe** is a melon.

A. Write a vocabulary word for each sentence.

1. A light fragrance was made in Cologne, Germany.
   _____

2. A runner raced 26 miles to Athens with news of victory at the Battle of Marathon in ancient Greece.
   _____

3. A composer gained fame for his songs at Vau-de-Vire in France.
   _____

4. Men in Tuxedo, New York, wore a new style of dinner jacket in the late 1800s.
   _____

5. Delicious melons were first grown on an estate named Cantalopo in Italy.
   _____

6. A small, saltwater fish was found near the island of Sardinia.
   _____

B. Draw a line to match each word with its name story.

1. **bikini**

2. **tarantula**

3. **bologna**

4. **tangerine**

a. A sweet fruit was first found in Tangiers in Africa.

b. Bologna, a city in Italy, is where a lightly smoked meat sausage was made.

c. People on the island of Bikini in the Pacific Ocean wear few clothes because of the warm climate.

d. Taranto, Italy, is known for its spiders.

| sardines | tuxedo | vaudeville | bikini | marathon |
| cologne | bologna | tarantula | tangerine | cantaloupe |

Read each list of words. Write a vocabulary word to go with each group.

1. _____

      towel
      lotion
      umbrella

2. _____

      lemon
      grapefruit
      orange

3. _____

      prom
      wedding
      ball

4. _____

      ham
      salami
      pastrami

5. _____

      distance
      challenge
      race

6. _____

      hairy
      legs
      poison

7. _____

      perfume
      lipstick
      rouge

8. _____

      ocean
      net
      food

9. _____

      concert
      play
      opera

10. _____

      honeydew
      rind
      watermelon

Many words in English come from the languages of **other cultures.**

alligator	bandit	syrup	pajamas	okra
barbecue	magazine	sheik	kimono	impala

Words From Spanish An **alligator** is a large reptile with leathery skin.

A **barbecue** is an outdoor grill for cooking meat.

Words From Arabic A **bandit** is a robber.

A **magazine** is a publication for reading.

Syrup is a sweet, thick liquid, such as molasses.

A **sheik** is the chief or head of a tribe.

Word From Persian **Pajamas** are clothes worn for sleeping.

Word From Japanese A **kimono** is a long outer garment worn in Japan.

Words From Africa **Okra** is a vegetable used in stew or soup.

Impala is a kind of antelope from Africa.

A. Write *Arabic, Japanese, African,* or *Persian* to tell where the word for each picture is from.

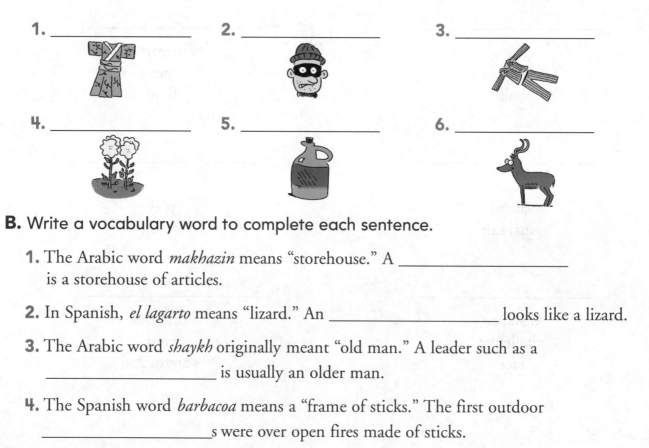

1. _____

2. _____

3. _____

4. _____

5. _____

6. _____

B. Write a vocabulary word to complete each sentence.

1. The Arabic word *makhazin* means "storehouse." A _____ is a storehouse of articles.

2. In Spanish, *el lagarto* means "lizard." An _____ looks like a lizard.

3. The Arabic word *shaykh* originally meant "old man." A leader such as a _____ is usually an older man.

4. The Spanish word *barbacoa* means a "frame of sticks." The first outdoor _____s were over open fires made of sticks.

alligator	bandit	syrup	pajamas	okra
barbecue	magazine	sheik	kimono	impala

Read the clues. Write the word next to the clue.
Then find and circle each word in the puzzle.

```
B D J T M Q A V C M X P S
A L L I G A T O R L O W Y
R F R E K W H K I M O N O
B A N D I T Y R S E U B X
E H S Z M A G A Z I N E D
C N I O P A J A M A S G I
U X J N A V M X K R Y T V
E C T Y L Q S O H Z R A N
W U K P A E B E N C U P J
S H E I K I Z T Q L P O R
```

1. an outlaw _____

2. a thick-skinned reptile _____

3. a backyard cooker _____

4. worn under a bathrobe _____

5. sometimes comes from maple trees _____

6. a weekly or monthly publication _____

7. an antelope's relative _____

8. loose clothing worn with a sash _____

9. an ingredient in gumbo soup _____

10. head of a village or tribe _____

A **clip** is a word that has been shortened, or clipped.

fridge	taxi	ref	limo	champ
grad	mike	fan	curio	rev

A **fridge** is an appliance used to keep food and drinks cold.

A **grad** is a student who has earned a diploma at a school.

A **taxi** is a car for hire.

A **mike** is an instrument that magnifies sound.

A **ref** is a judge in a sports event.

When you're a **fan**, you're a supporter of someone.

A clip for *limousine* is **limo**.

A **curio** is a strange or novel object.

If you're a **champ**, you're a winner.

A **rev** is a rotation.

A. Draw a line to match each clip with the word from which it comes.

1. **mike**   **a.** revolution

2. **grad**   **b.** fanatic

3. **ref**   **c.** champion

4. **champ**   **d.** microphone

5. **rev**   **e.** graduate

6. **curio**   **f.** referee

7. **fan**   **g.** curiosity

B. Write the clip for each word.

1. refrigerator   2. taxicab   3. limousine

_____   _____   _____

fridge	taxi	ref	limo	champ
grad	mike	fan	curio	rev

A. Write the best word from the box for each sentence.

1. The _____ called a foul on one of the players.

2. Grace put the leftovers from dinner in the _____ .

3. My aunt was driven to her wedding in a white _____ .

4. The explorer brought back a _____ from her travels.

5. The speaker used a _____ so everyone could hear her.

6. Some _____ students came back to the campus for a reunion.

7. When it comes to competitive skating, Ali is the _____ .

8. Oscar checked the meter of his _____ as he drove a passenger home.

9. Chris is a big _____ of that band.

10. The _____ of the motor increased as Carl gave it more gas.

B. Read each question. Choose the best answer.

1. Which one is a person?   ❏ mike   ❏ fan   ❏ rev

2. Which one provides a service?   ❏ taxi   ❏ curio   ❏ champ

3. Which one makes decisions?   ❏ rev   ❏ ref   ❏ limo

4. What does a singer need?   ❏ hike   ❏ bike   ❏ mike

A **blend** is a word formed when parts of two words are combined or blended together. A blend is also called a *portmanteau* word. A portmanteau is a suitcase with two sides.

splatter	squiggle	squawk	paratroops	flurry
glimmer	medevac	spacelab	telethon	flare

If you **splatter** something, you spray it around.

A **glimmer** is a gleam.

A **squiggle** is a twist or curve.

A **medevac** is a helicopter for transporting wounded people.

A **squawk** is a loud, harsh sound.

A **spacelab** is a laboratory in space.

Paratroops are military units that use parachutes to descend behind enemy lines.

A TV program that lasts many hours is a **telethon**.

A **flurry** is a sudden gust or movement.

When candles **flare**, they flame up quickly.

A. Write the blend formed from each pair of words.

1. squall and squeak _____

2. television and marathon _____

3. splash and spatter _____

4. medical and evacuation _____

5. parachute and troops _____

6. squirm and wiggle _____

7. gleam and shimmer _____

8. flame and glare _____

B. Write the vocabulary word for each clue.

1. I'm a place where research goes on.

2. I sometimes arrive in the form of snow.

_____   _____

| splatter | squiggle | squawk | paratroops | flurry |
| glimmer | medevac | spacelab | telethon | flare |

Use the clues to complete the puzzle.

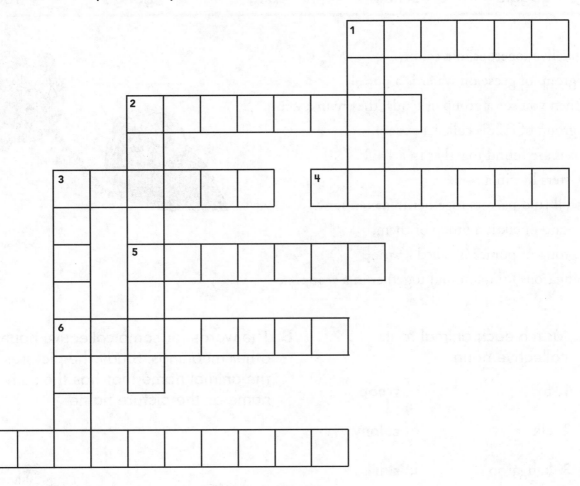

Across

1. a sudden outburst
2. a place where observations occur
3. what a parrot does
4. evacuation aircraft
5. a kind of glow
6. a lengthy show
7. highly trained jumpers

Down

1. what a fire does
2. not a straight line
3. a messy sprinkle

A **collective noun** names a group of animals, people, or things. A collective noun can have a singular or plural verb depending on how it is used in a sentence.

colony	knot	skulk	company	string
gaggle	school	bed	gang	troop

Ants live together in a **colony**.

A group of geese on water is a **gaggle**.

When you see a group of toads, they're in a **knot**.

A group of fish is called a **school**.

Foxes are found together in a **skulk**.

Oysters live in a **bed**.

You'll find parrots together in a **company**.

A **gang** of elk is a group of them.

A group of ponies is called a **string**.

Kangaroos jump around together in a **troop**.

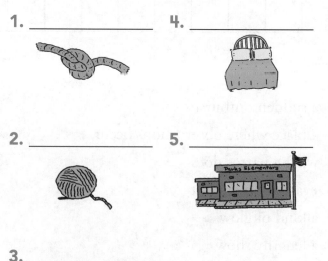

A. Match each animal to its collective noun.

1. fox   a. **troop**

2. elk   b. **colony**

3. kangaroo   c. **skulk**

4. geese   d. **gang**

5. ant   e. **gaggle**

B. The words for some collective nouns have other meanings. Study the pictures. Write the animal name that has the same group name as the picture name.

1. _____

2. _____

3. _____

4. _____

5. _____

Staw Hat Company

colony	knot	skulk	company	string
gaggle	school	bed	gang	troop

A. Write the best word from the box to complete each sentence.

1. You have to go to Australia to see a _____ of kangaroos.

2. The divers looked for a _____ of oysters.

3. In the rain forest, a _____ of parrots lives in the trees.

4. A _____ of geese honked as we drove up to the farm.

5. There's a _____ of ants out on the patio.

6. The cowboy led a _____ of ponies across the road.

7. Down by the pond, there's a _____ of toads.

8. A _____ of tuna swam by the boat.

9. Watch out for the _____ of foxes in the woods.

10. We saw a _____ of elk in the mountains out west.

B. Read each question. Choose the best answer.

1. Which group can fly?   ❏ colony   ❏ knot   ❏ gaggle

2. Which group has scales?   ❏ skulk   ❏ school   ❏ string

3. What's found in a bed?   ❏ pear   ❏ peanut   ❏ pearl

4. Which group has a joey?   ❏ company   ❏ gang   ❏ troop

Special words name different landforms and bodies of water in **geography**.

| isthmus | peninsula | strait | delta | oasis |
| tributary | valley | gorge | plateau | archipelago |

An **isthmus** is a narrow strip of land that connects two large areas of land.

A branch of a river is called a **tributary**.

A **peninsula** is an area of land surrounded by water on three sides.

A **valley** is the land that lies between mountains or hills.

A **strait** is a narrow channel that connects two larger bodies of water.

A **gorge** is a deep, narrow valley that often has a stream running through it.

A **delta** is the dirt and sand that collect at the mouth of a river.

A **plateau** is a large area of high, flat land.

An **oasis** is a fertile place in a desert where there are water, trees, and other plants.

A chain of islands is called an **archipelago**.

A. Write the name for each picture.

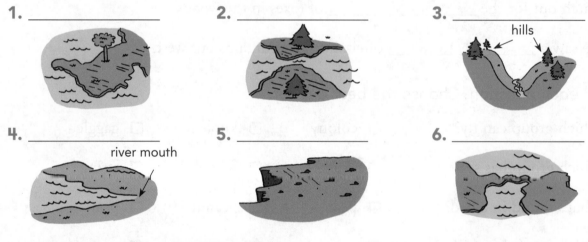

1. _____

2. _____

3. _____
hills

4. _____
river mouth

5. _____

6. _____

B. Write a vocabulary word for each clue.

1. I'm like a branch but not on a tree trunk. _____

2. It's fun to island-hop through me. _____

3. I'm a good place to stop in the desert. _____

4. Another word for me is *canyon*. _____

| isthmus | peninsula | strait | delta | oasis |
| tributary | valley | gorge | plateau | archipelago |

Read the clues. Then complete the puzzle.

1. found in a river mouth

2. land between mountains

3. a narrow passage of water

4. higher than a plain and flatter than a hill

5. a land link

6. a string of islands over a wide area

7. an arm of land that extends into the water

8. something like a deep canyon

9. a branch of a river

10. desert destination

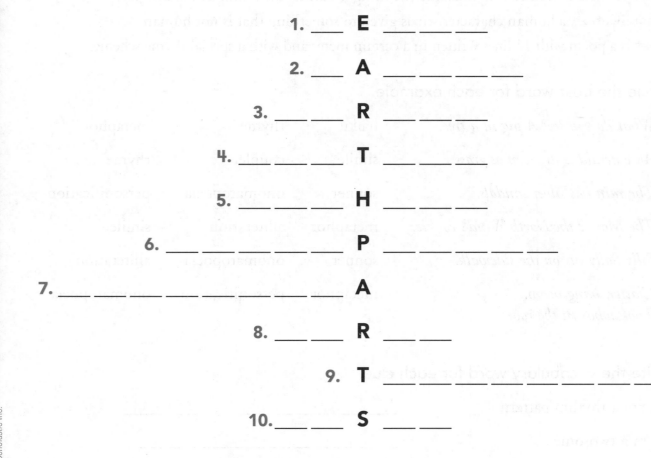

1. ___ E ___ ___ ___

2. ___ A ___ ___ ___ ___

3. ___ ___ R ___ ___ ___

4. ___ ___ ___ T ___ ___ ___

5. ___ ___ ___ H ___ ___

6. ___ ___ ___ ___ ___ P ___ ___ ___ ___

7. ___ ___ ___ ___ ___ ___ A

8. ___ ___ R ___ ___

9. T ___ ___ ___ ___ ___ ___ ___ ___

10. ___ ___ S ___ ___

Special words are used in **poetry**.

rhyme	meter	simile	couplet	personification
haiku	metaphor	alliteration	onomatopoeia	sonnet

Words that **rhyme** have the same ending sound.

A **haiku** is a three-line poem in which the first and third lines have five syllables and the middle line has seven.

Meter is the arrangement of beats in a line of poetry.

A **metaphor** is a comparison of two unlike things.

A **simile** uses the words *like* or *as* to compare two unlike things.

Alliteration is the repetition of the first sound of several words in a poem.

A **couplet** is two lines of poetry that usually rhyme.

Onomatopoeia is a word that sounds like the thing it names; for example, *buzz* or *pop*.

In **personification**, a human characteristic is given to something that is not human.

A **sonnet** is a poem with 14 lines written in a certain meter and with a special rhyme scheme.

A. Circle the best word for each example.

1. *What do you see? A pig in a tree.*   haiku   rhyme   metaphor

2. *An emerald is as green as grass.*   simile   couplet   rhyme

3. *The rain has silver sandals.*   sonnet   onomatopoeia   personification

4. *The Moon's the North Wind's cookie.*   metaphor   alliteration   simile

5. *Silly Sally sits on the sidewalk.*   sonnet   onomatopoeia   alliteration

6. *Clatter, bang boom.*
   Look who's in the room.   metaphor   personification   onomatopoeia

B. Write the vocabulary word for each clue.

1. I am a rhythm pattern. _____

2. I'm a twosome. _____

3. Shakespeare wrote many of me. _____

4. I am a poem but do not rhyme. _____

| rhyme | meter | simile | couplet | personification |
| haiku | metaphor | alliteration | onomatopoeia | sonnet |

Use the vocabulary words to fill in the map.
Then add other poetry words that you know.

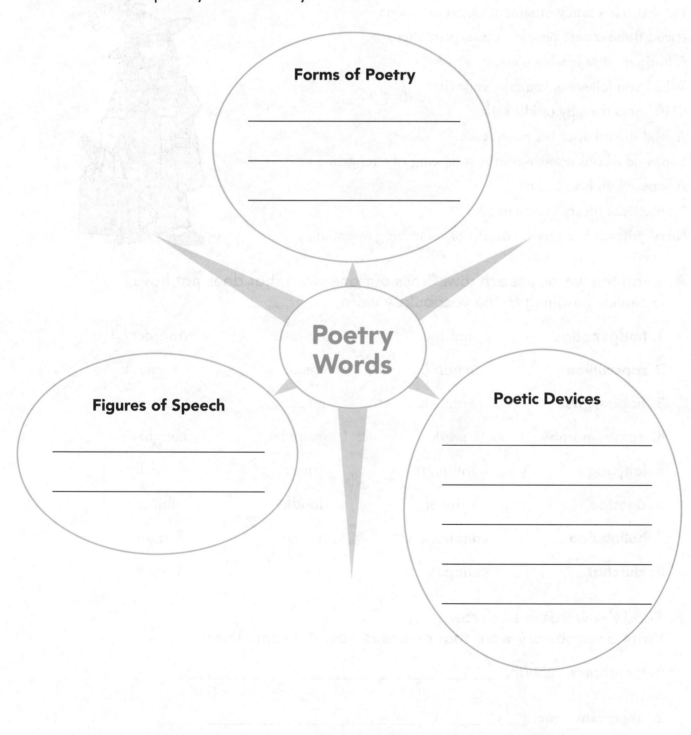

Forms of Poetry

_____

_____

_____

Poetry Words

Figures of Speech

_____

_____

Poetic Devices

_____

_____

_____

_____

_____

Some words are fun to know and use because they sound or look **unusual**.

doodad	hodgepodge	chitchat	namby-pamby	fiddlesticks
flabbergast	lollygag	hullabaloo	rapscallion	nitty-gritty

Her hat has a fancy ornament called a **doodad**.

If you **flabbergast** people, you surprise them.

A **hodgepodge** is a big mess.

When you **lollygag**, you take your time.

Chitchat is friendly or idle talk.

A loud disturbance is a **hullabaloo**.

Someone who is **namby-pamby** is lacking in strength.

A **rapscallion** is a scamp.

Fiddlesticks means "nonsense."

Nitty-gritty is the specific details of something essential.

A. Read the words in each row. Cross out one word that does not have a similar meaning to the vocabulary word.

1. **hodgepodge**	jumble	hogwash	disorder
2. **rapscallion**	ragtime	rascal	rogue
3. **flabbergast**	astonish	amaze	flatter
4. **namby-pamby**	weak	insipid	naughty
5. **lollygag**	lollipop	fritter	dillydally
6. **doodad**	trinket	doodle	object
7. **hullabaloo**	commotion	uproar	humor
8. **chitchat**	chimpanzee	gossip	rumor

B. Read the words in each row.
Write a vocabulary word that means almost the same thing.

1. foolishness, rubbish, _____

2. important, core, _____

doodad	hodgepodge	chitchat	namby-pamby	fiddlesticks
flabbergast	lollygag	hullabaloo	rapscallion	nitty-gritty

Play a game of Move On. Find a word in the first box that does not have the same meaning as the other three words. Move that word to the next box by writing it on the blank line. Continue until you reach the last box. Complete the sentence in that box.

Start here.

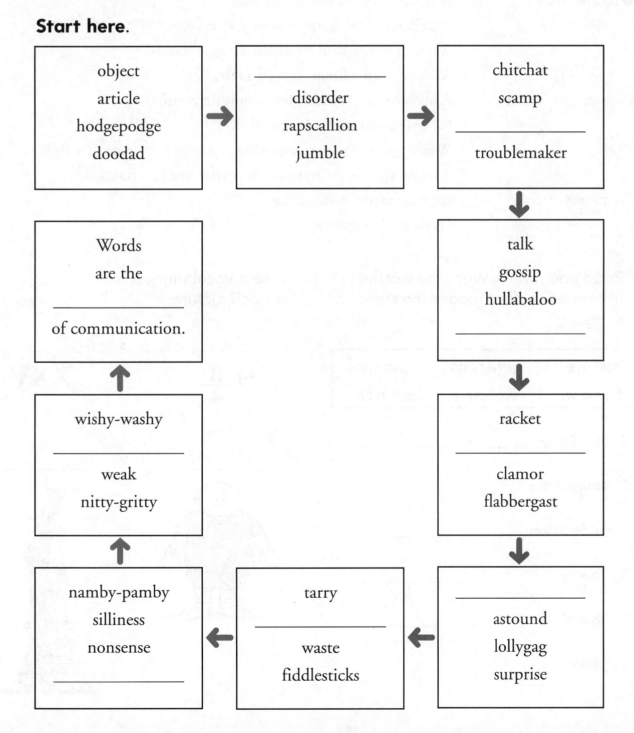

object
article
hodgepodge
doodad

→

_____
disorder
rapscallion
jumble

→

chitchat
scamp
_____
troublemaker

↓

talk
gossip
hullabaloo
_____

↓

racket
_____
clamor
flabbergast

↓

_____
astound
lollygag
surprise

←

tarry
_____
waste
fiddlesticks

←

namby-pamby
silliness
nonsense
_____

↑

wishy-washy
_____
weak
nitty-gritty

↑

Words
are the
_____
of communication.

Many words have **Latin roots**.

ped**al**	ped**estal**	**numer**al	e**numer**ate	**liber**al
pedestrian	bi**ped**	**numer**ous	**numer**ator	**liber**ty

Root:

Ped means "foot."

A **pedal** is a lever worked by a foot.

A **pedestrian** is someone who goes on foot.

A **pedestal** is a base on which a statue stands.

A **biped** is an animal with two feet.

Numer means "number."

A **numeral** is a symbol that stands for a number.

Numerous means "a great many."

When you **enumerate** something, you go over it step-by-step.

A **numerator** is the number above the line in a fraction.

Liber means "free."

Liberal means "giving freely."

Liberty is freedom.

A. Read each word. Write the word(s) from the box that means the same thing.

restate	generous	plenty
freedom	walker	foot bar

1. **numerous** _____

2. **enumerate** _____

3. **pedestrian** _____

4. **liberty** _____

5. **liberal** _____

6. **pedal** _____

B. Write a vocabulary word for each picture.

1. _____   3. _____

$$\rightarrow \frac{3}{4}$$

XXV

2. _____   4. _____

pedal	pedestal	numeral	enumerate	liberal
pedestrian	biped	numerous	numerator	liberty

Read the clues. Then complete the puzzle.

1. ample
2. used to make a bicycle move
3. a holder for a statue
4. a two-footed creature
5. to count out

6. used in zip codes
7. several or more
8. above a denominator
9. independence
10. someone who strides

1. **L** __ __ __ __ __ __
2. __ __ __ **A** __
3. __ __ __ __ __ **T** __ __
4. __ **I** __ __ __
5. __ **N** __ __ __ __ __ __
6. __ __ __ **R** __ __
7. __ __ __ __ __ **O** __ __
8. __ __ __ __ __ __ **O** __
9. __ __ __ __ __ **T** __
10. __ __ __ **S** __ __ __ __

Many words have **Latin roots**.

clarity	clarify	clarion	predict	diction
declare	declaration	dictate	dictator	dictionary

Root:

Clar means "clear." **Clarity** is clearness.

When you **declare** something, you make it known.

If you **clarify** something, you make it clear.

A **declaration** is an announcement.

A **clarion** is a clear, shrill sound.

Dict means "say." If you **dictate** something, you say it aloud for someone to write down.

When you **predict** something, you say what will happen next.

A **dictator** is a person who rules with total authority.

Diction is a person's manner of speaking.

A **dictionary** is a book of alphabetized words, their meanings, and pronunciations.

A. Read the vocabulary word.
  Find and circle two other words that mean almost the same thing.

1. **diction**	wording	phrasing	opinion
2. **clarify**	interpret	inquire	explain
3. **predict**	prevent	foretell	prophesy
4. **declare**	proclaim	announce	demand
5. **clarity**	obviousness	hidden	clearness
6. **declaration**	statement	delay	proclamation
7. **dictator**	ruler	despot	citizen

B. Underline the root in each word.

1. **clarion**   2. **dictate**   3. **dictionary**

clarity	clarify	clarion	predict	diction
declare	declaration	dictate	dictator	dictionary

Write the vocabulary word for each clue. Then write the circled letters on the correct numbered lines at the bottom of the page to answer the riddle.

Where can you always find money?

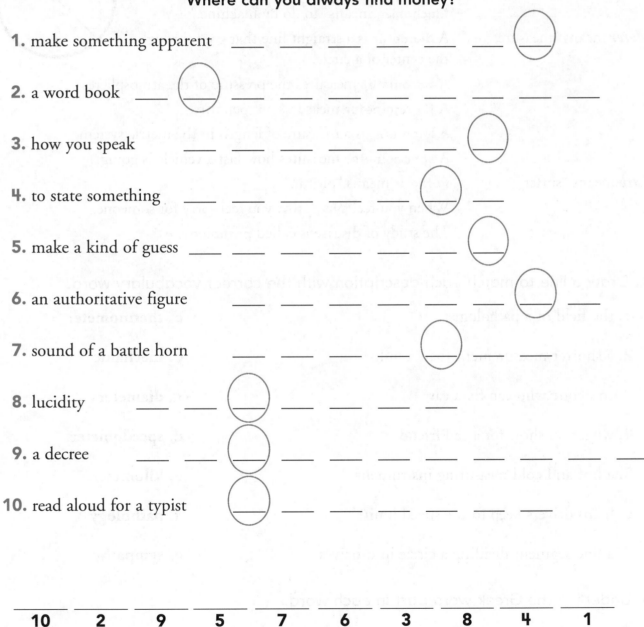

1. make something apparent

2. a word book

3. how you speak

4. to state something

5. make a kind of guess

6. an authoritative figure

7. sound of a battle horn

8. lucidity

9. a decree

10. read aloud for a typist

____ ____ ____ ____ ____ ____ ____ ____ ____
10   2   9   5   7   6   3   8   4   1

Many English words have **Greek word parts.**

mech**anic**	dia**meter**	thermo**meter**	speedo**meter**	sym**path**y
mechanize	baro**meter**	kilo**meter**	**path**etic	**path**ology

Word Part:

Mech means "machine."   A **mechanic** is someone who repairs machines.
Mechanize means "to do by machine."

Meter means "measure."   A **diameter** is a straight line that goes through the center of a circle.

A **barometer** measures the pressure of the atmosphere.

A **thermometer** measures temperature.

A **kilometer** is a measure of length in the metric system.

A **speedometer** measures how fast a vehicle is going.

Path means "suffer."   **Pathetic** means "pitiful."

When you feel **sympathy**, you feel sorry for someone.

The study of disease is called **pathology**.

A. Draw a line to match each description with the correct vocabulary word.

1. the field of a pathologist   **a. thermometer**

2. a shorter measurement than a mile   **b. mechanic**

3. someone who can fix a car   **c. diameter**

4. what you show for a sad friend   **d. speedometer**

5. a hot and cold measuring instrument   **e. kilometer**

6. helps drivers keep to the speed limit   **f. pathology**

7. a line segment dividing a circle into halves   **g. sympathy**

B. Underline the Greek word part in each word.

1. **pathetic**   2. **mechanize**   3. **barometer**

| mechanic | diameter | thermometer | speedometer | sympathy |
| mechanize | barometer | kilometer | pathetic | pathology |

Use the clues to complete the puzzle.

Across

2. woeful
4. motorize
5. its abbreviation is km
7. compassion
9. a measuring instrument for temperature

Down

1. people who know how machines work
2. examination of illness
3. a speed reader
6. twice the radius of a circle
8. pressure gauge

An **acronym** is a word made from the first letters of a phrase.

scuba	radar	modem	quasar	canola
zip	sonar	laser	snafu	veep

Scuba gear enables a diver to breathe underwater.

A **zip** code is a way of identifying places in the United States for mail delivery.

Radar is an instrument that uses radio waves to determine the distance, direction, and speed of unseen objects.

Sonar is a device that uses sound waves to locate objects underwater.

A **modem** is a device that converts digital information.

A **laser** produces a strong, narrow beam of light.

A heavenly object that lets off powerful radio waves is a **quasar**.

If something turns into a big disorganized mess, it's a **snafu**.

Canola is a kind of oil used for cooking.

A **veep** is a vice president.

A. Draw a line to match each phrase to the correct acronym.

1. radio detecting and ranging   **a. quasar**

2. modulator and demodulator   **b. zip**

3. Canada oil—low acid   **c. laser**

4. sound navigation ranging   **d. snafu**

5. self-contained underwater breathing apparatus   **e. radar**

6. light amplification by stimulated emission of radiation   **f. modem**

7. quasi stellar   **g. canola**

8. zone improvement plan   **h. scuba**

9. situation normal all fouled up   **i. sonar**

B. What word do the letters V.P. spell? _____

scuba	radar	modem	quasar	canola
zip	sonar	laser	snafu	veep

Read the clues. Write the word next to the clue.
Then find and circle each word in the puzzle.

```
S  W  H  S  B  E  J  X  A  C  V
C  A  N  O  L  A  T  Q  R  K  E
U  C  F  N  M  P  D  S  N  G  E
B  V  D  A  F  Y  L  B  Z  I  P
A  U  J  R  A  D  A  R  A  Q  W
E  N  Z  G  W  C  S  X  G  U  I
M  X  Q  M  O  D  E  M  L  A  R
T  V  S  I  L  B  R  O  T  S  H
D  K  Y  M  N  X  K  E  C  A  A
S  N  A  F  U  V  O  J  Z  R  F
```

1. an underwater breathing tank _____

2. a yellow vegetable oil _____

3. second in command _____

4. sound wave equipment _____

5. a postal sorting system _____

6. radio wave equipment _____

7. a powerful light beam _____

8. a computer has one _____

9. a distant, powerful object in space _____

10. a botched situation _____

Some English words have different meanings in **Britain** than they do in the United States.

pram	larder	flat	underground	chemist
lift	cupboard	holiday	nappy	cutlery

A **pram** is a baby carriage.

If you ride in a **lift**, you take an elevator.

A **larder** is a pantry.

A **cupboard** is a closet.

If you rent a **flat**, you rent an apartment.

When you go on **holiday**, you take a vacation.

The **underground** is a subway.

A diaper is called a **nappy** by the British.

A **chemist** is a pharmacist.

When you set the table with **cutlery**, you use silverware.

A. Write a vocabulary word for each picture.

1. _____

2. _____

3. _____

4. _____

5. _____

6. _____

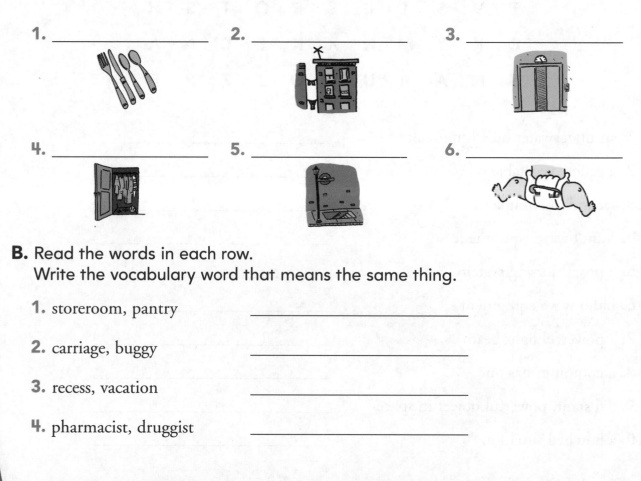

B. Read the words in each row.
Write the vocabulary word that means the same thing.

1. storeroom, pantry _____

2. carriage, buggy _____

3. recess, vacation _____

4. pharmacist, druggist _____

pram	larder	flat	underground	chemist
lift	cupboard	holiday	nappy	cutlery

A. Write the best word from the box to complete each sentence.

1. Mother brought an extra _____ for the baby when we went out.

2. Harriet looked in the _____ for something to eat.

3. A customer called the _____ to get his prescription filled.

4. The commuters took the _____ to get to their jobs.

5. Will the Marks take their dog when they go on _____ ?

6. Push the button for the _____ if you're going to the tenth floor.

7. Olivia placed _____ on the table for lunch.

8. Mrs. Elliot put the infant in the _____ so she could go for a walk.

9. The doors to the _____ were open, and clothes spilled out.

10. Malcolm rented a _____ for the year he would live in London.

B. Read each question. Choose the best answer.

1. Which one can you ride? ❑ underneath ❑ underweight ❑ underground

2. Which one's for a baby? ❑ prom ❑ prim ❑ pram

3. Which one moves vertically? ❑ sift ❑ lift ❑ rift

4. Which one's for living? ❑ float ❑ flit ❑ flat

Many words have interesting **stories** about their origin.

album	ketchup	leotard	cyclone	dahlia
oxygen	manuscript	academy	zany	volcano

An **album** is a book with blank pages for holding photos or other collections.

Oxygen is a colorless gas in the air that people, animals, and plants need to breathe.

Ketchup is a tomato sauce.

Manuscript is the text of a book or paper.

A **leotard** is a bodysuit that dancers wear.

An **academy** is a school.

A **cyclone** is a violent, rotating windstorm.

If someone is **zany**, that person is clownish.

A **dahlia** is a kind of flower.

A **volcano** is a cone-shaped mountain that is formed by lava erupting from a crack in Earth's surface.

A. Write a vocabulary word for each word story.

1. The Greek word *kyklos* refers to a circle. _____

2. The Italian word *zanni* means a "clown." _____

3. In ancient Rome, public notices were posted on blank tablets named from the Latin word *albus*, meaning "white." _____

4. The Greek philosopher Plato taught students in a grove called Akademeia. _____

5. Long ago, people in China made a pickled fish sauce called *ke-tsiap*. _____

6. Two Latin words, *manu* and *scriptus*, mean "hand" and "write." _____

B. Draw a line from each vocabulary word to the person associated with the word.

1. oxygen　　　　**a.** Vulcan was the Roman god of fire.

2. volcano　　　　**b.** Anders Dahl was a Swedish botanist in the 1700s.

3. leotard　　　　**c.** French chemist Antoine Laurent Lavoisier first used this word after an important element was identified in the 18th century.

4. dahlia　　　　**d.** Jules Léotard was a French tightrope walker.

album	ketchup	leotard	cyclone	dahlia
oxygen	manuscript	academy	zany	volcano

Read each list of words. Write a vocabulary word to go with each group.

1. _____

foolish
clownish
loony

6. _____

edit
write
revise

2. _____

tornado
typhoon
damage

7. _____

spicy
hamburger
reddish

3. _____

mountain
lava
eruption

8. _____

garden
water
blossom

4. _____

stamp
autograph
wedding

9. _____

gymnast
acrobat
dancer

5. _____

school
college
university

10. _____

nitrogen
carbon
hydrogen

A **prefix** is a word part that has been added to the beginning of a word and changes the word's meaning.

retro- means "backward"	*ir-* means "not"
mal- means "bad"	*inter-* means "between"
ab- means "from"	

retroactive	**ir**responsible	**mal**function	**inter**section	**ab**duct
retrospective	**ir**rational	**mal**formed	**inter**pose	**ab**stain

A law that is **retroactive** applies to events before the law was passed.

A **retrospective** is a survey of past experiences.

If you are **irresponsible**, you are not responsible.

When someone is **irrational**, that person is not thinking clearly.

When machines **malfunction**, they don't work.

Malformed means "poorly shaped."

An **intersection** is where one thing crosses another.

To **interpose** means "to come between things."

Abduct means "to carry off by force."

If you **abstain** from something, you do without it.

A. Read each word.
   Write a vocabulary word that means almost the same thing.

1. untrustworthy _____

2. refrain _____

3. intervene _____

4. misshapen _____

5. kidnap _____

6. illogical _____

B. Add the correct prefix to each word to form a new word.
   Use the meaning clue in parentheses to help you.

1. *(backward)* _____active

2. *(between)* _____section

3. *(bad)* _____function

4. *(backward)* _____spective

retroactive	irresponsible	malfunction	intersection	abduct
retrospective	irrational	malformed	interpose	abstain

A. Write the best word from the box to complete each sentence.

1. Bria found it very hard to _____ from chocolate.

2. That tree has a _____ and twisted trunk.

3. To reach the library, turn right at the next _____ .

4. In the story, a dragon tries to _____ the princess.

5. There will be a _____ of the artist's work at the
   gallery next week.

6. Ming tried to _____ her ideas into the conversation.

7. It was _____ of Ryan to leave your bike out all night.

8. Let's hope the washing machine doesn't _____ because
   we have a lot of laundry.

9. Heavy traffic can make some drivers upset and _____ .

10. The tax increase will be _____ to the first of the year.

B. Read each question. Choose the best answer.

1. Which one's an intersection? ☐ circle ☐ curve ☐ cross

2. What does a dieter do? ☐ abduct ☐ abstain ☐ absurd

3. What can malfunction? ☐ rock ☐ rocket ☐ rocky

4. When might you intervene? ☐ fight ☐ field ☐ fiction

A **prefix** is a word part that has been added to the beginning of a word and changes the word's meaning.

bi- means "two" **com-** means "with"

il- means "not" **hydro-** means "water"

mono- means "single"

bivalve	**com**miserate	**il**legal	**hydro**plane	**mono**tone
biannual	**com**pile	**il**literate	**hydro**electric	**mono**syllable

A **bivalve** is a shell with two parts that hinge together.

A **biannual** event occurs twice a year.

If you **commiserate** with someone, you feel sorrow for his or her trouble.

When you **compile** things, you collect them.

Something that is **illegal** is against the law.

A person who does not know how to read or write is **illiterate**.

A **hydroplane** can land or take off on water.

Electricity made from waterpower is **hydroelectric**.

Monotone means "sameness of tone or style."

A **monosyllable** is a word with one syllable.

A. Read each word. Write the word from the box that means almost the same thing.

compile	commiserate
illiterate	illegal
monotone	hydroplane

1. unlearned _____

2. seaplane _____

3. pity _____

4. unlawful _____

5. assemble _____

6. drone _____

B. Add the correct prefix to each word to form a new word. Use the meaning clue in parentheses to help you.

1. (*two*) _____valve

2. (*single*) _____syllable

3. (*water*) _____electric

4. (*two*) _____annual

Play the Word Building game. Add one of the prefixes on the list to the roof of each house. Then write the new word on the line below. Use a dictionary to check your words. On another piece of paper, write a sentence using each new word.

Prefixes: *hydro-   il-   com-   bi-   mono-*

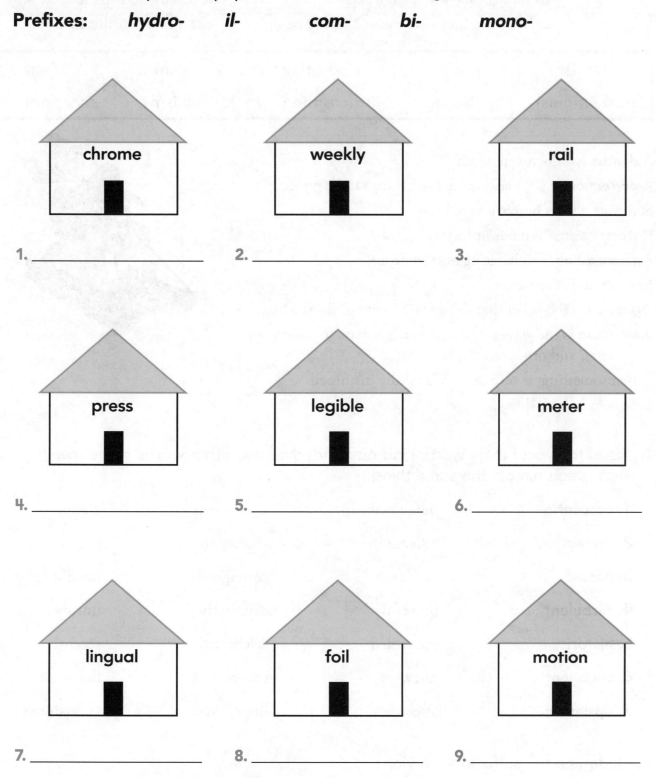

chrome

weekly

rail

1. _____

2. _____

3. _____

press

legible

meter

4. _____

5. _____

6. _____

lingual

foil

motion

7. _____

8. _____

9. _____

A **suffix** is a word part that is added to the end of a word and changes the meaning of the word.

-ist means "one who practices"	*-ic* means "relating to"
-ation, *-tion* and *-ism* mean "state of being"	*-ent* means "inclined to"

dent**ist**	hero**ic**	accusa**tion**	optim**ism**	turbul**ent**
perfection**ist**	histor**ic**	recrea**tion**	journal**ism**	succul**ent**

A **dentist** is a doctor for teeth.

A **perfectionist** is a person who likes things to be perfect.

Someone who is **heroic** is very brave.

Historic means "famous in history."

An **accusation** is a charge against someone.

Recreation is amusement.

Optimism is the belief that things will turn out for the best.

Journalism is the gathering and reporting news for newspapers, magazines, and other media.

When something is **turbulent**, it is wildly disturbed.

Succulent means "juicy."

A. Read the vocabulary word. Find and underline two other words in the row that mean almost the same thing.

1. **accusation**	denouncement	assortment	charge
2. **recreation**	reflection	relaxation	play
3. **heroic**	noble	courageous	horrible
4. **turbulent**	peaceful	disorderly	unruly
5. **historic**	renowned	celebrated	recent
6. **succulent**	juicy	tough	fleshy
7. **optimism**	affection	hopefulness	cheerfulness

B. Underline the suffix in each word.

1. **dentist**   2. **journalism**   3. **perfectionist**

| dent**ist** | hero**ic** | accusa**tion** | optim**ism** | turbul**ent** |
| perfection**ist** | histor**ic** | recrea**tion** | journal**ism** | succul**ent** |

A. Write the best word from the box to complete each sentence.

1. After work, Simon likes to play basketball for _____ .

2. The _____ examined Corey's teeth for cavities.

3. During the storm, the water was choppy and _____ .

4. Our class visited a _____ part of town for a social studies project.

5. Isabel's good spirits and _____ help her get through difficult situations.

6. Matsu hopes to get a job in _____ when she finishes school.

7. Alberto slowly bit into a _____ piece of meat.

8. The student was a _____ who tried to get everything right.

9. The firefighters were _____ in their efforts to rescue people.

10. The _____ against the offender was serious.

B. Read each question. Choose the best answer.

1. Which one is turbulent? ❒ chair ❒ air ❒ stair

2. Which one is fun? ❒ delegation ❒ accusation ❒ recreation

3. Which one is upbeat? ❒ optimism ❒ pessimism ❒ realism

4. What's a peach? ❒ turbulent ❒ succulent ❒ tolerant

Here are some vocabulary words you learned.
Use at least twelve of these words to write a story below.

Word Bank

veto	bewildered
compliment	heedless
spellbound	fowl
invalid	sardines
okra	limo
flare	skulk
valley	sonnet
lollygag	numerous
dictate	mechanic
snafu	flat
cyclone	retroactive
compile	heroic

_____

_____

_____

_____

_____

_____

_____

_____

_____

_____

_____

_____

_____

_____

_____

Write the number that is 1,000 *more*.

1. 277,350 _____

2. 1,222,357 _____

3. 309,177,030 _____

4. 9,662,000,000 _____

Write the number that is 1,000 *less*.

5. 2,500,000 _____

6. 1,555,799,000 _____

7. 300,020,000 _____

8. 7,000,500,000 _____

Write the number 100,000 *less*.

9. 600,000 _____

10. 9,000,000 _____

11. 1,000,000 _____

Write the number 100,000 *more*.

12. 23,400,000 _____

13. 54,799,662 _____

14. 9,000,000,000 _____

A magic square is an ancient math puzzle.
The Chinese first made the puzzle over 2,600 years ago.

Use each of the numbers from the number bank once to complete the magic square.
The sum of each row, column, and diagonal must be 390.

90			105
97	103	92	
	91		
		95	93

Number Bank

94   96   98   99
100   101   102   104

Examine the number square.
Find and circle the four numbers that add to 100.

Hint: They may be anywhere in the square.

46	17	22	97
2	45	38	55
77	12	90	39
6	84	68	23

It's your turn! Make your own number puzzle and ask a friend to solve it!

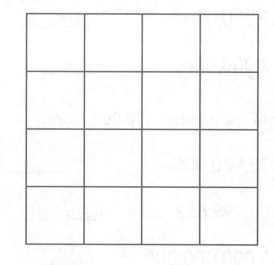

Add. Circle the answer that is a palindrome.

$$\begin{array}{r} 329 \\ 3,475 \\ +29 \\ \hline \end{array}$$
$$\begin{array}{r} 738 \\ 5,018 \\ +52 \\ \hline \end{array}$$
$$\begin{array}{r} 4,125 \\ 7,099 \\ +375 \\ \hline \end{array}$$

$$\begin{array}{r} 1,425 \\ 7,059 \\ +3,275 \\ \hline \end{array}$$
$$\begin{array}{r} 5,126 \\ 369 \\ +4,375 \\ \hline \end{array}$$
$$\begin{array}{r} 2,134 \\ 8,054 \\ +273 \\ \hline \end{array}$$

$$\begin{array}{r} 3,134 \\ 22 \\ +5,656 \\ \hline \end{array}$$
$$\begin{array}{r} 157 \\ 6,032 \\ +555 \\ \hline \end{array}$$
$$\begin{array}{r} 417 \\ 4,171 \\ +417 \\ \hline \end{array}$$

$$\begin{array}{r} 746 \\ 522 \\ +392 \\ \hline \end{array}$$
$$\begin{array}{r} 2,382 \\ 3,691 \\ +6,724 \\ \hline \end{array}$$
$$\begin{array}{r} 7,459 \\ 1,359 \\ 813 \\ +5,231 \\ \hline \end{array}$$

$$\begin{array}{r} 452 \\ 8,064 \\ +791 \\ \hline \end{array}$$
$$\begin{array}{r} 5,661 \\ 1,185 \\ +1,602 \\ \hline \end{array}$$
$$\begin{array}{r} 12,996 \\ 5,691 \\ 2,567 \\ +5,994 \\ \hline \end{array}$$

Subtract. Circle any answer whose digits add to 20.

7,464 3,127	808 − 657	6,575 − 2,943
6,345 812	50,328 − 42,660	928,015 − 425,444
4,000 784	9,000 − 1,784	58,000 − 1,283
6,600 2,237	7,020 − 4,721	50,810 − 3,294
7,308 4,616	55,432 − 8,612	787,218 − 392,009

When evaluating several numbers using different operations, remember PMDAS: parentheses, multiplication, division, addition, and subtraction.

Use the order of operations to solve.

$(5 + 4) \times 6 =$ _____

$21 - 9 \times 2 =$ _____

$14 + 12 \times 3 =$ _____

$50 - 6 \times 8 =$ _____

$22 - 16 \div 8 =$ _____

$12 \times (16 \div 8) =$ _____

$7 \times 4 + 32 =$ _____

$75 \div 3 \times 15 =$ _____

$16 - 8 \times 2 =$ _____

$(86 - 32) \div 9 =$ _____

$25 \times (36 \div 9) =$ _____

$55 + (6 + 8) \times 2 =$ _____

$55 \div 11 \times 13 =$ _____

$9 - 2 + 6 \times 7 =$ _____

$(48 + 16) \times 3 =$ _____

$18 \times (21 - 17 + 5) =$ _____

Write the value of the underlined digit.

1. 20,<u>5</u>58,007 _____

2. 3<u>2</u>,007,585 _____

3. 1,2<u>9</u>4,000,052 _____

4. <u>1</u>5,000,040,312 _____

5. 8,75<u>6</u>,039 _____

6. 7,<u>5</u>68,943,060 _____

Write each number in standard form.

7. three hundred thousand fifteen _____

8. twenty-nine million four hundred thirty-seven _____

9. six hundred forty-three million _____

10. eighty-two billion one hundred eleven _____

Write each number in word form.

11. 225,431,000 _____

_____

12. 309,254 _____

_____

13. 38,260,806,007 _____

_____

Write the short word name for each number. The first one has been done for you.

1. 4,000,000   <u>4 million</u>

2. 80,000,000 _____

3. 12,000,000 _____

4. 7,000,000,000 _____

5. 59,000,000,000 _____

6. 13,000,000 _____

Write the short word name for the number that is 1,000,000 *less*.

7. 6,000,000 _____

8. 90,000,000 _____

9. 1,000,000,000 _____

Write the short word name for the number that is 1,000,000 *more*.

10. 800,000,000 _____

11. 50,000,000 _____

12. 999,000,000 _____

Complete the table.

Number	In Thousands	In Hundreds	In Tens	In Ones
30,000	30	300	3,000	
600,000			60,000	
1,800,000				1,800,000
29,000,000		290,000		
31,500,000				

Write the number of:

1. tens in one million   _____

2. hundreds in one hundred million   _____

3. hundreds in one billion   _____

4. tens in five hundred million   _____

Complete the table.

Number	Millions	Thousands	Hundreds
30 million	30	30,000	
900 million			9,000,000
1 billion			
20 billion		20,000,000	

Write each number in expanded form. The first one has been done for you.

1. 2,382,000 2,000,000 + 300,000 + 80,000 + 2,000

2. 400,306,000 _____

3. 8,000,000,700 _____

4. 76,432,987 _____

5. 419,582,665 _____

6. 55,082,006,500 _____

7. 20,375,000,120 _____

8. 15,200,063,542 _____

9. 367,509,000,001 _____

10. 900,000,567,200 _____

Compare. Write **<**, **=**, or **>**.

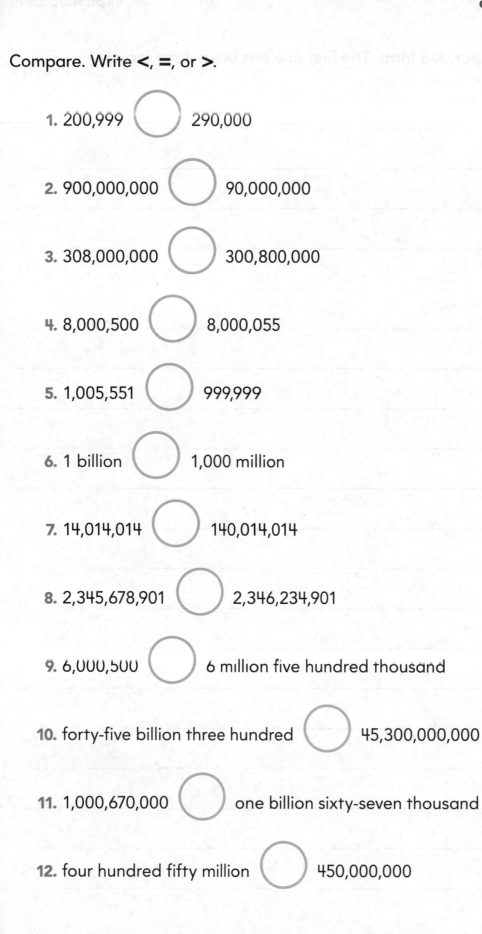

1. 200,999 ◯ 290,000

2. 900,000,000 ◯ 90,000,000

3. 308,000,000 ◯ 300,800,000

4. 8,000,500 ◯ 8,000,055

5. 1,005,551 ◯ 999,999

6. 1 billion ◯ 1,000 million

7. 14,014,014 ◯ 140,014,014

8. 2,345,678,901 ◯ 2,346,234,901

9. 6,000,500 ◯ 6 million five hundred thousand

10. forty-five billion three hundred ◯ 45,300,000,000

11. 1,000,670,000 ◯ one billion sixty-seven thousand

12. four hundred fifty million ◯ 450,000,000

Order each set of numbers from *least* to *greatest*.

1. 4,190,000   1,409,000   140,409

_____

2. 12,007,000   210,700,000   1,210,707,000

_____

3. 80,850,000,000   805,000,000   8,850,500,805

_____

Find the greatest and least numbers in each set.
Then find their difference.

4. 38,745   39,547   37,845   39,845

_____ − _____ = _____

5. 481,414   418,144   418,441   484,141

_____ − _____ = _____

6. 9,562,677   9,526,767   9,767,526   9,775,266

_____ − _____ = _____

Round each number to the nearest 1,000 *and* 100,000.

Number	Nearest 1,000	Nearest 100,000
389,900		
1,844,938		
24,061,562		

Round each number to its *greatest* place.

788,148 _____   1,435,456 _____

179,861,007 _____   92,000,999 _____

8,650,000,000 _____   277,005 _____

Round to the place of the underlined digit.

20,548,007 _____   92,807,585 _____

1,286,000,052 _____   33,000,040,300 _____

6,726,739 _____   7,528,903,080 _____

Use all the numbers in the number bank to form:

Number Bank

3   5   8   2

7   6   1   4   9

1. the *greatest* number   _____

2. the *least* number   _____

3. the greatest *even* number   _____

4. the greatest *odd* number   _____

Use all the numbers in the number bank to form:

Number Bank

3   5   8   2

7   6   1   4   9

5. the number closest to 1 billion   _____

6. the number closest to 900 million   _____

7. the number closest to 100 million   _____

8. the least even number   _____

Use the digits 1–8 to make the smallest 8-digit even number you can.
The number must have a 5 in the millions place and a 4 in the hundreds place.

9. What is the number?   ____ ____ ____ ____ ____ ____ ____ ____

Find the product. Then express as an exponent.
The first one has been done for you.

> When you multiply 10s together, you can express the product as an exponent. The exponent gives the number of times that 10 is used as a factor.
>
> For example, $10 \times 10 \times 10 = 10^3$. Notice how the exponent equals the number of zeroes in the factors.

1. 10×10 = _100_

   = _10^2_

2. $10 \times 10 \times 10$ = _____

   = _____

3. $10 \times 10 \times 10 \times 10$ = _____ = _____

4. 100×100 = _____ = _____

5. $1{,}000 \times 1{,}000$ = _____ = _____

Express as whole numbers.

6. 10^2 = _____

7. 10^4 = _____

8. 10^6 = _____

9. 10^7 = _____

10. 10^3 = _____

Multiply.

11. 3×10^2 = _____

12. 2×10^3 = _____

13. 5×10^4 = _____

14. 18×10^5 = _____

15. 45×10^6 = _____

16. 57×10^4 = _____

Fill in the Venn diagram. Write factors of 24 in one part, factors of 40 in one part, and factors of both 24 and 40 in the overlapping part.

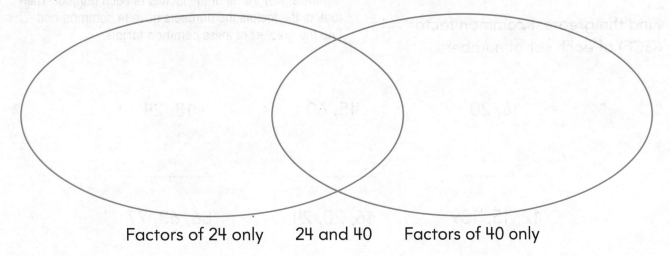

Factors of 24 only   24 and 40   Factors of 40 only

List all the factors of each number.
Write *P* or *C* to show whether the number is prime or composite.

4	19	60
21	53	70
47	81	38

Find the greatest common factor
(GCF) of each set of numbers.

To find the **greatest common factor (GCF)** of a set of
numbers, first list all of the factors of each number. Then
look at the factors the numbers have in common and
find the greatest of these common factors.

16, 20   45, 60   18, 24

_____   _____   _____

12, 15, 189   16, 20, 24   56, 63, 77

_____   _____   _____

Find the least common multiple
(LCM) of each set of numbers.

To find the **least common multiple (LCM)** of a set of
numbers, make a list of each number's multiples. Then
look at the multiples the numbers have in common and
find the smallest of these common multiples.

6 and 8   9 and 12   3, 4, and 9

_____   _____   _____

4 and 10   3 and 6   2, 5, and 8

_____   _____   _____

16 and 20   12 and 18   10, 12, and 15

_____   _____   _____

Circle all numbers divisible by 3.

| 9 | 16 | 28 | 45 | 213 | 3,519 |

Circle all numbers divisible by 4.

| 16 | 42 | 96 | 422 | 9,416 | 3,820 |

Circle all numbers divisible by 6.

| 84 | 91 | 1,029 | 396 | 5,415 | 72,144 |

Circle all numbers divisible by 9.

| 54 | 71 | 109 | 702 | 2,421 | 62,100 |

Solve It

I am a number between 200 and 300. I am divisible by 6 and 4, but not by 5 or 8. The sum of my digits is 9. What number am I?

Show your work.

_____

Use mental math to find each product.

1. $5 \times 600 =$ _____

2. $5 \times 8,000 =$ _____

3. $4 \times 90,000 =$ _____

4. $30 \times 200 =$ _____

5. $7 \times 4,000 =$ _____

6. $4 \times 80 =$ _____

7. $60 \times 70 =$ _____

8. $70 \times 60,000 =$ _____

9. $300 \times 40,000 =$ _____

10. $8,000 \times 8,000 =$ _____

Solve It

Show your work.

A theater has 3 sections in the orchestra level. Each section has 30 rows, and each row has 20 seats. How many seats are there in all in the orchestra level?

_____

Estimate the product by rounding the larger factor to its greatest place.

$219 \times 3 =$ _____ $568 \times 7 =$ _____

$946 \times 4 =$ _____ $6{,}741 \times 8 =$ _____

$2{,}299 \times 5 =$ _____ $6{,}980 \times 6 =$ _____

Find each product. Circle the two products that round to 40,000.

1,109	9,205	6,043
× 3	× 5	× 4

9,060	5,180	6,089
× 4	× 7	× 8

Chances are you won't know the answers to these wacky facts!
Multiply and then write the product in the blank.
What you find out may surprise you!

1. Even without its head, a cockroach can live up to _____ days.
   (10 × 1)

2. When you sneeze, the air rushes through your

   nose at about _____ miles per hour.
   (50 × 2)

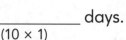

3. A cheetah can run up to _____ miles an hour.
   (10 × 6)

4. If you weigh 100 pounds on Earth, you would weigh _____

   (19 × 2)

   pounds on Mars.

5. The top speed for a sailfish has been recorded

   at _____ miles per hour.
   (17 × 4)

6. A large order of French fries has about _____ calories.
   (120 × 3)

7. The figure of the Statue of Liberty is about _____ feet high
   (30 × 5)

   from base to torch.

8. There are about _____ muscles in the body.
   (128 × 5)
   These muscles make up about _____ percent of the body weight.
   (10 × 4)

Round each factor to its greatest place. Estimate the product.

$11 \times 698 =$ _____ $32 \times 431 =$ _____

$43 \times 791 =$ _____ $58 \times 378 =$ _____

$62 \times 279 =$ _____ $93 \times 527 =$ _____

$21 \times 807 =$ _____ $37 \times 915 =$ _____

Find each product.

$$\begin{array}{r} 429 \\ \times \quad 27 \\ \hline \end{array}$$ $$\begin{array}{r} 3,693 \\ \times \quad 50 \\ \hline \end{array}$$

$$\begin{array}{r} 804 \\ \times \quad 47 \\ \hline \end{array}$$ $$\begin{array}{r} 7,853 \\ \times \quad 39 \\ \hline \end{array}$$

Multiply to find your way out of the river rapids. If the path is correct, the answer to the first multiplication sentence will be the first factor in the next sentence, and so on.

Find the value of *n*. Use basic facts to help you.

$240 \div 8 = n$

$n =$ _____

$280 \div 4 = n$

$n =$ _____

$480 \div 6 = n$

$n =$ _____

$810 \div 9 = n$

$n =$ _____

$180 \div 30 = n$

$n =$ _____

$490 \div 70 = n$

$n =$ _____

$630 \div 7 = n$

$n =$ _____

$560 \div 70 = n$

$n =$ _____

$350 \div 5 = n$

$n =$ _____

Compare. Write **<**, **=**, or **>**.

$3,600 \div 6$ ◯ $4,000 \div 8$

$45,000 \div 90$ ◯ $25,000 \div 50$

$2,700 \div 3$ ◯ $4,500 \div 5$

$16,000 \div 20$ ◯ $1,600 \div 2$

$7,200 \div 9$ ◯ $5,400 \div 6$

$6,300 \div 7$ ◯ $5,600 \div 8$

$32,000 \div 4$ ◯ $48,000 \div 8$

$36,000 \div 20$ ◯ $18,000 \div 10$

Round each dividend to estimate each quotient.
The first one has been done for you.

1. $1,957 \div 4$ = $\underline{\quad 2,000 \div 4 = 500 \quad}$

2. $8,076 \div 9$ = _____

3. $4,813 \div 6$ = _____

4. $62,904 \div 7$ = _____

5. $3,951 \div 5$ = _____

6. $2,379 \div 8$ = _____

7. $62,792 \div 9$ = _____

8. $3,507 \div 7$ = _____

Find each quotient.

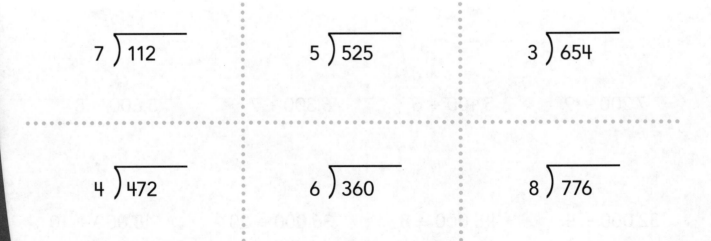

$7\overline{)112}$ $5\overline{)525}$ $3\overline{)654}$

$4\overline{)472}$ $6\overline{)360}$ $8\overline{)776}$

Find each quotient and remainder.

$3 \overline{)\ 568}$ $8 \overline{)\ 907}$ $5 \overline{)\ 3,964}$

$7 \overline{)\ 3,048}$ $8 \overline{)\ 50,519}$ $7 \overline{)\ 93,712}$

$2 \overline{)\ 806}$ $7 \overline{)\ 749}$ $6 \overline{)\ 6,246}$

$4 \overline{)\ 8,360}$ $7 \overline{)\ 7,630}$ $6 \overline{)\ 72,186}$

Many Americans will change careers during their lives. Even presidents of the United States have had different jobs!

What careers do you think these presidents had before they moved into the White House? Your job is to find out! First, take a guess. Then divide, match the quotient, and see if your guess is correct.

Divide:

1. Andrew Jackson

   $75 \div 6 =$ _____

2. Woodrow Wilson

   $193 \div 4 =$ _____

3. Ronald Reagan

   $462 \div 7 =$ _____

4. John F. Kennedy

   $469 \div 5 =$ _____

5. Andrew Johnson

   $432 \div 8 =$ _____

6. Lyndon Johnson

   $843 \div 9 =$ _____

7. Jimmy Carter

   $72 \div 2 =$ _____

8. Thomas Jefferson

   $755 \div 5 =$ _____

Quotient and Career:

66   Actor

151   Writer

93 R6   Teacher

12 R3   Soldier

36   Peanut Farmer

54   Tailor

48 R1   Professor

93 R4   Newspaperman

Many women have done deeds that have made history, but we don't always hear about it! Here's your chance to find out more.

Read about the deed in the first column. Then find the sentence in the second column that continues the story. Divide the number in the first column by the number in the second column and match the quotient to find the accomplished woman.

Elizabeth Blackwell 2,958
Nellie Bly 4,232
Lydia Pinkham 4,319
Ida B. Wells 6,307
Sarah Edmonds 1,065

This woman was called "the best reporter in America." (12,696)

_____

This woman disguised herself as a man to fight in the Civil War. (2,130)

_____

About 20,000 people came to watch her become the first woman to receive an M.D. (a doctor's degree). (14,790)

_____

When she was 22, this woman was forced to leave a train because she wouldn't sit in the "colored only" section. (18,921)

_____

In 1873, this woman started selling an herbal medicine and offering advice about women's health. (25,914)

_____

Her medicine sales started earning $300,000 a year! (6)

When she couldn't find an American hospital that would hire her, she began her own hospital. (5)

She wrote a book about her war adventures, titled *Nurse and Spy in the Union Army*. (2)

Once she pretended to be mentally ill so she could write a news story about mental hospitals. (3)

She sued the railroad and continued to write about problems in the South. (3)

Find each quotient.

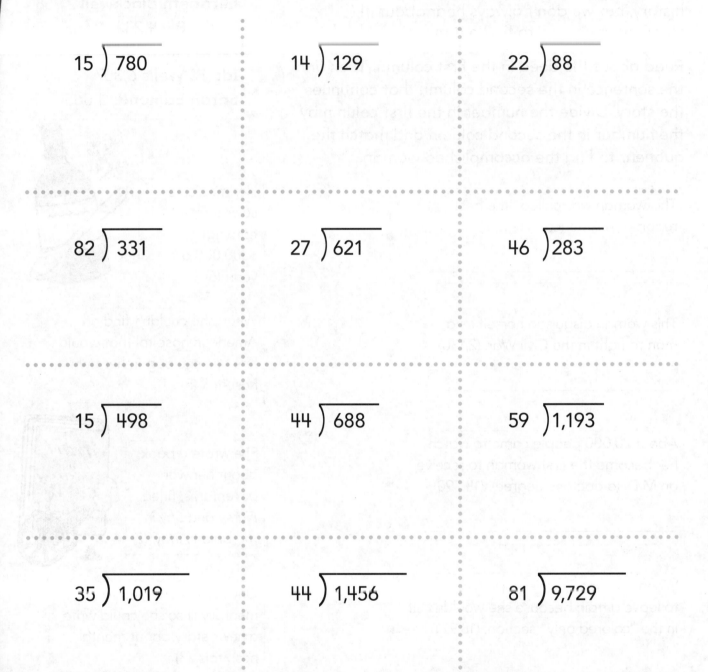

15) 780

14) 129

22) 88

82) 331

27) 621

46) 283

15) 498

44) 688

59) 1,193

35) 1,019

44) 1,456

81) 9,729

These food facts may or may not be true! Divide and decide if the quotient is odd or even. If the quotient is odd, then oddly enough, the fact is true!

1. The shape of a pretzel was invented by a monk who gave "pretzels" to children when they memorized prayers.

   $18,543 \div 21 =$ _____ True False

2. Cracker Jack were the brainchild of a man named Jack Cracker, who invented the snack after some popcorn got stuck in his tooth.

   $25,546 \div 53 =$ _____ True False

3. Hot dogs can be traced back 3,500 year ago, when Babylonians stuffed animal intestines with spicy meat.

   $19,703 \div 61 =$ _____ True False

4. Pasta was first made in China from rice and bean flour.

   $9,845 \div 11 =$ _____ True False

5. Ketchup became popular when Alice White dropped a tomato and dipped some french fries in the juice.

   $9,204 \div 78 =$ _____ True False

6. In 1902, American children received their first boxes of animal cookies. They were to hang the circus box with a string on their Christmas trees.

   $28,035 \div 45 =$ _____ True False

7. Frank Fleer's first try at creating bubble gum was called Blibber-Blubber Bubble Gum.

   $43,097 \div 71 =$ _____ True False

A fraction is in **simplest form** when the only common factor its numerator and denominator have is 1. To find a fraction's simplest form, divide the numerator and denominator by the greatest common factor.

For example, let's take the fraction 12/15. The greatest common factor 12 and 15 have is 3. If we divide both the numerator and denominator by 3, we see that the fraction's simplest form is 4/5.

Circle each fraction that is in simplest form.

$$\frac{9}{12} \qquad\qquad \frac{7}{16} \qquad\qquad \frac{2}{8}$$

$$\frac{4}{15} \qquad\qquad \frac{21}{30} \qquad\qquad \frac{3}{10}$$

Write each fraction in simplest form.

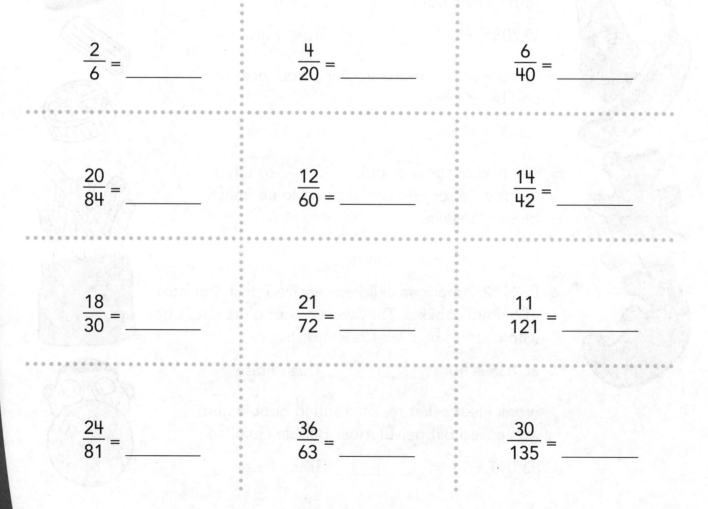

$$\frac{2}{6} = \underline{\hspace{2cm}} \qquad \frac{4}{20} = \underline{\hspace{2cm}} \qquad \frac{6}{40} = \underline{\hspace{2cm}}$$

$$\frac{20}{84} = \underline{\hspace{2cm}} \qquad \frac{12}{60} = \underline{\hspace{2cm}} \qquad \frac{14}{42} = \underline{\hspace{2cm}}$$

$$\frac{18}{30} = \underline{\hspace{2cm}} \qquad \frac{21}{72} = \underline{\hspace{2cm}} \qquad \frac{11}{121} = \underline{\hspace{2cm}}$$

$$\frac{24}{81} = \underline{\hspace{2cm}} \qquad \frac{36}{63} = \underline{\hspace{2cm}} \qquad \frac{30}{135} = \underline{\hspace{2cm}}$$

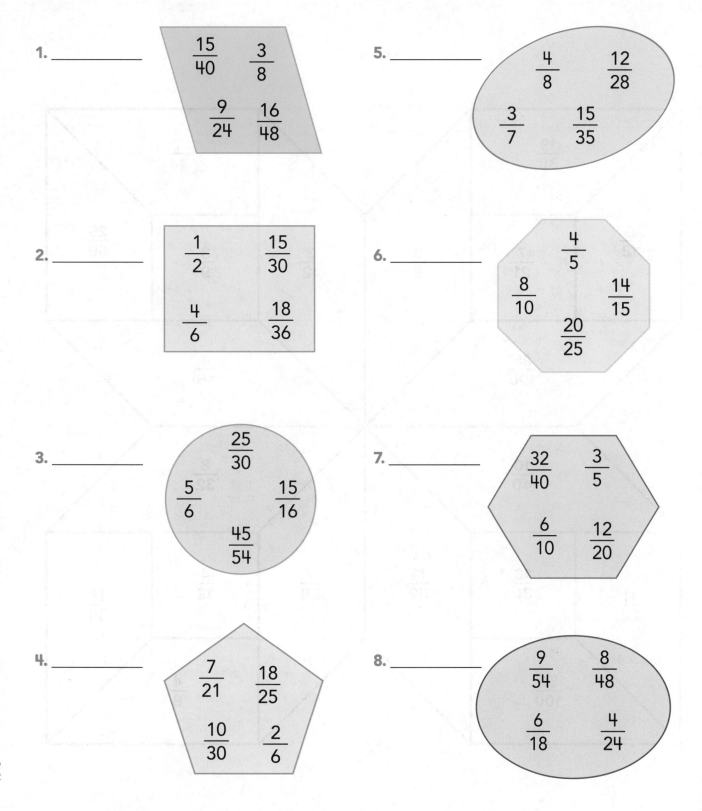

equivalent fractions

In each shape, cross out the fraction that does *not* belong.
Then, write one that *does* belong on the line next to the shape.

1. _____

$\dfrac{15}{40}$ $\dfrac{3}{8}$

$\dfrac{9}{24}$ $\dfrac{16}{48}$

5. _____

$\dfrac{4}{8}$ $\dfrac{12}{28}$

$\dfrac{3}{7}$ $\dfrac{15}{35}$

2. _____

$\dfrac{1}{2}$ $\dfrac{15}{30}$

$\dfrac{4}{6}$ $\dfrac{18}{36}$

6. _____

$\dfrac{4}{5}$

$\dfrac{8}{10}$ $\dfrac{14}{15}$

$\dfrac{20}{25}$

3. _____

$\dfrac{25}{30}$

$\dfrac{5}{6}$ $\dfrac{15}{16}$

$\dfrac{45}{54}$

7. _____

$\dfrac{32}{40}$ $\dfrac{3}{5}$

$\dfrac{6}{10}$ $\dfrac{12}{20}$

4. _____

$\dfrac{7}{21}$ $\dfrac{18}{25}$

$\dfrac{10}{30}$ $\dfrac{2}{6}$

8. _____

$\dfrac{9}{54}$ $\dfrac{8}{48}$

$\dfrac{6}{18}$ $\dfrac{4}{24}$

Color the fractions equivalent to $\frac{1}{2}$ dark blue. Color the fractions equivalent to $\frac{1}{3}$ red. Color the fractions equivalent to $\frac{1}{4}$ light blue.

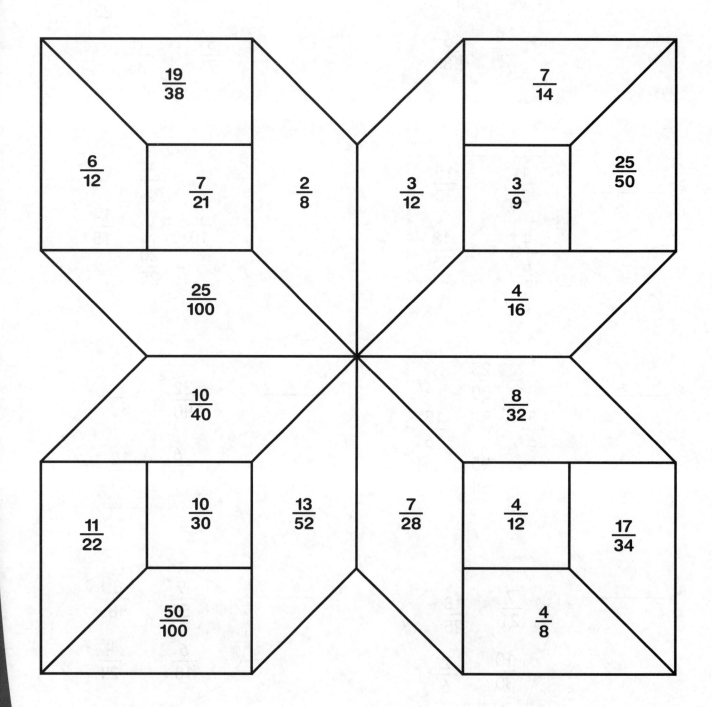

Compare each pair of fractions.
Use **<**, **=**, or **>**. The first one
has been done for you.

Here's a quick way to compare two fractions: First, multiply the denominator of the second fraction with the numerator of the first fraction and write the product above the first fraction. Then, multiply the denominator of the first fraction with the numerator of the second fraction and write the product above the second fraction. Finally, compare the first product with the second product to see if the first fraction is greater than, less than, or equal to the second fraction.

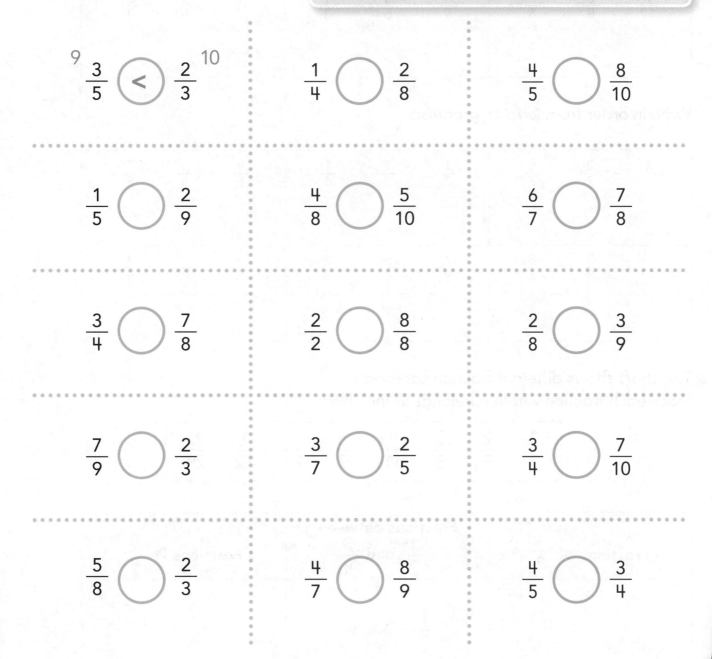

$^9\ \dfrac{3}{5}\ \boxed{<}\ \dfrac{2}{3}\ ^{10}$ $\dfrac{1}{4}\ \bigcirc\ \dfrac{2}{8}$ $\dfrac{4}{5}\ \bigcirc\ \dfrac{8}{10}$

$\dfrac{1}{5}\ \bigcirc\ \dfrac{2}{9}$ $\dfrac{4}{8}\ \bigcirc\ \dfrac{5}{10}$ $\dfrac{6}{7}\ \bigcirc\ \dfrac{7}{8}$

$\dfrac{3}{4}\ \bigcirc\ \dfrac{7}{8}$ $\dfrac{2}{2}\ \bigcirc\ \dfrac{8}{8}$ $\dfrac{2}{8}\ \bigcirc\ \dfrac{3}{9}$

$\dfrac{7}{9}\ \bigcirc\ \dfrac{2}{3}$ $\dfrac{3}{7}\ \bigcirc\ \dfrac{2}{5}$ $\dfrac{3}{4}\ \bigcirc\ \dfrac{7}{10}$

$\dfrac{5}{8}\ \bigcirc\ \dfrac{2}{3}$ $\dfrac{4}{7}\ \bigcirc\ \dfrac{8}{9}$ $\dfrac{4}{5}\ \bigcirc\ \dfrac{3}{4}$

Write in order from *greatest* to *least*.

$\frac{2}{9}$ $\frac{7}{9}$ $\frac{5}{9}$	$\frac{1}{5}$ $\frac{1}{3}$ $\frac{1}{8}$	$\frac{3}{5}$ $\frac{3}{4}$ $\frac{3}{8}$
$\frac{7}{12}$ $\frac{3}{4}$ $\frac{5}{6}$	$\frac{4}{9}$ $\frac{5}{6}$ $\frac{1}{3}$	$\frac{2}{5}$ $\frac{9}{10}$ $\frac{3}{4}$

Write in order from *least* to *greatest*.

$\frac{3}{7}$ $\frac{2}{7}$ $\frac{4}{7}$	$\frac{1}{2}$ $\frac{1}{3}$ $\frac{1}{6}$	$\frac{4}{5}$ $\frac{1}{4}$ $\frac{7}{8}$
$\frac{11}{12}$ $\frac{3}{8}$ $\frac{5}{6}$	$\frac{7}{9}$ $\frac{5}{6}$ $\frac{2}{3}$	$\frac{4}{5}$ $\frac{7}{10}$ $\frac{3}{4}$

The chart shows different fraction categories.
Place each fraction where it belongs in the chart.

$$\frac{2}{3} \quad \frac{2}{5} \quad \frac{3}{5} \quad \frac{4}{11} \quad \frac{5}{7} \quad \frac{9}{10} \quad \frac{1}{12} \quad \frac{21}{24}$$

Fractions $< \frac{1}{2}$	Fractions between $\frac{1}{2}$ and $\frac{3}{4}$	Fractions $> \frac{3}{4}$

This quilt is made of 16 square sections sewn together.
The quilt represents one whole.

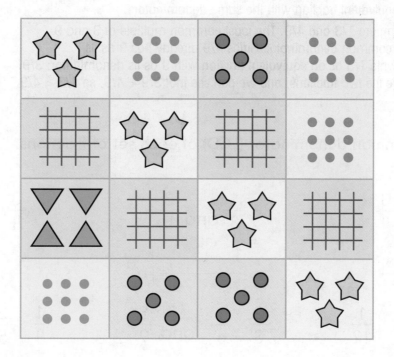

Write the fraction or mixed number represented by each description.

1. The starred sections   _____

2. The circle sections   _____

3. The dotted, starred, and triangle sections   _____

4. 1 quilt and 3 dotted sections   _____

5. 2 quilts plus the crossed sections   _____

6. 1 quilt plus all the sections   _____

When evaluating fractions with different denominators, first find the least common denominator (or least common multiple of both denominators), then rewrite each fraction as an equivalent fraction with the same denominators.

For example, let's compare 1/3 and 4/9. The least common multiple of 3 and 9 is 9—that's the least common denominator. Since 4/9 already has 9 as its denominator, let's rewrite 1/3 as an equivalent fraction with 9 as its denominator: 3/9. Now we can compare the two fractions, and we can see that 3/9 < 4/9, so 1/3 < 4/9.

Find the least common denominator (LCD) of each set of fractions.

$\dfrac{1}{2}$ and $\dfrac{3}{4}$

$\dfrac{1}{3}$ and $\dfrac{3}{5}$

$\dfrac{3}{4}$ and $\dfrac{9}{20}$

_____

_____

_____

$\dfrac{1}{3}$, $\dfrac{5}{6}$, and $\dfrac{1}{12}$

$\dfrac{2}{3}$, $\dfrac{1}{6}$, and $\dfrac{5}{9}$

$\dfrac{1}{4}$, $\dfrac{2}{5}$, and $\dfrac{1}{8}$

_____

_____

_____

Find each sum. Write answers in simplest form.

$\dfrac{2}{3} + \dfrac{1}{8} =$

$\dfrac{1}{3} + \dfrac{4}{9} =$

$\dfrac{1}{6} + \dfrac{2}{5} =$

$\dfrac{5}{6} + \dfrac{5}{9} =$

$\dfrac{3}{8} + \dfrac{1}{4} =$

$\dfrac{4}{7} + \dfrac{5}{6} =$

$\dfrac{3}{7} + \dfrac{1}{5} + \dfrac{7}{10} =$

$\dfrac{2}{3} + \dfrac{1}{5} + \dfrac{3}{10} =$

$\dfrac{5}{6} + \dfrac{7}{8} + \dfrac{1}{4} =$

Subtract. Give answers in simplest form.

$\dfrac{7}{8} - \dfrac{1}{2} =$ $\dfrac{7}{9} - \dfrac{2}{3} =$ $\dfrac{7}{8} - \dfrac{1}{8} =$

$\dfrac{2}{3} - \dfrac{8}{15} =$ $\dfrac{3}{4} - \dfrac{5}{12} =$ $\dfrac{8}{15} - \dfrac{1}{3} =$

$\dfrac{5}{6} - \dfrac{4}{5} =$ $\dfrac{4}{5} - \dfrac{1}{6} =$ $\dfrac{8}{9} - \dfrac{3}{4} =$

$\dfrac{3}{7} - \dfrac{1}{14} =$ $\dfrac{9}{10} - \dfrac{2}{5} =$ $\dfrac{2}{5} - \dfrac{2}{7} =$

$\dfrac{19}{21} - \dfrac{4}{7} =$ $\dfrac{1}{2} - \dfrac{1}{8} =$ $\dfrac{9}{10} - \dfrac{1}{5} =$

Teachers never want to see these animals in their classes, unless, of course, they can watch them every minute of the day. Which animals aren't trustworthy?

Add or subtract the fractions. Rename if necessary. Next to the answer space is a letter. When you find your answer in the riddle box, place that letter above it to solve the riddle.

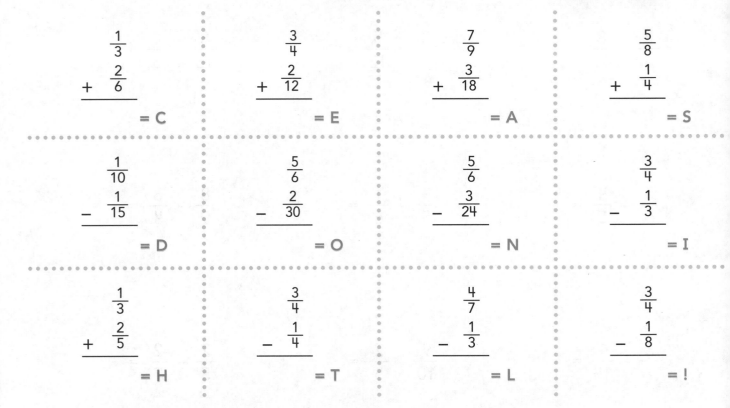

$$\frac{1}{3}$$
$$+ \frac{2}{6}$$
_____ = C

$$\frac{3}{4}$$
$$+ \frac{2}{12}$$
_____ = E

$$\frac{7}{9}$$
$$+ \frac{3}{18}$$
_____ = A

$$\frac{5}{8}$$
$$+ \frac{1}{4}$$
_____ = S

$$\frac{1}{10}$$
$$- \frac{1}{15}$$
_____ = D

$$\frac{5}{6}$$
$$- \frac{2}{30}$$
_____ = O

$$\frac{5}{6}$$
$$- \frac{3}{24}$$
_____ = N

$$\frac{3}{4}$$
$$- \frac{1}{3}$$
_____ = I

$$\frac{1}{3}$$
$$+ \frac{2}{5}$$
_____ = H

$$\frac{3}{4}$$
$$- \frac{1}{4}$$
_____ = T

$$\frac{4}{7}$$
$$- \frac{1}{3}$$
_____ = L

$$\frac{3}{4}$$
$$- \frac{1}{8}$$
_____ = !

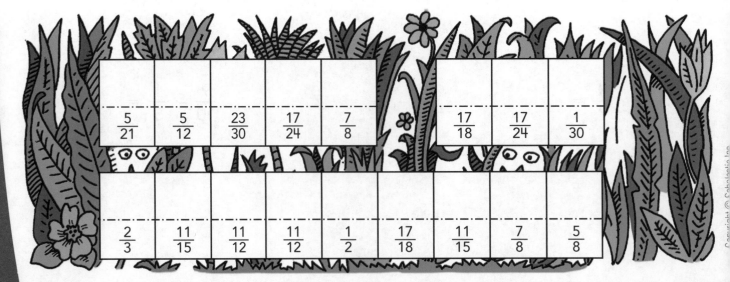

| $\frac{5}{21}$ | $\frac{5}{12}$ | $\frac{23}{30}$ | $\frac{17}{24}$ | $\frac{7}{8}$ | | $\frac{17}{18}$ | $\frac{17}{24}$ | $\frac{1}{30}$ |

| $\frac{2}{3}$ | $\frac{11}{15}$ | $\frac{11}{12}$ | $\frac{11}{12}$ | $\frac{1}{2}$ | $\frac{17}{18}$ | $\frac{11}{15}$ | $\frac{7}{8}$ | $\frac{5}{8}$ |

Convert these mixed numbers to improper fractions.

To convert a mixed number to an improper fraction, multiply the denominator of the fraction with the whole number (to see how many fractional parts are in the whole number), then add the numerator (to find the total number of parts).

For example, let's convert 2 1/4. First, multiply the denominator by the whole number (4 x 2), then add the numerator (1): 2 1/4 = 9/4.

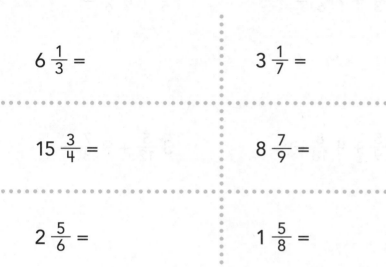

$6\frac{1}{3} =$ $3\frac{1}{7} =$ $4\frac{5}{12} =$

$15\frac{3}{4} =$ $8\frac{7}{9} =$ $5\frac{3}{5} =$

$2\frac{5}{6} =$ $1\frac{5}{8} =$ $7\frac{2}{3} =$

Convert these improper fractions to mixed numbers.

To convert an improper fraction to a mixed number, simply divide the numerator by the denominator. The remainder is the numerator of the fraction.

For example, let's take 5/2. 5 divided by 2 equals 2 R1. So 5/2 = 2 1/2.

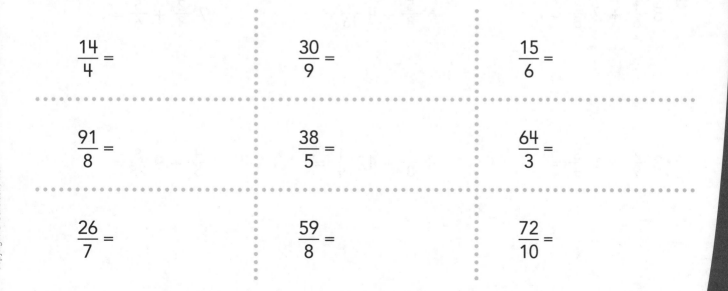

$\frac{14}{4} =$ $\frac{30}{9} =$ $\frac{15}{6} =$

$\frac{91}{8} =$ $\frac{38}{5} =$ $\frac{64}{3} =$

$\frac{26}{7} =$ $\frac{59}{8} =$ $\frac{72}{10} =$

Find each sum in simplest form.

To add mixed numbers and fractions, first rewrite them as improper fractions with the same denominators. Then solve and rewrite the sum in simplest form.

$10 \frac{3}{5} + 3 =$

$4 \frac{1}{3} + 7 \frac{1}{6} =$

$\frac{4}{5} + 8 \frac{1}{6} =$

$4 \frac{3}{4} + 2 \frac{7}{20} =$

$7 \frac{5}{9} + 4 \frac{8}{18} =$

$3 \frac{5}{12} + 9 \frac{7}{8} =$

$5 \frac{7}{12} + 3 \frac{2}{3} =$

$\frac{5}{8} + 1 \frac{1}{4} =$

$8 \frac{1}{2} + 4 \frac{1}{3} =$

$5 \frac{1}{6} + 2 \frac{3}{5} =$

$6 \frac{5}{8} + 4 \frac{9}{16} =$

$7 \frac{2}{3} + \frac{5}{6} =$

$3 \frac{2}{9} + 1 \frac{3}{4} =$

$8 \frac{1}{8} + 12 \frac{1}{4} =$

$\frac{4}{5} + 9 \frac{8}{25} =$

Write each difference in
simplest form.

To subtract mixed numbers and fractions, first rewrite
them as improper fractions with the same denominators.
Then solve and rewrite the difference in simplest form.

$3 \frac{2}{5}$
$- \ 2 \frac{1}{5}$

$5 \frac{7}{8}$
$- \ 1 \frac{3}{8}$

$8 \frac{5}{6}$
$- \ 2 \frac{1}{3}$

$7 \frac{15}{20}$
$- \ 4 \frac{3}{5}$

3
$- \ 1 \frac{1}{2}$

$6 \frac{1}{5}$
$- \ 2 \frac{2}{3}$

$6 \frac{4}{12}$
$- \ 5 \frac{1}{3}$

$7 \frac{1}{4}$
$- \ 4 \frac{2}{3}$

$9 \frac{3}{8}$
$- \ 2 \frac{5}{16}$

$5 \frac{5}{15}$
$- \ 2 \frac{3}{10}$

$10 \frac{7}{16}$
$- \ 8 \frac{1}{4}$

$12 \frac{3}{12}$
$- \ 2 \frac{6}{18}$

Find each product in simplest form.

Multiplying fractions is as simple as multiplying the numerators first, then multiplying the denominators.

$\frac{4}{5} \times \frac{1}{4} =$ _____

$\frac{1}{5} \times \frac{2}{3} =$ _____

$\frac{5}{6} \times \frac{1}{3} =$ _____

$\frac{5}{8} \times \frac{4}{9} =$ _____

$\frac{3}{10} \times \frac{2}{5} =$ _____

$0 \times \frac{1}{9} =$ _____

$\frac{6}{7} \times \frac{3}{4} =$ _____

$\frac{4}{7} \times \frac{8}{11} =$ _____

$\frac{5}{6} \times \frac{8}{10} =$ _____

Compare. Write **<**, **=**, or **>**.

$\frac{2}{5} \times \frac{1}{4} \bigcirc \frac{1}{4} \times \frac{2}{3}$

$\frac{5}{6} \times \frac{9}{10} \bigcirc \frac{1}{2} \times \frac{4}{5}$

$\frac{7}{8} \times \frac{1}{6} \bigcirc \frac{1}{6} \times \frac{7}{8}$

$\frac{3}{8} \times \frac{1}{4} \bigcirc \frac{1}{4} \times \frac{3}{16}$

$\frac{1}{4} \times \frac{2}{5} \bigcirc \frac{1}{5} \times \frac{5}{6}$

$\frac{4}{9} \times \frac{3}{5} \bigcirc \frac{3}{6} \times \frac{3}{5}$

To multiply mixed numbers and fractions, first
convert the mixed number to an improper fraction.
Then multiply both fractions.

Find each product in simplest form.

$\frac{4}{5} \times 40 =$

$12 \times \frac{2}{3} =$

$\frac{5}{6} \times 48 =$

$2\frac{2}{5} \times \frac{5}{6} =$

$\frac{6}{7} \times 2\frac{1}{3} =$

$3\frac{3}{5} \times 1\frac{2}{3} =$

$8\frac{1}{2} \times \frac{1}{3} =$

$\frac{5}{8} \times 3\frac{3}{4} =$

$4\frac{2}{3} \times \frac{1}{7} =$

$9 \times \frac{3}{5} =$

$2\frac{1}{2} \times \frac{4}{5} =$

$\frac{5}{7} \times 6 =$

$\frac{2}{3} \times 2\frac{5}{6} =$

$1\frac{1}{10} \times 3\frac{2}{3} =$

$1\frac{1}{2} \times \frac{1}{2} =$

Dividing fractions is as easy as multiplying fractions. Simply multiply the number by the reciprocal of the divisor.

For example, let's take 5 ÷ 1/2. The reciprocal of 1/2 is 2/1 or 2. Multiply that by 5 and the answer is 10. So 5 ÷ 1/2 = 10.

Divide.

$3 \div \frac{1}{2} =$

$4 \div \frac{1}{3} =$

$6 \div \frac{1}{8} =$

$12 \div \frac{1}{2} =$

$\frac{1}{3} \div 4 =$

$\frac{1}{4} \div 6 =$

$\frac{1}{6} \div 5 =$

$\frac{1}{2} \div 8 =$

$9 \div \frac{1}{5} =$

$\frac{2}{5} \div 4 =$

$3 \div \frac{4}{5} =$

$10 \div \frac{1}{2} =$

$\frac{7}{8} \div 2 =$

$15 \div \frac{3}{4} =$

$\frac{2}{3} \div 6 =$

Write the decimal.

1. three tenths _____

2. four hundredths _____

3. sixty-one hundredths _____

4. sixteen thousandths _____

5. nine thousandths _____

6. two and three tenths _____

Write the word form.

7. 0.5 _____

8. 0.67 _____

9. 1.025 _____

10. Circle each number that has a 6 in the tenths place.

　6.5　　　　　　　　7.63　　　　　　　　24.06　　　　　　　　60.623

11. Circle each number that has a 6 in the hundredths place.

　623.05　　　　　　7.16　　　　　　　　26.26　　　　　　　　30.67

12. Circle each number that has a 6 in the thousandths place.

　6.615　　　　　　　7.162　　　　　　　84.006　　　　　　　10.326

Approach this activity with caution—
it's been known to produce high levels of
fun and learning! Each digit can occupy only
one place to make the whole puzzle fit
together perfectly.

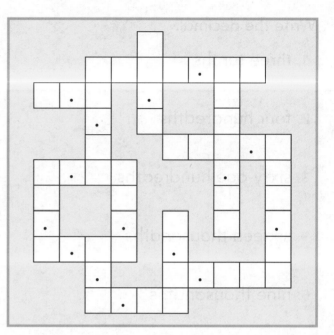

Write each decimal in standard form on the
lines below. Fit the number into the puzzle.
The decimal points occupy one space and
are already written in the puzzle.

1. three and forty-four hundredths

_____

2. four and six tenths

_____

3. forty-one and seven tenths

4. four thousand sixteen and thirty-two hundredths

5. nine hundred forty-seven and thirty-six hundredths

6. six and five tenths

7. fifty-six and four tenths

8. one and thirty-five hundredths

9. one and six thousandths

10. forty-five and sixty-three hundredths

11. fifteen and three tenths

12. three hundred seventeen and nine tenths

13. three thousand seven and fifty-five hundredths

14. six and nineteen hundredths

15. six and ninety-nine hundredths

Write as a decimal.

$\frac{3}{10}$ = _____

$\frac{7}{10}$ = _____

$\frac{1}{100}$ = _____

$\frac{6}{100}$ = _____

$\frac{173}{1,000}$ = _____

$\frac{4}{1,000}$ = _____

Write a decimal equivalent to each fraction.
Circle the greatest and least decimals.

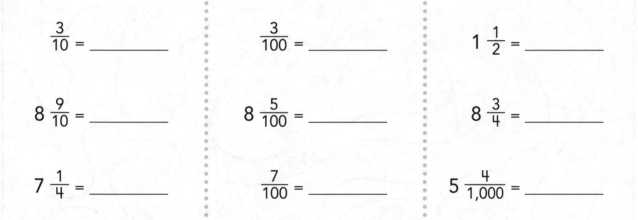

$\frac{3}{10}$ = _____

$\frac{3}{100}$ = _____

$1\frac{1}{2}$ = _____

$8\frac{9}{10}$ = _____

$8\frac{5}{100}$ = _____

$8\frac{3}{4}$ = _____

$7\frac{1}{4}$ = _____

$\frac{7}{100}$ = _____

$5\frac{4}{1,000}$ = _____

Write an equivalent fraction or mixed number.

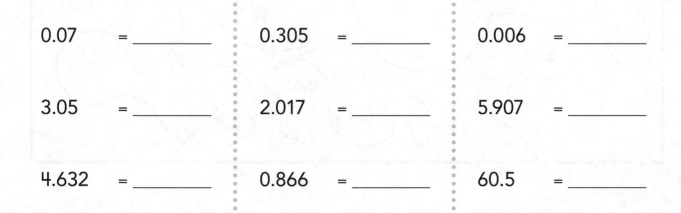

0.07 = _____

0.305 = _____

0.006 = _____

3.05 = _____

2.017 = _____

5.907 = _____

4.632 = _____

0.866 = _____

60.5 = _____

What do Wearie Willie and the man Emmett Kelly have in common? They're different names for the same person. Emmett Kelly spent hours putting on makeup to magically transform himself into the sad circus clown known as Wearie Willie.

Create your own transformation. Match the fractions in the data bank with the equivalent decimals in the picture puzzle and then shade them. The first one has been done for you.

Data Bank

$\frac{3}{10}$ $\frac{25}{100}$

$16\frac{5}{10}$ $1\frac{2}{10}$

$\frac{14}{100}$ $4\frac{49}{100}$

$\frac{7}{10}$ $\frac{7}{100}$

$15\frac{8}{10}$ $3\frac{3}{10}$

$\frac{71}{100}$ $33\frac{9}{10}$

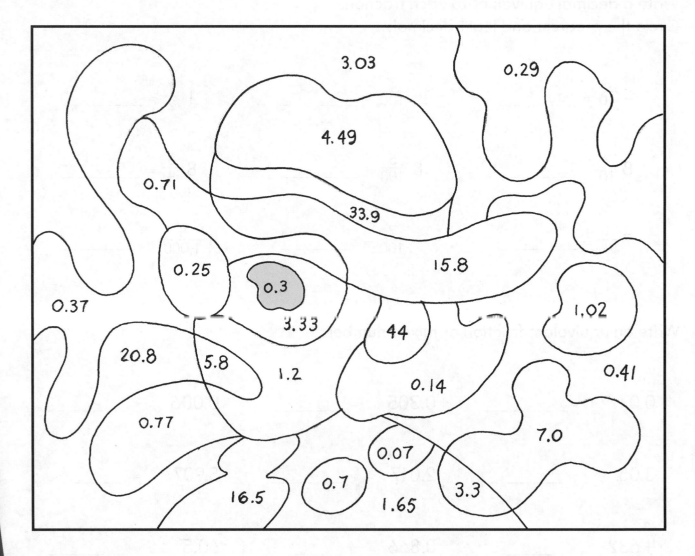

Compare. Write **<**, **=**, or **>**.

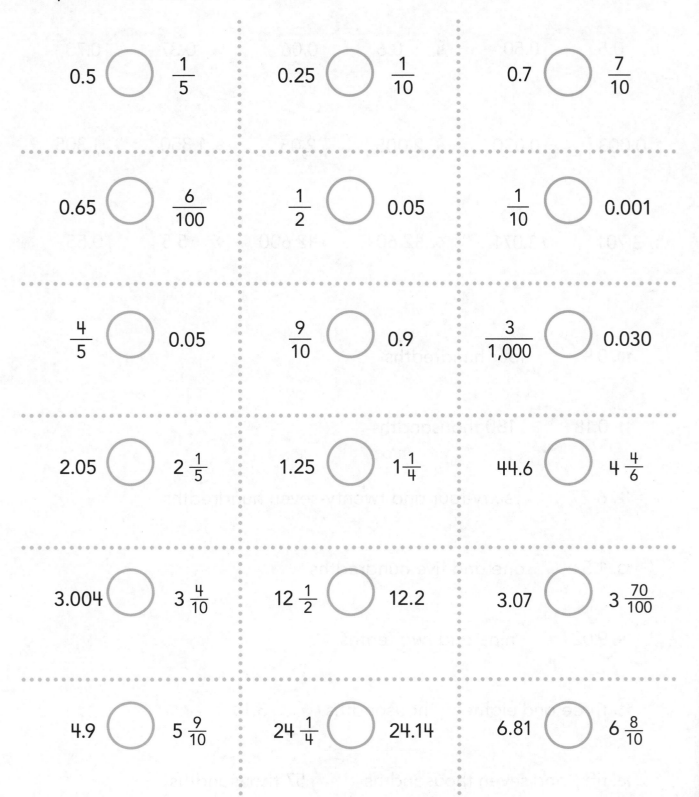

0.5 ◯ $\frac{1}{5}$

0.25 ◯ $\frac{1}{10}$

0.7 ◯ $\frac{7}{10}$

0.65 ◯ $\frac{6}{100}$

$\frac{1}{2}$ ◯ 0.05

$\frac{1}{10}$ ◯ 0.001

$\frac{4}{5}$ ◯ 0.05

$\frac{9}{10}$ ◯ 0.9

$\frac{3}{1,000}$ ◯ 0.030

2.05 ◯ $2\frac{1}{5}$

1.25 ◯ $1\frac{1}{4}$

44.6 ◯ $4\frac{4}{6}$

3.004 ◯ $3\frac{4}{10}$

$12\frac{1}{2}$ ◯ 12.2

3.07 ◯ $3\frac{70}{100}$

4.9 ◯ $5\frac{9}{10}$

$24\frac{1}{4}$ ◯ 24.14

6.81 ◯ $6\frac{8}{10}$

Compare. Write **<**, **=**, or **>**.

1. 0.5 ◯ 0.50

2. 0.003 ◯ 0.030

3. 3.701 ◯ 3.071

4. 0.6 ◯ 0.06

5. 2.005 ◯ 2.05

6. 42.60 ◯ 42.600

7. 0.37 ◯ 0.73

8. 1.350 ◯ 1.305

9. 5.5 ◯ 0.55

10. 0.4 ◯ four hundredths

11. 0.18 ◯ 180 thousandths

12. 6.27 ◯ sixty-four and twenty-seven hundredths

13. 1.5 ◯ one and five hundredths

14. 9.02 ◯ nine and two tenths

15. three and eighteen thousandths ◯ 3.18

16. fifty and seven thousandths ◯ 57 thousandths

Order the decimals from *least* to *greatest*.

1. 0.6   0.2   0.9   0.5

_____

2. 0.04   0.4   0.004   4.0

_____

3. 6.703   6.73   6.307   6.037

_____

4. 0.42   0.029   0.32

_____

5. 0.603   0.2   0.432

_____

Order the decimals from *greatest* to *least*.

6. 0.4   0.004   0.444

_____

7. 0.75   0.507   0.57

_____

8. 0.1   0.19   0.91   0.09

_____

9. 0.7   0.07   0.77   0.077

_____

10. 10.001   10.901   10.909   10.009

_____

When you weigh yourself, you're really measuring how much gravity pulls on you. If you weigh 100 pounds on Earth, you'd weigh only 38 pounds on Mars. That's because the pull of gravity is less on Mars.

The table lists the pull of gravity on the other planets as compared to Earth's. Use it to answer the "weighty" problems that follow.

Planet	Gravitational Pull
Mercury	0.38 times Earth's
Venus	0.91 times Earth's
Earth	1.00 times Earth's
Mars	0.38 times Earth's
Jupiter	2.36 times Earth's
Saturn	1.06 times Earth's
Uranus	0.89 times Earth's
Neptune	1.13 times Earth's

1. Order the decimals from least to greatest. Write the name of the planet next to the decimal.

a. _____

b. _____

c. _____

d. _____

e. _____

f. _____

g. _____

h. _____

2. On which planet would you weigh the most? _____

3. On which planets would you weigh the least? _____

4. On which planets would you weigh the same? _____

5. The pull of gravity on the sun is 27 times Earth's. A person who weighs 100 pounds on Earth would weigh _____ pounds on the sun.

Hold on to your hat, this roundup is guaranteed
to have your head spinning in circles.

Use the digits **6**, **7**, **1**, **4**, and **9** to make each sentence true.
Use all five digits in each number.
Place the decimal point in one of the answer boxes.

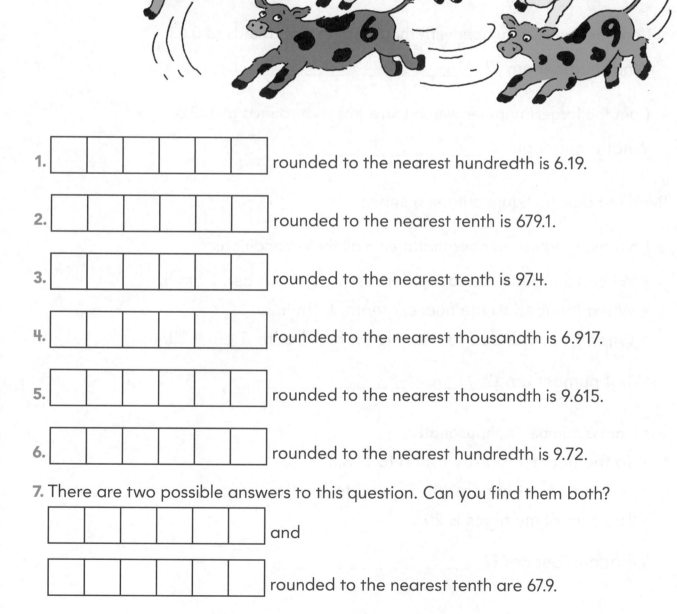

1. [   ][   ][   ][   ][   ] rounded to the nearest hundredth is 6.19.

2. [   ][   ][   ][   ][   ] rounded to the nearest tenth is 679.1.

3. [   ][   ][   ][   ][   ] rounded to the nearest tenth is 97.4.

4. [   ][   ][   ][   ][   ] rounded to the nearest thousandth is 6.917.

5. [   ][   ][   ][   ][   ] rounded to the nearest thousandth is 9.615.

6. [   ][   ][   ][   ][   ] rounded to the nearest hundredth is 9.72.

7. There are two possible answers to this question. Can you find them both?

[   ][   ][   ][   ][   ] and

[   ][   ][   ][   ][   ] rounded to the nearest tenth are 67.9.

Round each decimal to the nearest tenth *and* hundredth.

Number	Nearest Tenth	Nearest Hundredth
6.157		
10.052		
3.336		

Solve the riddles.

1. I am the smallest number with thousandths that rounds to 0.63.

   What number am I? _____

2. I am the largest number with hundredths that rounds to 122.6.

   What number am I?_____

Read the clues to figure out the number.

3. I am the greatest number that meets all these conditions:

   • When you round me to the nearest whole number, I am 4.
   • When rounded to the nearest tenth, I am 4.2.
   • When I am rounded to the nearest hundredth, I am 4.23.

   What number am I? _____

4. • I am a number in thousandths.
   • To the nearest tenth, I round to 243.5.
   • To the nearest hundredth, I round to 243.46.
   • The sum of my digits is 20.

   What number am I? _____

Write the correct number from the number bank.

Number Bank

3.5   9.05   9.5

0.05   4.9

10.05   10.5   10.6

0.50   4.5

1. It is the greatest number. _____

2. It is a number equal to 0.5. _____

3. They are numbers that round to 10. _____

4. It is a number that is less than 0.1. _____

Use all the digits in the number bank and a decimal point to form the following numbers. The decimal point must have at least one number before it or after it.

Number Bank

2   6   1   4

5. the greatest number _____

6. the least number _____

7. a number less than 2 with a 4 in hundredths place _____

Write the decimal from the number bank that fits each clue.

Number Bank

4.075   4.34   4.75

8.50   8.005

8. _____ is much nearer to 4 than to 5.

9. _____ is halfway between 8 and 9.

10. _____ is the same as four and three fourths.

11. _____ is a little more than 8.

12. Which number is not used? _____

Use the models to add the decimal amounts shown.
The first one has been done for you.

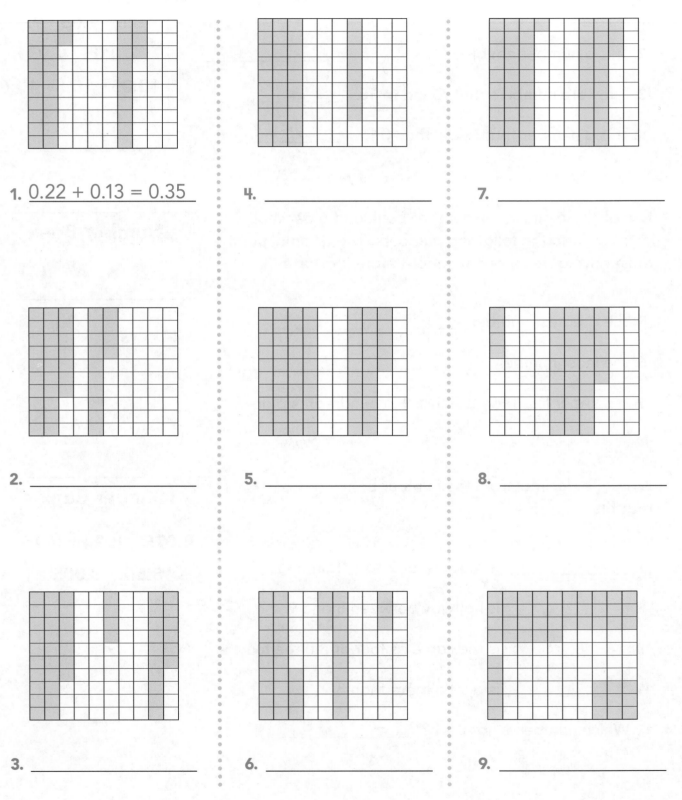

1. 0.22 + 0.13 = 0.35

4. _____

7. _____

2. _____

5. _____

8. _____

3. _____

6. _____

9. _____

Add the decimals.

2.3 + 56.4 =

100 + 3.09 =

2.4 + 68.05 =

3.07 + 28.5 =

5.25 + 603.8 =

4.99 + 38.1 =

5.32 + 26.4 =

1.05 + 462 =

25 + 0.63 =

52.3 + 5.23 =

71.04 + 5.2 =

3.7 + 25.86 =

16.2 + 0.4 + 285.3 =

2.6 + 58.32 + 0.08 =

2.55 + 68.3 + 702.9 =

Each model represents decimal subtraction. Write the subtraction equation below each model. The first one has been done for you.

1. $0.76 - 0.24 = 0.52$

4. _____

7. _____

2. _____

5. _____

8. _____

3. _____

6. _____

9. _____

Subtract the decimals.

12.5 – 7.3 =	8.54 – 2.91 =	6.4 – 3.25 =
45.1 – 2.69 =	83 – 2.5 =	69 – 68.48 =
32.68 – 5.1 =	9.94 – 7.11 =	53.2 – 5.23 =
6.98 – 2.51 =	73 – 0.4 =	562.3 – 28.5 =
85.216 – 23.95 =	115.3 – 23.58 =	29.4 – 16 =

Use the models to multiply the given decimals.

1. 0.46 × 2 = _____

2. 0.81 × 2 = _____

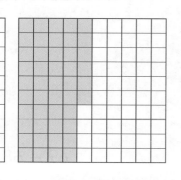 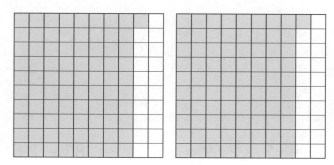

Multiply to find the product.

4 × 0.3 = _____   0.6 × 8 = _____   0.3 × 9 = _____

0.8 × 0.3 = _____   0.7 × 0.7 = _____   0.3 × 0.3 = _____

5 × 0.03 = _____   0.09 × 7 = _____   0.04 × 8 = _____

0.6 × 0.07 = _____   0.03 × 0.2 = _____   0.05 × 0.3 = _____

Use the models to divide the given decimals.

1. 0.18 ÷ 2 = _____

2. 0.56 ÷ 2 = _____

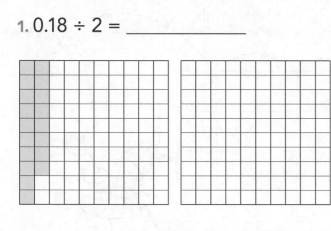 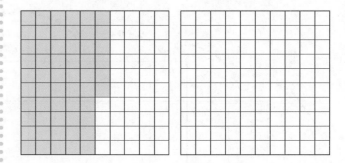

Divide the decimals by the whole numbers.

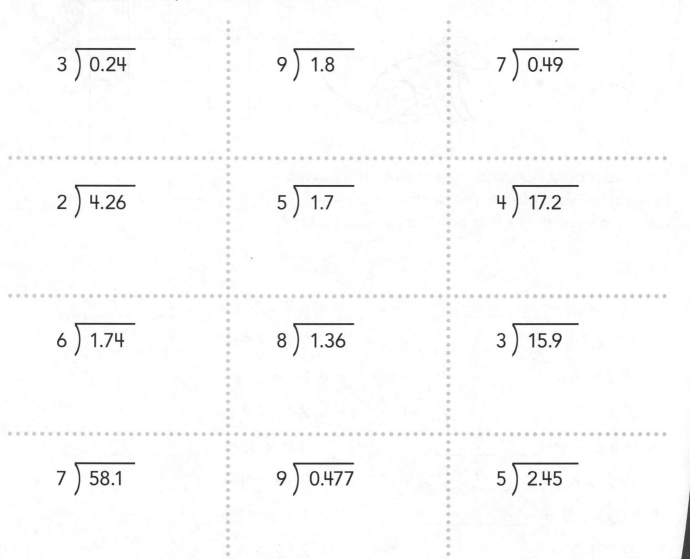

$3 \overline{)0.24}$ $9 \overline{)1.8}$ $7 \overline{)0.49}$

$2 \overline{)4.26}$ $5 \overline{)1.7}$ $4 \overline{)17.2}$

$6 \overline{)1.74}$ $8 \overline{)1.36}$ $3 \overline{)15.9}$

$7 \overline{)58.1}$ $9 \overline{)0.477}$ $5 \overline{)2.45}$

Can you find the decimal point in each of these answers?
This crossword puzzle is sure to sharpen your skills and point
you toward success with multiplication and division of decimals.

Find the product or quotient and write the answer
in the crossword puzzle. The decimal point will
occupy a square. The first one has been done for you.

Across

1. $5.9 \times 6.2 =$ _____

3. $3.3 \times 3.8 =$ _____

4. $28.2 \div 6 =$ _____

5. $19.6 \div 2 =$ _____

6. $162.6 \div 6 =$ _____

7. $49.2 \div 6 =$ _____

8. $87.03 \div 3 =$ _____

11. $27.2 \div 2 =$ _____

Down

1. $6.7 \times 5.1 =$ _____

2. $26.4 \div 3 =$ _____

3. $8.1 \times 2.2 =$ _____

4. $2.14 \times 2 =$ _____

5. $4.8 \times 1.9 =$ _____

9. $36.4 \div 4 =$ _____

10. $1.4 \times 1.2 =$ _____

12. $22.2 \div 6 =$ _____

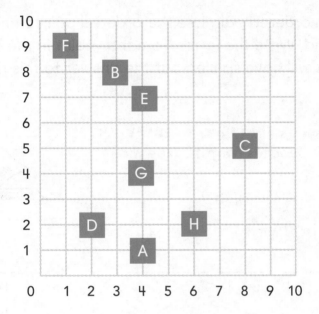

The coordinate grid shows some places in Trina's town:

A   School   B   Gas Station

C   Train Station   D   Pharmacy

E   Paint Store   F   Supermarket

G   Book Shop   H   Clothing Store

Name the ordered pair for each point.

1. A _____   3. H _____

2. D _____   4. F _____

Name the point and the place it represents.

5. (3, 8) _____   7. (2, 2) _____

6. (4, 4) _____   8. (4, 7) _____

Under each blank is an ordered pair. Use the ordered pair to find the correct point on the grid. Write the letter from that point in the blank. When you're done, you will have spelled out the answer to this riddle:

Why did the algebra teacher send back the box of peaches he got in the mail?

Answer:

___	___	___	___	___	___	___		___	___
(2, –3)	(3, 3)	(–5, –2)	(1, 1)	(–1, 1)	(–2, 3)	(3, 3)		(4, 1)	(3, 3)

___ ___ ___   ___ ___ ___ ___ ___ ___ ___
(4, 1) (1, 1) (3, –5)   (5, –3) (–3, –3) (3, –5) (3, 3) (–3, –3) (3, 3) (3, –5)

___ ___ ___ ___ ___!   (___ ___ ___ ___ ___)
(–3, –5) (1, 1) (–4, 1) (–3, –3) (–2, 3)   (–3, –5) (3, 3) (1, 1) (–3, –3) (–2, 3)

1. Figure out the rule. Then draw its graph on the coordinate grid.

   Rule _____

x	y
1	4
2	5
3	6
4	7
5	8

2. Read the rule. Then complete the table.

   The rule is $y = 2x - 1$

x	y
1	1
2	3
3	
	7
5	

   The rule is $y = 3x - 2$

x	y
4	10
5	13
6	
	19
8	

3. Make up your own rule. Record it in the input/output table. Then draw a graph on the coordinate grid to show your rule.

   Rule

   _____

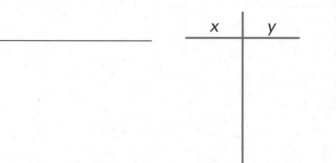

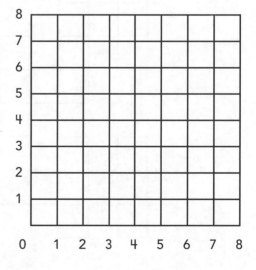

All the clues in this puzzle are about units of customary measure. Along with the puzzle grid, you'll also need the clues, which are on the next page.

ACROSS

1. 1,000 years

4. 12 inches

7. 365.25 days

8. Units for measuring temperature

10. 26 weeks is this part of a year

12. 100 years

13. 12:00 A.M.

15. Abbreviation for weight equivalent to 16 ounces

16. A typical cat might weigh 10 _____.

19. There are 60 _____ in a minute.

21. Number of years in a decade

23. Unit of weight for gems and precious stones

24. There are 24 _____ in a day.

27. There are 60 _____ in an hour.

DOWN

2. There are 12 _____ in a year.

3. 2 pints

5. There are 3,600 seconds in _____ hour.

6. 36 inches

8. There are 7 _____ in a week.

9. 4 quarts

11. 1 square mile = 640 _____

13. 5,280 feet

14. 2,000 pounds

16. There are 8 _____ in a gallon.

17. There are 52 _____ in a year.

18. 1/12th of a foot

20. 10 years

22. 1/16th of a pound

25. Half a dozen

26. 8 ounces (liquid measurement)

Show your work.

1. The area of a rectangular field is 4,800 ft². The length of the field is 80 ft. What is the perimeter of the field?

   _____

2. Alma's room is a rectangle. Its length is 5 yards and its width is 12 feet. It has a 9-foot ceiling. What is the perimeter of her room?

   _____

3. What is the perimeter of Ira's studio apartment?

   _____

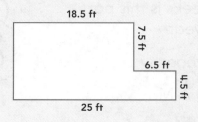

18.5 ft

7.5 ft

6.5 ft

4.5 ft

25 ft

4. Find the area of the shaded figure.

   _____

   What is its perimeter?

   _____

These rectangles have fractional side lengths.
Determine the number of square units in each shape.

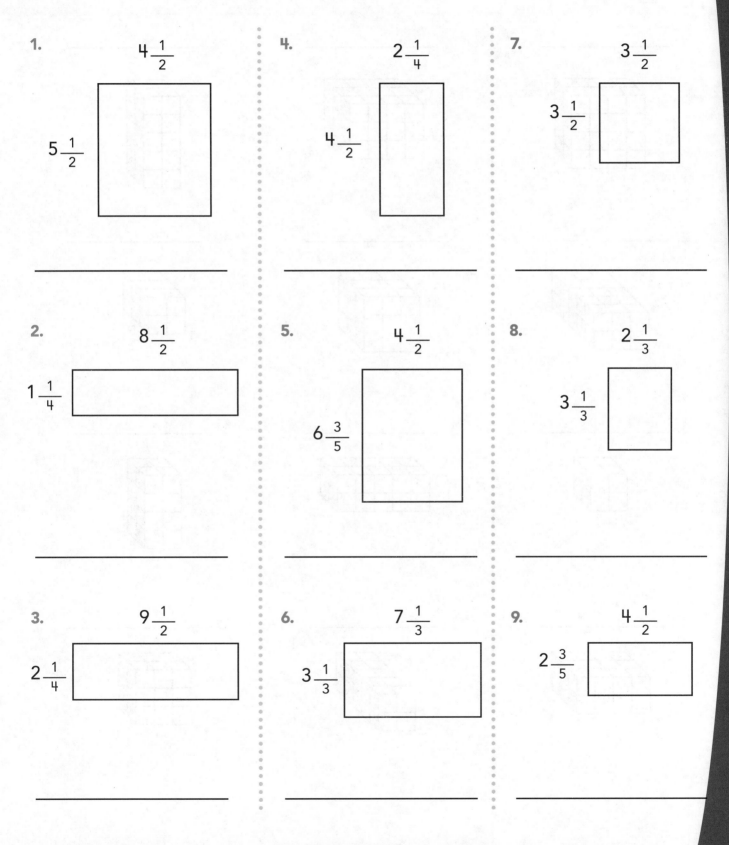

1. $4\frac{1}{2}$

$5\frac{1}{2}$

_____

2. $8\frac{1}{2}$

$1\frac{1}{4}$

_____

3. $9\frac{1}{2}$

$2\frac{1}{4}$

_____

4. $2\frac{1}{4}$

$4\frac{1}{2}$

_____

5. $4\frac{1}{2}$

$6\frac{3}{5}$

_____

6. $7\frac{1}{3}$

$3\frac{1}{3}$

_____

7. $3\frac{1}{2}$

$3\frac{1}{2}$

_____

8. $2\frac{1}{3}$

$3\frac{1}{3}$

_____

9. $4\frac{1}{2}$

$2\frac{3}{5}$

_____

Determine the number of cubic units in each right rectangular prism.

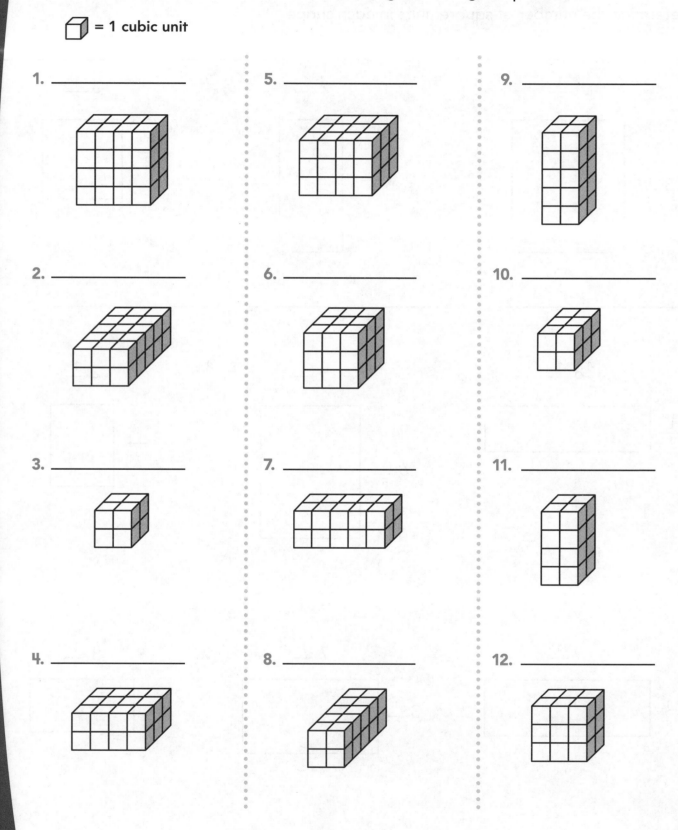

= 1 cubic unit

1. _____

2. _____

3. _____

4. _____

5. _____

6. _____

7. _____

8. _____

9. _____

10. _____

11. _____

12. _____

Determine the number of cubic units in each shape.

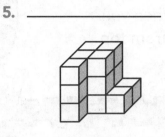 = 1 cubic unit

1. _____

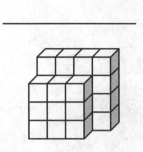

2. _____

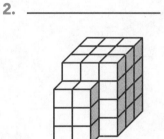

3. _____

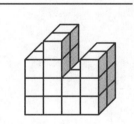

4. _____

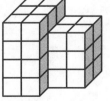

5. _____

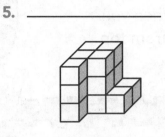

6. _____

7. _____

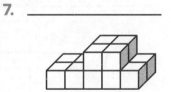

8. _____

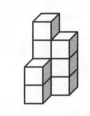

9. _____

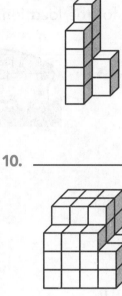

10. _____

11. _____

12. _____

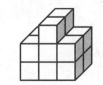

Where is the world's first castle found?

To find out, unscramble each geometry word.
Write the correctly spelled word in the spaces
provided—one letter per space. When you
finish, read the highlighted letters from top
to bottom for the location.

1. NESTMEG ___ ___ [ ] ___ ___ ___ ___

2. NECO ___ [ ] ___ ___

3. ELMOVU ___ ___ ___ [ ] ___ ___

4. CRINAPPLERUDE ___ ___ ___ [ ] ___ ___ ___ ___ ___ ___ ___ ___ ___

5. AYR ___ [ ] ___

6. GLEAN ___ ___ [ ] ___ ___

7. YAMDRIP ___ ___ ___ [ ] ___ ___ ___

8. PESHER ___ ___ ___ [ ] ___ ___

9. MIRPS ___ ___ ___ ___ [ ]

10. REXVET ___ ___ ___ [ ] ___ ___

11. PINTO ___ ___ ___ ___ [ ]

The table shows the area, in square miles, of some of the world's larger islands.

Large Islands Around the World	
Island	**Area (mi²)**
Cuba	42,804
Greenland	840,004
Borneo	288,869
New Guinea	303,381
Honshu	88,982

Source: www.worldatlas.com

Use the data in the table to answer the questions.

1. How much smaller than New Guinea is Borneo? _____

2. Which island is about twice the size of Cuba? _____

3. Which two islands together have an area of about 378,000 square miles when each area is rounded to the nearest thousand?

_____

4. Which two have a difference in area of about 750,000 square miles?

_____

Bonus: Earth's total surface area is about 510 million square kilometers. About 362,000,000 km² are covered by water. How much of the surface is covered by land?

_____

Complete the chart about teens who have part-time jobs.
Then answer the questions.

Teen	Income	Expenses		Savings
		Travel	Food/Fun	
Alex	$70	$6.00	$22.50	
Irma	$54	$4.50		$28.75
Tyrone		$5.30	$18.75	$30.95
Felicia	$86	$7.75	$42.00	

1. Who saved the most money? _____

2. How much more than Irma did Alex save? _____

3. Whose expenses were lowest? _____

4. Who saved less than half of his/her salary? _____

5. How much did the teens save all together? _____

The menu shows today's lunch specials at Bill's Burger Barn.
Use the menu to answer the questions.

Bill's Burger Barn
TODAY'S LUNCH SPECIALS

Bistro Burger With Brie	$7.95
Bacon Buffalo Burger	$5.95
Ostrich Burger (feathers extra)	$9.50
Chipotle Cheeseburger	$6.25
All Desserts (apple pie only)	$4.95
All Sides (salad only)	$1.75
All Drinks	$2.00

1. Dan orders the Ostrich Burger, a side, and a drink. He pays with a $20 bill.
What will his change be?

_____

2. Oliver orders the most expensive burger and a side. He has $15.
Can he also buy a dessert? Explain.

_____

_____

3. Annie spent $13 on her meal, including a $1.30 tip. She ordered three things.
What did she order?

_____

_____

It is noon in New York on March 1.
The table shows times in some other cities around the world.

Use the information in the table to answer the questions.

City	Time	City	Time
Barcelona, Spain	6:00 P.M.	London, England	5:00 P.M.
Cairo, Egypt	7:00 P.M.	Buenos Aires, Argentina	2:00 P.M.
San Juan, Puerto Rico	1:00 P.M.	Tokyo, Japan	2:00 A.M.*
Honolulu, Hawaii	7:00 A.M.	Sydney, Australia	4:00 A.M.*

*the following day

1. If it is 3:00 P.M. in New York, what time is it in

San Juan? _____

Barcelona? _____

Cairo? _____

2. If it is 7:00 A.M. in New York, what time is it in

Tokyo? _____

Sydney? _____

Honolulu? _____

3. If it is 8:00 P.M. in Buenos Aires, what time is it in

New York? _____

San Juan? _____

London? _____

The table shows how long it took three students to do their homework.

Homework Time

	Marcus	Kendra	Leon
Math	$\frac{1}{2}$ h	$\frac{3}{4}$ h	$\frac{5}{6}$ h
Reading	$\frac{4}{5}$ h	$\frac{1}{2}$ h	$\frac{3}{4}$ h
Science	$\frac{3}{4}$ h	$\frac{5}{6}$ h	$\frac{1}{2}$ h

Use the data to answer the questions.

1. Who spent the least amount of time on reading work? _____

   How many minutes was that? _____

2. How many hours did it take Marcus to finish all his homework? _____

3. How many minutes did it take Leon to finish his math and science homework? _____

4. How many minutes longer than Marcus did Kendra spend on her science homework? _____

5. Which two students spent the same amount of time to finish all their homework? _____

   How many minutes was that? _____

All the students at Calloway School named their favorite musical instrument.

The results for the top five answers are shown.

Favorite Musical Instruments	
Instrument	Votes
Guitar	321
Piano	169
Violin	93
Drums	114
Triangle	19

Use the data to answer the questions.

1. Which instrument got about $\frac{1}{5}$ as many votes as violin? _____

2. Which instrument got about $\frac{3}{7}$ of all the votes? _____

3. Which instrument got a bit less than $\frac{1}{4}$ of all votes? _____

   Which one got about $\frac{2}{3}$ the votes that one got? _____

4. Which 3 instruments together got about $\frac{3}{4}$ of all votes? _____

   _____

The graph shows how the top three baseball teams in the National League West finished in one year.

Use the data to answer the questions.

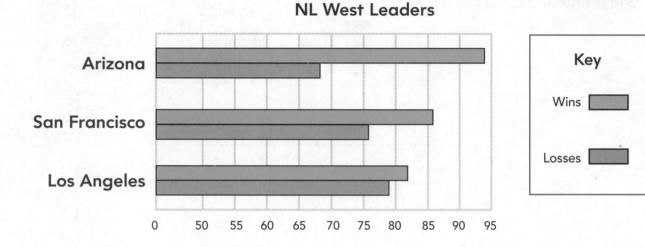

NL West Leaders

Key

Wins

Losses

1. What information does the graph compare?

_____

_____

2. Which bar represents how many games a team won? _____

3. Which team won 10 more games than it lost? _____

4. Which team lost about 10 fewer games than Los Angeles did?

_____

5. About how many more games did Arizona win than lose?

_____

The table shows sports teams' records for two consecutive years.

Display the data in a horizontal double-bar graph. Make a key. Give your graph a title and label the data.

Team	2014 Wins	2015 Wins
Soccer	12	15
Basketball	10	18
Baseball	14	11
Tennis	16	16
Golf	4	6

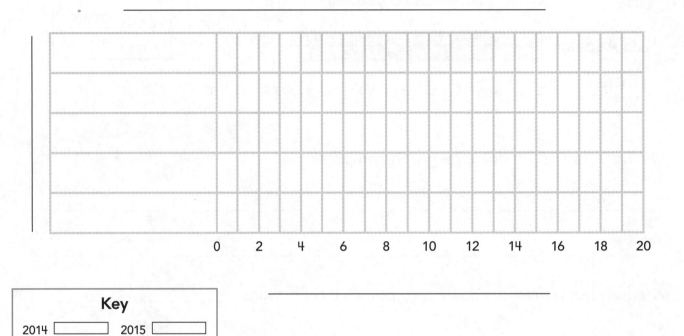

0   2   4   6   8   10   12   14   16   18   20

Key

2014 ☐   2015 ☐

Summarize what your table shows about the teams. _____

_____

_____

The circle graph shows how Hallie's Hamster, Dave, spends his day.

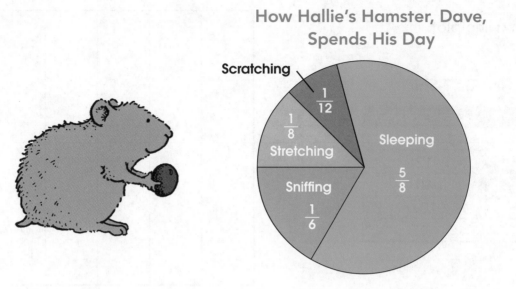

How Hallie's Hamster, Dave,
Spends His Day

Scratching
$\frac{1}{12}$
$\frac{1}{8}$
Stretching
Sleeping
$\frac{5}{8}$
Sniffing
$\frac{1}{6}$

Use the data to answer the questions.

1. On which activity does Dave spend
   the least amount of time each day?

   _____

2. How many hours each day does Dave sleep? _____

3. What does Dave spend 4 hours
   doing each day?

   _____

4. How many more hours does Dave spend
   sleeping than stretching each day?

   _____

5. How many more hours does Dave spend
   scratching and sniffing than stretching?

   _____

A music teacher ordered T-shirts for the chorus.
The table shows the different sizes she got.

Show the data in a line plot.

Chorus T-Shirts

Sizes	Shirts Ordered
S	7
M	12
L	10
XL	0
XXL	1

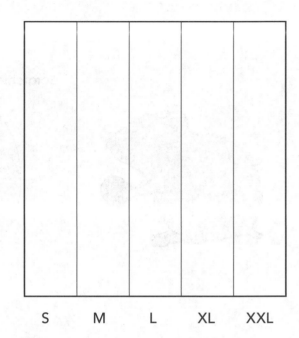

S   M   L   XL   XXL

Summarize what your line plot shows about T-shirt size data.

Use the words *mode, range,* and *outlier.*

_____

_____

Many teams took part in Field Day events.
The line plot shows the number of medals teams won.

Use the data to answer the questions.

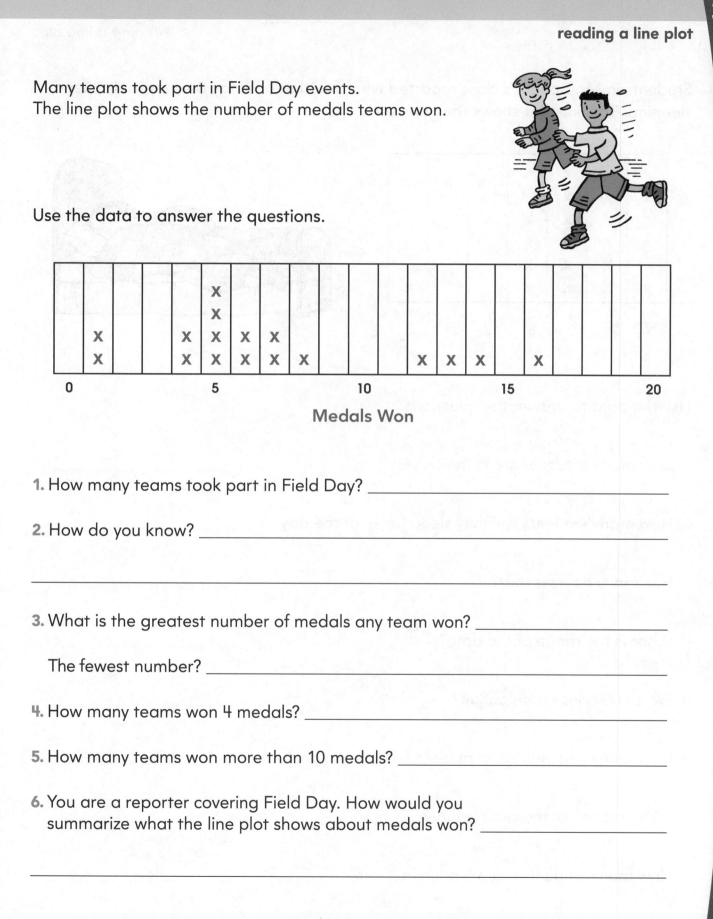

Medals Won

1. How many teams took part in Field Day? _____

2. How do you know? _____

_____

3. What is the greatest number of medals any team won? _____

The fewest number? _____

4. How many teams won 4 medals? _____

5. How many teams won more than 10 medals? _____

6. You are a reporter covering Field Day. How would you
summarize what the line plot shows about medals won? _____

_____

_____

Students in Ms. Spright's class reported what fraction of a day they typically spend sleeping. The line plot shows their answers.

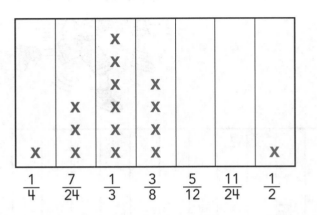

| $\frac{1}{4}$ | $\frac{7}{24}$ | $\frac{1}{3}$ | $\frac{3}{8}$ | $\frac{5}{12}$ | $\frac{11}{24}$ | $\frac{1}{2}$ |

Use the data to answer the questions.

1. How many students are in the class? _____

2. How many students say they sleep for $\frac{1}{4}$ of the day? _____

   How many hours is that? _____

3. What is the range of the data? _____

4. Which response is an outlier? _____

5. How many students sleep at least 8 hours a night? _____

   What fraction of the class is that? _____

6. How many students sleep 9 hours a night? _____

The line plot shows heights of students in Ms. Schortle's class.
Use the data to answer the questions.

Students' Heights

						X			
						X			X
				X		X	X		X
				X	X	X	X		X
X			X	X	X	X	X	X	X
1.45	1.46	1.47	1.48	1.49	1.50	1.51	1.52	1.53	1.54

Heights in Meters

1. How many students are in the class? _____

2. What is the tallest height in the class? _____

3. What is the range of the data? _____

4. What is the mode of the data? _____

5. How many students are 1.50 meters or taller? _____

6. What fraction of the class is 1.53 meters or taller? _____

7. What height in the class is an outlier? _____

The stem-and-leaf plot shows how fifth graders scored on a social studies test.

Stems show tens digits; leaves show ones digits. The lowest score shown is 52. Do you see why?

Use the data to answer the questions.

Test Scores	
Stem	Leaf
5	2 3 5 8
6	0 0 3 4 6
7	0 1 1 7
8	0 0 0 2 8 8
9	1 3 5 5 9

1. How many test scores were in the 50s? _____

2. How many students scored 71? _____

3. What is the greatest score anyone earned? _____

4. How many students took the test? _____

5. What is the range of the scores? _____

6. What is the mode of the test scores? _____

Answer Key

READING COMPREHENSION

p. 11
1. C 2. C 3. D 4. B 5. C

p. 13
1. A 2. D 3. B 4. B 5. C

p. 15
1. C 2. A 3. B 4. D 5. B

p. 17
1. C 2. A 3. D 4. B 5. D

p. 19
1. C 2. D 3. D 4. B 5. D

p. 21
1. A 2. D 3. C 4. B 5. A

p. 23
1. B 2. B 3. C 4. D 5. C

p. 25
1. B 2. D 3. B 4. B 5. A

p. 27
1. C 2. D 3. D 4. A 5. D

p. 29
1. A 2. C 3. C 4. A 5. B

p. 31
1. C; Sample answer: In the story, *feline* refers to the enemy, which is a cat. The only animal on the list that is a kind of cat is the leopard (lines 1–2, 5–7).
2. B; Sample answer: The young mouse's idea sounds great until a wiser mouse pointed out how dangerous it would be to put into action (lines 19–27).
3. Sample answer: The cat approaches so quietly and sneakily that the mice have no time to escape (lines 11–13).
4. Sample answer: A cat wearing a bell would make life safer for the mice, but it could be deadly for any mouse to attempt to put a bell on a cat.
5. Sample answer: The mice realize that they had cheered too soon. The question made them see how impossible it would be to bell the cat, so they were still in danger (lines 19–24).

p. 33
1. D; Sample answer: I figured out that adjacent means "next to." I read each choice, and the most likely thing to be next to a couch is an end table (lines 8–10).
2. A; Sample answer: I know the word *woe* means troubles, so I figure that a woebegone dog house would need

fixing up (lines 1–4).
3. Sample answer: She was intrigued by the idea of a talking dog for sale and wanted to learn more (lines 1–6).
4. Sample answer: Like a tall tale, there are ridiculously unbelievable events that characters in the story accept without question (lines 12–28).
5. Sample answer: The owner doesn't think it's unusual that the dog talks, but acts more annoyed that Max doesn't tell the truth (lines 32–36).

p. 35
1. C; Sample answer: The title tells me that the story is set on a dark and stormy night. *Calm* would be a good antonym for *turbulent*, and the closest choice to that is *serene*, so I picked C (lines 1–2).
2. B; Sample answer: Their car broke down, and it was dangerous to be out in the storm, so they decided to stay in the shack (lines 2–3, 9–10).
3. Sample answer: It means that nobody had been in the shack for a long time; it was abandoned (lines 3–8, 27–29).
4. Sample answer: I think she's there to be the link to the past, to reveal the sad story of the lost young sailor whose sad parents moved away (lines 24–32).
5. Sample answer: It's a ghost story, but ghosts aren't real. There are unexplainable things, like green glowing skin (lines 14–15), a salty puddle but no footprints (lines 18–19), and the recollection of a sailor lost at sea (lines 29–32). It is set in 1923 (the past), and the weird events were probably passed down by word of mouth.

p. 37
1. B; Sample answer: I reread the first paragraph and found that Michaela had originally been named Mabinty Bangura (lines 1–10).
2. D; Sample answer: I reread the paragraph about Earliest Memories. I know that nutrition is the healthy stuff your body gets from the food you eat, so I picked D (lines 16–20).
3. Sample answer: She had been dreaming of being a dancer for nearly her entire life, and refused to give up a lifelong dream. She believes that dance is part of who she is (lines 21–31).
4. Sample answer: She might mean that she lived in a terrible orphanage and that she was in a bad place emotionally because she was sick, lonely, unhappy, and lacked opportunities (lines 13–24).
5. Sample answer: I think they must be

very generous, caring, dedicated, and supportive people to have adopted a sick child from another country. They changed Michaela's life in every way, and must have supported her interest in and passion for dance to enable her to get so far (lines 7–10, 19–20, 30–31).

p. 39
1. C; Sample answer: I know that *routine* means by habit or on a repeating pattern. The word most opposite is *unscheduled* (lines 9–11).
2. D; Sample answer: I reread the paragraph about Jack London's life. Each choice is true, but the one that best explains his ability to write about adventure is that he had adventures himself (lines 22–25).
3. Sample answer: Tyler loves reading realistic stories like London's with challenging and unexpected turns, and that explore big ideas like loyalty, survival, and overcoming hardships (lines 7–9, 28–29).
4. Sample answer: I think it means that Tyler's mind was taken off the problems of an injury by the even greater problems Buck faced in his difficult life (lines 12–21).
5. Sample answer: Tyler was entertained and moved by reading *Call of the Wild*, and maybe used the letter to express appreciation. It's like a writer's response essay with some details about Jack London, which tells me that Tyler did some research. OR maybe it was a school assignment, like a book report (lines 2–9, 30–32).

p. 41
1. D; Sample answer: I chose D because it is the only choice that does not appear in the piece (lines 9–14).
2. A; Sample answer: I wasn't sure what *compulsory* meant when I first read it, but after I finished the piece and looked back over it, I figured it out. It means the same as *mandatory* (lines 4–5, 29–30).
3. Sample answer: The writer gives information from the National Highway Traffic Safety Administration that says that it's 40 times safer to ride in a school bus than in a car (lines 15–17).
4. Sample answer: The writer puts some words in italics, uses bold-faced words to begin most paragraphs, and calls out short summaries along the side to reinforce ideas (lines 1, 8, 18, 21–22, 25, graphics).
5. Sample answer: Three facts: 23 million children ride school buses every weekday (lines 2–3); seats have 4 inches of foam padding (lines

12–13); putting in seat belts takes up space (lines 22–24). Three opinions: Making seat belts compulsory is a tough sell (lines 4–5); cost issues must be considered (lines 18–20); adding seat belts would have minimal, if any, impact on safety (lines 20–22).

p. 43
1. B; Sample answer: *Los Reciclados* means "The Recycled Orchestra." The idea of an orchestra playing on instruments made from trash is really unique (lines 5–7).
2. C; Sample answer: I think that *ingenuity* means using your cleverness to make the best of what you have at hand. Cola showed amazing ingenuity by making the instruments (lines 12–19).
3. Sample answer: Favio had the idea of bringing music to the children of Cateura, and Cola had the skills to make instruments Favio needed for the children's use (lines 12–19).
4. Sample answer: What some people threw away, Favio and Cola were able to turn into playable musical instruments. What was junk to some people became sources of deep pride for others, like the guitar in the photo (photo, title, and lines 5–7, 16–24, 28–30).
5. Answers will vary, but should include something like this: Favio Chávez is creative, compassionate, encouraging, bold, resourceful, caring, and spirited. He saw problems and tried his best to find solutions (lines 8–18, 20–24).

p. 44
arid; parachute; confine; overhead; smother; appear
Think About It! First, smokejumpers parachute down, and then they dig a fire line. If that doesn't work, they clear branches and dig up dirt to contain and smother the fire. Finally, they crawl through the area, feeling the ground to make sure it isn't hot.

p. 45
badgered; department; candidates; winced; demonstrated
Think About It! Answers will vary.
Sample answer: Fact: Royal Pythons are not poisonous. Opinion: Snakes are magnificent!

p. 46
similar; Newborn; rodents; chief; hibernate
Think About It! Answers will vary.
Sample answer: Black bears and polar bears are alike in body shape, fur, and in the way that their newborns are raised. They are different in size, diet, and color. Also, black bears hibernate, while polar bears do not.

p. 47
Contrary; damage; according; division; likens; vacuum
Think About It! Fact: *Cracking your knuckles does no harm to them.* Opinion: *Cracking your knuckles feels good.*

p. 48
doubt; consume; expect; vanilla; popularity
Think About It! Opinion

p. 49
genius; inventor; puzzled; studied; mirror
Think About It! Da Vinci painted the famous *Mona Lisa*, but he also drew plans for inventions, like bicycles and airplanes, long before they were built.

p. 50
decorate; quality; insulation; oxygen; chemical
Think About It! Houseplants improve air quality and decorate homes and offices.

p. 51
spectacle; schedule; unpredictable; performance; reliability
Think About It! Old Faithful has earned its name by spouting off reliably on a predictable schedule, so you can count on it.

p. 52
spunky; released; suspended; scheme; antics; applause
Think About It! Answers will vary.
Sample answer: Casey Stengel was a fun-loving person who enjoyed pranks.

p. 53
business; promise; campaign; promptly; raccoons
Think About It! Answers will vary.
Sample answer: Pets make the White House a more interesting place because they are fun and unpredictable.

p. 54
comical; species; stomachs; evolved; sunlight
Think About It! Scientists think penguins developed a similar color pattern because it protects them from their enemies in the water.

LANGUAGE ARTS

p. 56
Sentence Mender: "I won first prize!" Kerry said with pride.
Analogy of the Day: D; A *bear* lives in a *den*, and a *spider* lives on a *web*.

p. 57
Sentence Mender: Jason's bruise on his leg caused him to limp.
Analogy of the Day: B; *Big* is the opposite of *small*, and *dry* is the opposite of *wet*.

p. 58
Sentence Mender: The new glass building on Spring Street sparkles like a diamond.
Analogy of the Day: C; When you are *sad*, you *frown*, and when you are *happy*, you *smile*.

p. 59
Sentence Mender: We should ask him to cease playing his drums so late at night.
Analogy of the Day: A; *Lunch* comes before *dinner*, and *afternoon* comes before *evening*.

p. 60
Sentence Mender: The Detroit Tigers played a doubleheader on Labor Day.
Analogy of the Day: D; *Instrument* is a category in which *trombone* belongs, and *tree* is a category in which *oak* belongs.

p. 61
Sentence Mender: What is the height, in feet, of that eight-story building?
Analogy of the Day: B; *Grass* has a characteristic of being *green*, and a *knife* has a characteristic of being *jagged*.

p. 62
Sentence Mender: The determined inventor would not concede defeat.
Analogy of the Day: B; A *toe* is part of a *foot*, and a *room* is part of a *house*.

p. 63
Sentence Mender: He's the oldest and biggest of the three brothers.
Analogy of the Day: D; A *sailor* is part of the *navy*, and a *student* is part of a *class*.

p. 64
Sentence Mender: The park ranger led us on the descent from the mountain.
Analogy of the Day: C; *Clean* is a lesser degree of *spotless*, and *large* is a lesser degree of *gigantic*.

p. 65
Sentence Mender: Dan and Iris went to Paris to take a French cooking class.
Analogy of the Day: B; *Cry* is the opposite of *laugh,* and *up* is the opposite of *down.*

p. 66
Sentence Mender: We visited South Carolina's first lighthouse.
Analogy of the Day: A; A *clock* makes the sound *tick,* and a *bee* makes the sound *buzz.*

p. 67
Sentence Mender: This morning, I had breakfast in my pajamas and spilled orange juice on them.
Analogy of the Day: A; An *apple* is a type of *fruit,* and a *shirt* is a type of *clothing.*

p. 68
Sentence Mender: What should we do about the worrisome leak in the kitchen?
Analogy of the Day: D; A *dessert* has the characteristic of being *tasty,* and *glue* has the characteristic of being *sticky.*

p. 69
Sentence Mender: The number has two sixes and three fours.
Analogy of the Day: B; A *car* is parked in a *garage,* and an *airplane* is parked in a *hangar.*

p. 70
Sentence Mender: Meg's teacher and her mom agree that Meg's handwriting is illegible.
Analogy of the Day: A; A *tornado* causes *destruction,* and *rain* causes *flooding.*

p. 71
Sentence Mender: It is easier to put a bridle on a horse than on a mule.
Analogy of the Day: D; A *drawer* is part of a *dresser,* and a *handle* is part of a *mug.*

p. 72
Sentence Mender: The track team's captain can run like a deer.
Analogy of the Day: D; An *athlete* is part of a *team,* and a *co-pilot* is part of a *crew.*

p. 73
Sentence Mender: That wonderful dog Gracie is the apple of her owner's eye.
Analogy of the Day: B; The sound of a *cow* is *moo,* and the sound of a *bell* is *ring.*

p. 74
Sentence Mender: Many cable customers have found the new service to be worse than it was before.
Analogy of the Day: C; You use an *airplane* to *travel,* and you use a *straw* to *drink.*

p. 75
Sentence Mender: Erin was upset when she learned that she couldn't go with her friends.
Analogy of the Day: B; *Ice* has the characteristic of being *cold,* and the *sky* has the characteristic of being *blue.*

p. 76
Sentence Mender: She was born in Troy, New York, on January 9, 2012.
Analogy of the Day: A; *Purple* is a kind of *color,* and *jazz* is a kind of *music.*

p. 77
Sentence Mender: Either Jack or Andrew will enter a muffin recipe in the contest.
Analogy of the Day: A; A *flame* has the characteristic of being *bright,* and a *candle* has the characteristic of being *waxy.*

p. 78
Sentence Mender: Hey, where are you going with my cell phone?
Analogy of the Day: D; *Peril* is a greater degree of *danger,* and *river* is a greater degree of *stream.*

p. 79
Sentence Mender: The chef realized that she needed more pepper, salt, and onion in the stew.
Analogy of the Day: C; A *star* is part of a *constellation,* and a *teacher* is part of the *faculty.*

p. 80
Sentence Mender: I finally got to play for the maestro, but he wasn't impressed with my efforts.
Analogy of the Day: B; You use a *ladder* to *reach,* and you use a *stove* to *cook.*

p. 81
Sentence Mender: After tripping on a gopher hole in the pasture, she could hardly walk.
Analogy of the Day: D; *Enemy* is the opposite of *friend,* and *calm* is the opposite of *tense.*

p. 82
Sentence Mender: The singer has now won an Oscar and a Grammy award.
Analogy of the Day: B; You *plant* before you *harvest,* and you *pour* before you *drink.*

p. 83
Sentence Mender: Both she and Nina missed the science test.
Analogy of the Day: C; A *train* travels on a *track,* and a *ship* travels on the *sea.*

p. 84
Sentence Mender: Miguel told Victor that he didn't need to practice anymore.
Analogy of the Day: A; A *screen* is part of a *television,* and a *classroom* is part of a *school.*

p. 85
Sentence Mender: First he poured the cereal, then he added fruit and milk.
Analogy of the Day: D; A *violin* is used by a *musician,* and a *club* is used by a *golfer.*

p. 86
Sentence Mender: Many people get sick from mosquito bites.
Analogy of the Day: C; *Exercise* causes *sweating,* and *sadness* causes *weeping.*

p. 87
Sentence Mender: Before Labor Day, we were happy and everything seemed perfect.
Analogy of the Day: B; A *terrier* is a kind of *dog,* and a *rose* is a kind of *flower.*

p. 88
Sentence Mender: "There are bear tracks ahead on the trail, so be careful," the ranger warned.
Analogy of the Day: A; *Annoy* is the opposite of *please,* and *love* is the opposite of *hate.*

p. 89
Sentence Mender: Henry wondered who won the World Series last year.
Analogy of the Day: B; *Bright* is a lesser degree of *brilliant,* and *delighted* is a lesser degree of *exhilarated.*

p. 90
Sentence Mender: I read an article called "How to Join Social Networks."
Analogy of the Day: B; *See* means the same as *view,* and *snooze* means the same as *sleep.*

p. 91

Sentence Mender: The Empire State Building is taller than the Chrysler Building.

Analogy of the Day: C; An *employee* is a member of a *company*, and a *whale* is a member of the group *mammal*.

p. 92

Sentence Mender: Matt Clark opened the door and stepped out.

Analogy of the Day: D; An *hour* is part of a *day*, and a *mattress* is part of a *bed*.

p. 93

Sentence Mender: The knight showed his bravery in battle and was rewarded with land and a title.

Analogy of the Day: C; *Silk* has the quality of being *soft*, and *sandpaper* has the quality of being *rough*.

p. 94

Sentence Mender: "We're going to the zoo when the new monkeys arrive!" said Max's sister.

Analogy of the Day: D; *Easy* is the opposite of *challenging*, and *simple* is the opposite of *tricky*.

p. 95

Sentence Mender: It used to be that few college graduates lived with their parents.

Analogy of the Day: A; You use a *shovel* to *dig*, and you use a *guitar* to make *music*.

p. 96

Sentence Mender: Ethan, Ellis, and Eli are the best tenors in the church choir.

Analogy of the Day: B; A *wrench* is a tool used by a *mechanic*, and a *brush* is a tool used by a *painter*.

p. 97

Sentence Mender: Marie Curie was a scientist who was ahead of her time.

Analogy of the Day: C; A *desk* can be found in an *office*, and a *submarine* can be found in the *ocean*.

p. 98

Sentence Mender: You and I should receive awards for spelling and grammar greatness.

Analogy of the Day: B; You use a *knife* to *cut*, and you use a *lamp* to *light*.

p. 99

Sentence Mender: It took me a long time to catch my first foul ball.

Analogy of the Day: D; *Abundant* means the same as *plentiful*, and *scared* means the same as *fearful*.

p. 100

Sentence Mender: One of our friends, Teresa, lost her house keys during the bus trip.

Analogy of the Day: D; A *leg* is a type of *limb*, and *pliers* are a type of *tool*.

p. 101

Sentence Mender: My Indian classmates speak English and Hindi.

Analogy of the Day: A; An *actor* is part of a *cast*, and a *city* is part of a *state*.

p. 102

Sentence Mender: My brother doesn't swim as fast as I can.

Analogy of the Day: C; An *engine* is part of a *truck*, and a *lens* is part of a *camera*.

p. 103

Sentence Mender: Grady and Rob are the two hosts of the party.

Analogy of the Day: C; *Warm* is a lesser degree of *sizzling*, and *weary* is a lesser degree of *exhausted*.

p. 104

Sentence Mender: Niko's dad really knows the ropes when it comes to sailing.

Analogy of the Day: D; *High* is the opposite of *low*, and *interested* is the opposite of *bored*.

GRAMMAR

p. 106

Answers will vary; check for proper capitalization and categories.

p. 107

1. B   2. A   3. A   4. C   5. B   6. D   7. A
8. A   9. A   10. A   11. B   12. D   13. C
14. D   15. A   16. C   17. C   18. A
19. B   20. A

p. 108

Answers may vary. Possible answers:
2. raincoat   3. Fuji   4. snare drum
5. flatbed   6. chocolate   7. horse
8. penguin   9. hammer   10. movie
11. food   12. reptile

p. 109

1. C   2. A   3. B   4. C   5. B   6. A
7. A   8. D

p. 110

1. A   2. B   3. C   4. A   5. C
6. C   7. C   8. C   9. A   10. B

p. 111

2. break   3. drew   4. hung   5. slept
6. spend   7. leave   8. grown   9. think
10. wrote

p. 112

Answers will vary. Sample answers:
1. dashed   2. chugged   3. tiptoed
4. yelled   5. dive   6. create   7. rested
8. wondered

p. 113

Answers will vary. Sample answers:
1. soft   2. blooming   3. adorable
4. horrible   5. terrific   6. enormous
7. tremendous   8. eye-opening
9. terrible   10. stupendous

p. 114

Answers will vary. Sample answers:
2. impatiently   3. sheepishly
4. loudly   5. sarcastically   6. angrily
7. pleadingly   8. worriedly   9. excitedly
10. seriously   11. breathlessly
12. sorrowfully

p. 115

1. B   2. C   3. A   4. B   5. A   6. A
7. D   8. D

p. 116

Answers will vary.

p. 117

Answers will vary.

p. 118

1. ax   2. break   3. ceiling   4. chili
5. coarse   6. fare   7. flour   8. hire
9. heard   10. petal   11. wring
12. soar

p. 119

2. We're; we are   3. might've; might have   4. it'll; it will   5. can't; cannot
6. I'm; I am   7. wouldn't; would not
8. needn't; need not   9. she'd; she would   10. you'd; you had   11. won't; will not   12. let's; let us

p. 120

1. A   2. B   3. C   4. No Error   5. C
6. B   7. B   8. C   9. B   10. C
11. No Error   12. A

p. 121

1. Six of the longest rivers in the world are the Nile in Africa, Congo in Central Africa, Lena in Russia, Amazon in South America, Mississippi in the USA, and the Yangtze in China. CLAM
2. Earth, Jupiter, Uranus, Mars, Pluto (a dwarf planet), Saturn, and Neptune are some of the planets in our solar system. JUMPS
3. William Shakespeare wrote many great plays like Hamlet, King Lear, Othello, As You Like It, Love's Labours Lost, and Macbeth. KOALA
4. Goslings, squibs, hatchlings, ephyrae, eyases, polliwogs, and fawns

are the names of baby geese, pigeons, dinosaurs, jellyfish, hawks, frogs, and deer. SHEEP

5. Some of the instruments in an orchestra are violins, horns, oboes, organs, flutes, saxophones, and drums. HOOFS

6. My favorite animated movies are Up, Ratatouille, Alice in Wonderland, Bambi, Beauty and the Beast, Ice Age, Toy Story, Shrek, and Happy Feet. RABBITS

p. 122
2. My goodness, rabbits can hop fast when they want to.
3. Gosh, all my licorice melted in the sun.
4. Yuck, cotton candy really sticks to your face, doesn't it?
6. Uh-oh, everybody just went out the wrong door.
7. Oops, Carl squirted ketchup on my new shirt.
8. Oh dear, a page from my homework just blew out the window.
9. Gee whiz, raccoons broke into the kitchen and ate Grandma's apple pie.
Riddle answer: RACECAR or RACE CAR

p. 123
Dear Grandma,
Although I've been here for only one week, I've already made a lot of new friends. Because kids come here from my school, I knew some of them already. Since this camp is right on a lake, we do a lot of water sports, like swimming and boating. Unless it's really raining, we're outside all day long. After the swim across the lake, we had a picnic. Before the talent show yesterday, I had to practice singing with my mouth full of pretzels. I won for funniest act! If you can come on visiting day, that would be awesome
Until I see you again, stay well.
Hug Fluffy for me.
Love,
Summer

p. 124
1. When the mosquitoes came out, in went the people.
2. While they were flying, nine planes flew in front of them.
3. Outside the bedroom, carpet the hallway.
4. Though we believe in recycling, our brother doesn't.
5. After you read the book, report on it to the class.

6. Please tell Paul, Revere is a city in Massachusetts.
7. When he began painting, everyone said he needed art lessons.
8. To make ice, chill water.
9. Before they finished eating, the chicken flew away.
10. To Abraham, Lincoln seemed like a good capital for Nebraska.
11. Inside, your grandpa's barn was noisy.
Riddle answer: INCORRECTLY

p. 125
What is full of holes, Amanda, but still holds water? A sponge, Justin.
Which weighs more, Steve, a pound of feathers or a pound of iron? Jane, they both weigh a pound.
Why didn't the skeleton go to the dance, Sophie? Because, Matt, he had no body to go with.
Dennis, why did Dracula's mother get him cough medicine? Because of his coffin, Lynda.

p. 126
What is that loud sound? Run! It's an erupting volcano! That was just my stomach rumbling.
A boa constrictor is crawling up my leg! It's a snake from Central and South America. How is that going to help me?
Is there a police station around here? There's one next to the Italian pastry shop. Help, someone stole my cannoli!
What act are you doing for the talent show? I'm dressing up as a duck and singing opera. That's amazingly fantastic!
I will not dance in the ballet tonight. Why not, madam? I refuse to wear that totally terrible tutu!
Here's the lion house at the zoo. How are you feeling, lion? Roar!
Do you hear that loud buzzing? It's just a bumblebee. Ow! It just stung my arm!
It's nice here in the woods. Did you hear that scary noise? It's Bigfoot!
Riddle answer: OGICURMT! (Oh gee, I see you are empty!)

p. 127
3. I am going to wave when it goes by.
5. It is. 7. I like turopoljes. 8. What are they? 9. They're spotted pigs.
10. I spotted one once. 13. You said you like asparagus. 14. I do.
19. That's just an elephant walking by.
20. Money doesn't grow on trees.
Answer: 100

p. 128
1. "Do you want to set up a clubhouse?" Fred asked Wayne.
2. Fred pointed to the old tool shed, the one that nobody used anymore.
3. "We could paint it, add rugs and pillows, and hang out there," said Fred.
4. So the boys began to clean out the shed, which took several long, dusty days.
5. "Yuck!" yelled Wayne, as he walked through sticky cobwebs.
6. After a few weeks, they barely recognized that old shed.
7. Fred's aunt gave them a rug. Wayne's mom gave them some old pillows.
8. They painted the door to say "F & W Club, Private! Stay Out!"
9. It's amazing how those boys turned that old shed into a perfect hideaway.
10. "Now all we need is room service," joked Wayne.

p. 129
Answers will vary. Sample answers:
1. The coach blows her whistle, so the game stops.
2. Gina loves hip-hop music, but Tony prefers salsa.
3. Arbor Day is in June, and Labor Day is in September.
4. I selected a purple bedspread because purple is my favorite color.
5. The traffic stops while the crossing guard escorts the children.
6. Abby enjoys writing poetry, such as limericks.

p. 130
1. A 2. D 3. B 4. C 5. C 6. A
7. D 8. B 9. B 10. C

p. 131
Sentences will vary. Sample answers:
1. When my parents saw the damage, they really got mad. 2. The theater usher was just kidding when he said to fasten my seat belt. 3. That new suit fits perfectly. 4. I'd really like to join you, but can I postpone until later?
5. Dad was sorry, but he said it would be so expensive. 6. She was feeling sick so she stayed home from school.

p. 132
1. C 2. A 3. C 4. C 5. A 6. A
7. B 8. D

WRITING

p. 134
Answers will vary.

p. 135
A. Explanations will vary. Sample answers: 1. typewriter = dinosaur; The typewriter is really old. 2. brother = couch potato; My brother sits around and isn't active. 3. meal = rock; The meal made my stomach feel full and heavy.
B. Answers will vary.

p. 136
Answers will vary.

p. 137
Answers will vary.

p. 138
A. 1. declarative 2. interrogative 3. exclamatory 4. imperative 5. interrogative 6. exclamatory 7. imperative
B. Answers will vary.

p. 139
A. simple 2. complex 3. compound 4. complex
B. Answers will vary.

p. 140
1. b 2. The Seattle Space Needle and the Tokyo Skytree are other famous towers. 3. Answers will vary.

p. 141
1. Although historians don't think that King Tut was an influential monarch in his day, a rare find in 1922 made him a celebrity. Carter died in 1939 at home in England.
2. Ancient Egypt was a land of many perils. The Nile River provided water, transportation, and fertile soil.
3. It normally took up to three months to bury a pharaoh after his death. Natron, a type of salt, was a primary ingredient in the process of mummification.

p. 142
1–4. Answers will vary.

p. 143
1. The writer asks a question to get readers interested and to encourage them to read more about fast driving.
2. Danica Patrick is one of the most influential drivers in race-car history.
3. Sentences will vary.

p. 144
Topic sentence: Scuba diving sounds fun and exciting, but it can be dangerous too. Conclusions will vary.

p. 145
1. Sentence (1) 2. The Panama Canal changed ocean travel. 3. Sentences will vary. 4. Sentence (6)

p. 146
1. So, For that reason, or As a result
2. Before 3. After
4. In addition, Also, or I should also mention (that)
Paragraphs will vary.

p. 147
1. also 2. For that reason
3. In addition 4. Although
5. Because of

p 148
5, 1, 3, 7, 4, 9, 2, 8, 10, 6

p. 149
1. next 2. After; Meanwhile
3. Answers will vary.

p. 150
Answers will vary.

p. 151
1. c 2. Answers will vary.

p. 152
Answers will vary.

p. 153
Answers will vary.

p. 154
Answers will vary.

p. 155
Answers will vary.

p. 156
1. D 2. C 3. A 4. B

p. 157
1. A 2. A 3. C 4. D

p. 159
1. B 2. A 3. D 4. B 5. C

p. 161
1. C 2. D 3. A 4. B 5. D

p. 163
1. D 2. B 3. C 4. D 5. B

p. 164
1. A 2. B 3. D 4. C

p. 165–166
1. D 2. B 3. A 4. B 5. C 6. D
7. A 8. C 9. B 10. D 11. C 12. C

VOCABULARY

p. 168
A. 1. tremble, shake, shiver 2. harmful, risky, dangerous 3. newcomer, beginner, learner 4. error, mistake, misjudgment 5. commonly, usually, mostly 6. notable, important, remarkable 7. foolhardy, reckless, careless 8. prohibit, forbid, ban
B. 1. variable 2. receptacle

p. 169
1. rash 2. veto 3. receptacle
4. hazardous 5. novice
6. outstanding 7. generally
8. blunder 9. quiver 10. variable

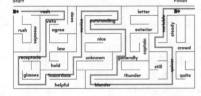

p. 170
A. 1. ceaseless 2. bewildered
3. treacherous 4. blissful 5. daunting
6. bountiful 7. valid 8. brutal
B. 1. cumbersome 2. dormant

p. 171
dormant, treacherous, bountiful, brutal, daunting, ceaseless, cumbersome, valid

p. 172
A. 1. firm 2. unmatched 3. permit
4. disapproval 5. prevent 6. energy
7. praise 8. weak
B. 1. exhaustion, vigor 2. allow, forbid
3. usual, unique 4. flimsy, sturdy

p. 173
A. 1. compliment 2. allow 3. vigor
4. ordinary 5. fatigue 6. substantial
7. prohibit 8. criticism 9. unique
10. flimsy
B. 1. house 2. compliment 3. jumping
4. original

p. 174
A. 1. inactive 2. settled 3. wise
4. boring 5. ridiculous 6. thoughtless
B. 1. unsettled, stable 2. lazy, playful
3. thoughtful, inconsiderate
4. dull, fascinating

p. 175
1. slow, sluggish, idle 2. absurd, rash, ridiculous 3. impermanent, unstable, temporary 4. dull, tiresome, uninteresting 5. inattentive, careless, heedless

p. 176
A. 1. windshield 2. guidebook
3. earthquake 4. blueprint
5. vineyard 6. whirlpool
7. masterpiece
B. 1. head, quarters 2. touch, down
3. spell, bound

p. 177
1. earthquake 2. windshield
3. masterpiece 4. vineyard
5. whirlpool 6. blueprint
7. touchdown 8. headquarters
9. spellbound 10. guidebook
Riddle answer: A staircase

p. 178
A. 1. bridle 2. foul 3. lute 4. cruise
B. 1. course 2. coarse

p. 179
1. A Bridle for My Horse 2. Planning
a Course for a Vacation Cruise 3. Tips
for Raising Fowl 4. How to Play the
Lute 5. Foul Play! The Story of Crews
That Loot Bridal Parties 6. Using
Burlap and Other Coarse Fabrics

p. 180
A. 1. a 2. b 3. b 4. b 5. a 6. a
B. 1. invalid 2. object 3. refuse
4. minute

p. 181
1. a 2. b 3. a 4. b 5. b 6. a 7. a
8. b 9. a 10. b

p. 182
A. 1. cologne 2. marathon
3. vaudeville 4. tuxedo 5. cantaloupe
6. sardines
B. 1. c 2. d 3. b 4. a

p. 183
1. bikini 2. tangerine 3. tuxedo
4. bologna 5. marathon 6. tarantula
7. cologne 8. sardines 9. vaudeville
10. cantaloupe

p. 184
A. 1. Japanese 2. Arabic 3. Persian
4. African 5. Arabic 6. African
B. 1. magazine 2. alligator 3. sheik
4. barbecue

p. 185

```
B D J T M Q A V C M X P S
A L L I G A T O R L O W Y
R F R E K W H K I M O N O
B A N D I T Y R S E U B X
E H S Z M A G A Z I N F D
C N I O P A J A M A S G I
U X J N A V M X K R Y T V
E C T Y L Q S O R Z R A N
W U K P A E B E N C U P J
S H E I K I Z T Q L P O R
```

1. bandit 2. alligator 3. barbecue
4. pajamas 5. syrup 6. magazine
7. impala 8. kimono 9. okra
10. sheik

p. 186
A. 1. d 2. e 3. f 4. c 5. a 6. g 7. b
B. 1. fridge 2. taxi 3. limo

p. 187
A. 1. ref 2. fridge 3. limo 4. curio
5. mike 6. grad 7. champ 8. taxi
9. fan 10. rev
B. 1. fan 2. taxi 3. ref 4. mike

p. 188
A. 1. squawk 2. telethon 3. splatter
4. medevac 5. paratroops
6. squiggle 7. glimmer 8. flare
B. 1. spacelab 2. flurry

p. 189
Across: 1. flurry 2. spacelab
3. squawk 4. medevac 5. glimmer
6. telethon 7. paratroops
Down: 1. flare 2. squiggle 3. splatter

p. 190
A. 1. c 2. d 3. a 4. e 5. b
B. 1. toads 2. ponies 3. parrots
4. oysters 5. fish

p. 191
A. 1. troop 2. bed 3. company
4. gaggle 5. colony 6. string 7. knot
8. school 9. skulk 10. gang
B. 1. gaggle 2. school 3. pearl
4. troop

p. 192
A. 1. peninsula 2. strait 3. valley
4. delta 5. plateau 6. isthmus
B. 1. tributary 2. archipelago
3. oasis 4. gorge

p. 193
1. delta 2. valley 3. strait
4. plateau 5. isthmus 6. archipelago
7. peninsula 8. gorge 9. tributary
10. oasis

p. 194
A. 1. rhyme 2. simile
3. personification 4. metaphor
5. alliteration 6. onomatopoeia
B. 1. meter 2. couplet 3. sonnet
4. haiku

p. 195
Forms of Poetry: sonnet, haiku, couplet
Figures of Speech: simile, metaphor
Poetic Devices: rhyme, meter,
alliteration, personification,
onomatopoeia

p. 196
A. 1. hogwash 2. ragtime 3. flatter
4. naughty 5. lollipop 6. doodle
7. humor 8. chimpanzee
B. 1. fiddlesticks 2. nitty-gritty

p. 197
hodgepodge, rapscallion, chitchat,
hullaballoo, flabbergast, lollygag,
fiddlesticks, namby-pamby, nitty-gritty

p. 198
A. 1. plenty 2. restate 3. walker
4. freedom 5. generous 6. foot bar
B. 1. numerator 2. biped 3. numeral
4. pedestal

p. 199
1. liberal 2. pedal 3. pedestal
4. biped 5. enumerate 6. numeral
7. numerous 8. numerator 9. liberty
10. pedestrian

p. 200
A. 1. wording, phrasing 2. interpret,
explain 3. foretell, prophesy
4. proclaim, announce 5. obviousness,
clearness 6. statement, proclamation
7. ruler, despot
B. 1. clarion 2. dictate 3. dictionary

p. 201
1. clarify 2. dictionary 3. diction
4. declare 5. predict 6. dictator
7. clarion 8. clarity 9. declaration
10. dictate
Riddle answer: Dictionary

p. 202
A. 1. f 2. e 3. b 4. g 5. a 6. d 7. c
B. 1. pathetic 2. mechanize
3. barometer

p. 203
Across: 2. pathetic 4. mechanize
5. kilometer 7. sympathy
9. thermometer
Down: 1. mechanics 2. pathology
3. speedometer 6. diameter
8. barometer

p. 204
A. 1. e 2. f 3. g 4. i 5. h 6. c 7. a
8. b 9. d
B. veep

p. 205

```
S W H S B E J X A C V
C A N O L A T Q R K E
U C F N M P D S N G E
B V D A F Y L B Z I P
A U J R A D A R A Q W
E N Z G W C S X G U I
M X Q M O D E M L A R
T V S I L B R O T S H
D K Y M N X K E C A A
S N A F U V O J Z R F
```

1. scuba 2. canola 3. veep 4. sonar
5. zip 6. radar 7. laser 8. modem
9. quasar 10. snafu

p. 206

A. 1. cutlery 2. flat 3. lift
4. cupboard 5. underground
6. nappy
B. 1. larder 2. pram 3. holiday
4. chemist

p. 207

A. 1. nappy 2. larder 3. chemist
4. underground 5. holiday 6. lift
7. cutlery 8. pram 9. cupboard
10. flat
B. 1. underground 2. pram 3. lift
4. flat

p. 208

A. 1. cyclone 2. zany 3. album
4. academy 5. ketchup 6. manuscript
B. 1. c 2. a 3. d 4. b

p. 209

1. zany 2. cyclone 3. volcano
4. album 5. academy 6. manuscript
7. ketchup 8. dahlia 9. leotard
10. oxygen

p. 210

A. 1. irresponsible 2. abstain
3. interpose 4. malformed 5. abduct
6. irrational
B. 1. retro 2. inter 3. mal 4. retro

p. 211

A. 1. abstain 2. malformed
3. intersection 4. abduct
5. retrospective 6. interpose
7. irresponsible 8. malfunction
9. irrational 10. retroactive
B. 1. cross 2. abstain 3. rocket
4. fight

p. 212

A. 1. illiterate 2. hydroplane
3. commiserate 4. illegal 5. compile
6. monotone
B. 1. bi 2. mono 3. hydro 4. bi

p. 213

Answers will vary. Possible answers:
1. mono 2. bi 3. mono 4. com 5. il
6. hydro 7. bi 8. hydro 9. com

p. 214

A. 1. denouncement, charge
2. relaxation, play 3. noble,
courageous 4. disorderly, unruly
5. renowned, celebrated 6. juicy,
fleshy 7. hopefulness, cheerfulness
B. 1. dent<u>ist</u> 2. journal<u>ism</u>
3. perfection<u>ist</u>

p. 215

A. 1. recreation 2. dentist
3. turbulent 4. historic 5. optimism
6. journalism 7. succulent
8. perfectionist 9. heroic
10. accusation
B. 1. air 2. recreation 3. optimism
4. succulent

p. 216

Check story for vocabulary words and
sense.

MATH

p. 218

1. 33; 38; 43 2. 132; 140; 148
3. 68; 84; 102 4. 790; 1,000; 1,240
5. 19 6. 100 7. 18 8. 1,023

1	2	5
2	4	7
3	6	9
4	8	11
5	10	13
6	12	15

p. 219

1. 278,350 2. 1,223,357
3. 309,178,030 4. 9,662,001,000
5. 2,499,000 6. 1,555,798,000
7. 300,019,000 8. 7,000,499,000
9. 500,000 10. 8,900,000
11. 900,000 12. 23,500,000
13. 58,899,662 14. 9,000,100,000

p. 220

90	96	99	105
97	103	92	98
101	91	104	94
102	100	95	93

17, 22, 38, 23
Number puzzles will vary.

p. 221

3,833	5,808	11,599
11,759	9,870	10,461
8,812	6,744	5,005
1,660	12,797	14,862
9,307	8,448	27,248

p. 222

4,337	151	3,632
5,533	7,668	502,571
3,216	7,216	56,717
4,363	2,299	47,516
2,692	46,820	395,209

p. 223

1. 286 − 1 2. 6 x 18 + 2
3. 68 x 21 4. 16 x 2 − 8
5. 816 x 2 6. 8,062 − 3
7. 2 x 803 + 6 8. 30 x 26 − 8
9. 280 + 36 or 286 + 30 10. 360 x 8 ÷ 2

p. 224

1. chili 2. corned beef hash 3. water
4. poached eggs on toast 5. crackers
6. orange juice

p. 225

54	3
50	2
20	24
60	375
0	6
100	83
65	49
192	162

p. 226

1. 500,000 2. 2,000,000
3. 90,000,000 4. 10,000,000,000
5. 6,000 6. 500,000,000
7. 300,015 8. 29,000,437
9. 643,000,000 10. 82,000,000,111
11. two hundred twenty-five million four
hundred thirty-one thousand 12. three
hundred nine thousand two hundred
fifty-four 13. thirty-eight billion two
hundred sixty million eight hundred six
thousand seven

p. 227

2. 80 million 3. 12 million 4. 7 billion
5. 59 billion 6. 13 million
7. 5 million 8. 89 million 9. 999
million
10. 801 million 11. 51 million
12. 1 billion

p. 228

Number	In Thousands	In Hundreds
30,000	30	300
600,000	600	6,000
1,800,000	1,800	18,000
29,000,000	29,000	290,000
31,500,000	31,500	315,000

Number	In Tens	In Ones
30,000	3,000	30,000
600,000	60,000	600,000
1,800,000	180,000	1,800,000
29,000,000	2,900,000	29,000,000
31,500,000	3,150,000	31,500,000

1. 100,000   2. 1,000,000
3. 10,000,000   4. 50,000,000

Number	Millions	Thousands	Hundreds
30 million	30	30,000	300,000
900 million	900	900,000	9,000,000
1 billion	1,000	1,000,000	10,000,000
20 billion	20,000	20,000,000	200,000,000

p. 229
2. 400,000,000 + 300,000 + 6,000
3. 8,000,000,000 + 700
4. 70,000,000 + 6,000,000 + 400,000 + 30,000 + 2,000 + 900 + 80 + 7
5. 400,000,000 + 10,000,000 + 9,000,000 + 500,000 + 80,000 + 2,000 + 600 + 60 + 5
6. 50,000,000,000 + 5,000,000,000 + 80,000,000 + 2,000,000 + 6,000 + 500
7. 20,000,000,000 + 300,000,000 + 70,000,000 + 5,000,000 + 100 + 20
8. 10,000,000,000 + 5,000,000,000 + 200,000,000 + 60,000 + 3,000 + 500 + 40 + 2
9. 300,000,000,000 + 60,000,000,000 + 7,000,000,000 + 500,000,000 + 9,000,000 + 1
10. 900,000,000,000 + 500,000 + 60,000 + 7,000 + 200

p. 230
1. <   2. >   3. >   4. >   5. >   6. =
7. <   8. <   9. <   10. <   11. >   12. =

p. 231
1. 140,409   1,409,000   4,190,000
2. 12,007,000   210,700,000   1,210,707,000
3. 805,000,000   8,850,500,805   80,850,000,000
4. 39,845 − 37,845 = 2,000
5. 484,141 − 418,144 = 65,997
6. 9,775,266 − 9,526,767 = 248,499

p. 232

Number	Nearest 1,000	Nearest 100,000
389,900	390,000	400,000
1,844,938	1,845,000	1,800,000
24,061,562	24,062,000	24,100,000

800,000	1,000,000
200,000,000	90,000,000
9,000,000,000	300,000

20,500,000	93,000,000
1,290,000,000	30,000,000,000
6,727,000	7,500,000,000

p. 233
1. 987,654,321   2. 123,456,789
3. 987,654,312   4. 987,654,321
5. 987,654,321   6. 897,654,321
7. 123,456,789   8. 123,456,798
9. 15,236,478

p. 234
2. $1,000 = 10^3$ 3. $10,000 = 10^4$
4. $10,000 = 10^4$ 5. $1,000,000 = 10^6$
6. 100   7. 10,000   8. 1,000,000
9. 10,000,000   10. 1,000
11. 300   12. 2,000   13. 50,000
14. 1,800,000   15. 45,000,000
16. 570,000

p. 235
Factors of 24 only: 3, 6, 12, 24
Factors of 40 only: 5, 10, 20, 40
Factors of 24 and 40: 1, 2, 4, 8

4 1, 2, 4 C	19 1, 19 P	60 1, 2, 3, 4, 5, 6, 10, 12, 15, 20, 30, 60 C
21 1, 3, 7, 21 C	53 1, 53 P	70 1, 2, 5, 7, 10, 14, 35, 70 C
47 1, 47 P	81 1, 3, 9, 27, 81 C	38 1, 2, 19, 38 C

p. 236

4	15	6
3	4	7

24	36	36
20	6	40
80	36	60

p. 237
Divisible by 3: 9; 45; 213; 3,519
Divisible by 4: 16; 96; 9,416; 3,820
Divisible by 6: 84; 396; 72,144
Divisible by 9: 54; 702; 2,421; 62,100
Solve It: 252

p. 238
1. 3,000   2. 40,000   3. 360,000
4. 6,000   5. 28,000   6. 320   7. 4,200
8. 4,200,000   9. 12,000,000
10. 64,000,000
Solve It: 1,800 seats

p. 239

600	4,200
3,600	56,000
10,000	42,000

3,327	46,025	24,172
36,240	36,260	48,712

p. 240
1. 10   2. 100   3. 60   4. 38   5. 68
6. 360   7. 150   8. 640, 40

p. 241

7,000	12,000
32,000	24,000
18,000	45,000
16,000	36,000

11,583	184,650
37,788	306,267

p. 242

p. 243

30	70	80
90	6	7
90	8	70

>	=
=	=
<	>
>	=

p. 244

2. 900 3. 800 4. 9,000 5. 800
6. 300 7. 7,000 8. 500

16	105	218
118	60	97

p. 245

189 R1	113 R3	792 R4
435 R3	6,314 R7	13,387 R3
403	107	1,041
2,090	1,090	12,031

p. 246

1. 12 R3, soldier   2. 48 R1, professor
3. 66, actor   4. 93 R4, newspaperman
5. 54, tailor   6. 93 R6, teacher
7. 36, peanut farmer   8. 151, writer

p. 247

Left column, top to bottom: Nellie Bly,
Sarah Edmonds, Elizabeth Blackwell,
Ida B. Wells, Lydia Pinkham

p. 248

52	9 R3	4
4 R3	23	6 R7
33 R3	15 R28	20 R13
29 R4	33 R4	120 R9

p. 249

1. 883, true   2. 482, false   3. 323, true
4. 895, true   5. 118, false   6. 623, true
7. 607, true

p. 250

Fractions in simplest form: 7/16, 4/15,
3/10

1/3	1/5	3/20
5/21	1/5	1/3
3/5	7/24	1/11
8/27	4/7	2/9

p. 251

1. 16/48   2. 4/6   3. 15/16   4. 18/25
5. 4/8   6. 14/15   7. 32/40   8. 6/18
Fractions that belong may vary, as
long as they're equivalent to the other
fractions in the group.

p. 252

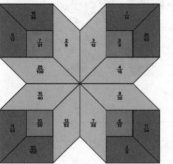

p. 253

<	=	=
<	=	<
<	=	<
>	>	>
<	<	>

p. 254

7/9, 5/9, 2/9	1/3, 1/5, 1/8	3/4, 3/5, 3/8
5/6, 3/4, 7/12	5/6, 4/9, 1/3	9/10, 3/4, 2/5
2/7, 3/7, 4/7	1/6, 1/3, 1/2	1/4, 4/5, 7/8
3/8, 5/6, 11/12	2/3, 7/9, 5/6	7/10, 3/4, 4/5

Fractions < 1/2	Fractions between 1/2 and 3/4	Fractions > 3/4
2/5, 4/11, 1/12	2/3, 5/7, 3/5	9/10, 21/24

p. 255

1. 4/16 or 1/4   2. 3/16   3. 9/16
4. 1 3/16   5. 2 4/16 or 2 1/4   6. 2

p. 256

4	15	20
12	9	40
19/24	7/9	17/30
25/18	5/8	59/42
93/70	7/6	47/24

p. 257

3/8	1/9	3/4
2/15	1/3	1/5
1/30	19/30	5/36
5/14	1/2	4/35
1/3	3/8	7/10

p. 258

2/3	11/12	17/18	7/8
1/30	23/30	17/24	5/12
11/15	1/2	5/21	5/8

Riddle answer: Lions and cheetahs!

p. 259

19/3	22/7	53/12
63/4	79/9	28/5
17/6	13/8	23/3
3 1/2	3 1/3	2 1/2
11 3/8	7 3/5	21 1/3
3 5/7	7 3/8	7 1/5

p. 260

13 3/5	11 1/2	8 29/30
7 1/10	12	13 7/24
9 1/4	1 7/8	12 5/6
7 23/30	11 3/16	8 1/2
4 35/36	20 3/8	10 3/25

p. 261

1 1/5	4 1/2	6 1/2
3 3/20	1 1/2	3 8/15
1	2 7/12	7 1/16
3 1/30	2 3/16	9 11/12

p. 262

1/5	2/15	5/18
5/18	3/25	0
9/14	32/77	2/3

<	>
=	>
<	<

p. 263

32	8	40
2	2	6
2 5/6	2 11/32	2/3
5 2/5	2	4 2/7
1 8/9	4 1/30	3/4

p. 264

6	12	48
24	1/12	1/24
1/30	1/16	45
1/10	3 3/4	20
7/16	20	1/9

p. 265

1. 0.3 2. 0.04 3. 0.61 4. 0.016
5. 0.009 6. 2.3
7. five tenths 8. sixty-seven hundredths
9. one and twenty-five thousandths
10. 7.63; 60.623 11. 7.16; 26.26
12. 84.006; 10.326

p. 266

1. 3.44 2. 4.6 3. 41.7 4. 4016.32
5. 947.36 6. 6.5 7. 56.4 8. 1.35
9. 1.006 10. 45.63 11. 15.3
12. 317.9 13. 3007.55 14. 6.19
15. 6.99

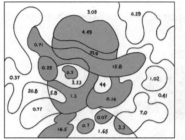

p. 267

0.3	0.7
0.01	0.06
0.173	0.004

0.3	(0.03)	1.5
(8.9)	8.05	8.75
7.25	0.07	5.004

7/100	305/1000	6/1000
3 5/100	2 17/1000	5 907/1000
4 632/1000	866/1000	60 1/2

p. 268

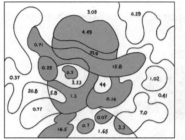

p. 269

>	>	=
>	>	>
>	=	<
<	=	>
<	>	<
<	>	>

p. 270

1. = 2. < 3. > 4. > 5. < 6. =
7. < 8. > 9. > 10. > 11. =
12. < 13. > 14. < 15. < 16. >

p. 271

1. 0.2 0.5 0.6 0.7
2. 0.004 0.04 0.4 4.0
3. 6.037 6.307 6.703 6.73
4. 0.029 0.32 0.42
5. 0.2 0.432 0.603
6. 0.444 0.4 0.004
7. 0.75 0.57 0.507
8. 0.91 0.19 0.1 0.09
9. 0.77 0.7 0.077 0.07
10. 10.909 10.901 10.009 10.001

p. 272

1. a. 0.38; Mercury b. 0.38; Mars
c. 0.89; Uranus d. 0.91; Venus
e. 1.00; Earth f. 1.06; Saturn
g. 1.13; Neptune h. 2.36; Jupiter
2. Jupiter 3. Mercury and Mars
4. Mercury and Mars 5. 2,700

p. 273

1. 6.1947 2. 679.14 3. 97.416
4. 6.9174 5. 9.6147 6. 9.7164
7. 67.914 and 67.941

p. 274

Number	Nearest Tenth	Nearest Hundredth
6.157	6.2	6.16
10.052	10.1	10.05
3.336	3.3	3.34

1. 0.625 2. 122.64 3. 4.234
4. 243.461

p. 275

1. 10.6 2. 0.50 3. 10.05 and 9.5
4. 0.05
5. 642.1 6. 1.246 7. 1.246 or 1.642
8. 4.075 9. 8.50 10. 4.75 11. 8.005
12. 4.34

p. 276

2. 0.27 + 0.14 = 0.41
3. 0.27 + 0.04 + 0.16 = 0.47
4. 0.3 + 0.08 = 0.38
5. 0.4 + 0.25 = 0.65
6. 0.24 + 0.13 + 0.03 = 0.4
7. 0.31 + 0.23 = 0.54
8. 0.04 + 0.36 = 0.4
9. 0.35 + 0.05 + 0.09 = 0.49

p. 277

58.7	103.09	70.45
31.57	609.05	43.09
31.72	463.05	25.63
57.53	76.24	29.56
301.9	61	773.75

p. 278
2. 0.34 – 0.16 = 0.18
3. 0.83 – 0.46 = 0.37
4. 0.98 – 0.33 = 0.65
5. 0.83 – 0.18 = 0.65
6. 0.34 – 0.03 = 0.31
7. 0.69 – 0.21 = 0.48
8. 0.68 – 0.26 = 0.42
9. 0.48 – 0.24 = 0.24

p. 279

5.2	5.63	3.15
42.41	80.5	0.52
27.58	2.83	47.97
4.47	72.6	533.8
61.266	91.72	13.4

p. 280
1. 0.92 2. 1.62

1.2	4.8	2.7
0.24	0.49	0.09
0.15	0.63	0.32
0.042	0.006	0.015

p. 281
1. 0.09 2. 0.28

0.08	0.2	0.07
2.13	0.34	4.3
0.29	0.17	5.3
8.3	0.053	0.49

p. 282
Across: 1. 36.58 3. 12.54 4. 4.7
5. 9.8 6. 27.1 7. 8.2 8. 29.01
11. 13.6
Down: 1. 34.17 2. 8.8 3. 17.82
4. 4.28 5. 9.12 9. 9.1 10. 1.68
12. 3.7

p. 283
1. (4,1) 2. (2,2) 3. (6,2) 4. (1,9)
5. B, Gas Station 6. G, Book Shop
7. D, Pharmacy 8. E, Paint Store

p. 284
Riddle answer: Because he had ordered pairs! (pears)

p. 285
1. Rule: $y = x + 3$

2. $y = 2x – 1$

x	y
1	1
2	3
3	5
4	7
5	9

$y = 3x – 2$

x	y
4	10
5	13
6	16
7	19
8	22

3. Answers will vary.

p. 286–287
Across: 1. millennium 4. foot 7. year
8. degrees 10. half 12. century
13. midnight 15. lb 16. pounds
19. seconds 21. ten 23. carat
24. hours 27. minutes
Down: 2. months 3. quart 5. one
6. yard 8. days 9. gallon 11. acres
13. mile 14. ton 16. pints 17. weeks
18. inch 20. decade 22. ounce
25. six 28. cup

p. 288
1. 280 feet 2. 54 feet or 18 yards
3. 74 feet 4. 44 square units, 34 units

p. 289
1. 24 3/4 square units
2. 10 5/8 square units
3. 21 3/8 square units
4. 10 1/8 square units
5. 29 7/10 square units
6. 24 4/9 square units
7. 12 1/4 square units
8. 7 7/9 square units
9. 11 7/10 square units

p. 290
1. 32 cubic units 2. 30 cubic units
3. 8 cubic units 4. 24 cubic units
5. 36 cubic units 6. 27 cubic units
7. 20 cubic units 8. 20 cubic units
9. 20 cubic units 10. 12 cubic units
11. 16 cubic units 12. 18 cubic units

p. 291
1. 25 cubic units 2. 42 cubic units
3. 24 cubic units 4. 36 cubic units
5. 17 cubic units 6. 18 cubic units
7. 14 cubic units 8. 9 cubic units
9. 11 cubic units 10. 39 cubic units
11. 9 cubic units 12. 14 cubic units

p. 292
1. segment 2. cone 3. volume
4. perpendicular 5. ray 6. angle
7. pyramid 8. sphere 9. prism
10. vertex 11. point
World's first castle: Gomdan, Yemen

p. 293
1. 14,512 square miles 2. Honshu
3. Borneo and Honshu 4. Greenland and Honshu Bonus: 148,000,000 square kilometers

p. 294

Teen	Income	Expenses		Savings
		Travel	Food/Fun	
Alex	$70	$6.00	$22.50	$41.50
Irma	$54	$4.50	$20.75	$28.75
Tyrone	$55.00	$5.30	$18.75	$30.95
Felicia	$86	$7.75	$42.00	$36.25

1. Alex 2. $12.75 3. Tyrone
4. Felicia 5. $137.45

p. 295
1. $6.75 2. No; after the burger and side, Oliver has only $3.75 left, and dessert is $4.95. 3. Bistro Burger With Brie, side, and a drink

p. 296
1. San Juan: 4:00 pm; Barcelona: 9:00 pm; Cairo: 10:00 pm 2. Tokyo: 9:00 pm; Sydney: 11:00 pm; Honolulu: 2:00 am 3. New York: 6:00 pm; San Juan: 7:00 pm; London 11:00 pm

p. 297
1. Kendra; 30 minutes 2. 2 hours (and 3 minutes) 3. 80 minutes 4. 5 minutes
5. Kendra and Leon; 125 minutes

p. 298
1. triangle 2. guitar 3. piano, drums
4. violin, drums, guitar

p. 299
1. wins and losses for three different teams   2. the green bar   3. San Francisco   4. Arizona   5. 25 games

p. 300

Summaries may vary; check that response is reasonable and reflects the data and graph.

p. 301
1. scratching   2. 15 hours   3. sniffing
4. 12 hours   5. 3 hours

p. 302

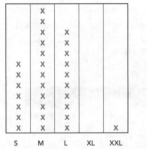

Summaries may vary. Sample answer: The line plot shows that the chorus has 30 members and that the data has a range of 11. The mode is size M, and size XXL is an outlier.

p. 303
1. 17   2. Counted 17 Xs.   3. 16; 1
4. 2 teams   5. 4 teams   6. Answers may vary. Sample answer: The number of medals won clusters toward the low end of the scale—between 4 and 7 medals.

p. 304
1. 15 students   2. 1 student; 6 hours
3. 1/4   4. 1/2   5. 11 students; 11/15
6. 4 students

p. 305
1. 20 students   2. 1.54 meters   3. 0.09
4. 1.51   5. 15 students   6. 1/4   7. 1.45 meters

p. 306
1. 4   2. 2 students   3. 99   4. 24 students   5. 47   6. 80

variable	novice
receptacle	outstanding
quiver	generally
blunder	hazardous
rash	veto
bountiful	treacherous

A **novice** is a beginner.

Something that is **variable** is likely to change.

Something that is **outstanding** is extremely good.

A **receptacle** is a container.

Generally means "usually."

If you **quiver**, you shake.

When something is **hazardous**, it is dangerous.

A **blunder** is a mistake.

If you **veto** something, you say no to it.

When you are careless, you are **rash**.

When someone is **treacherous**, that person cannot be trusted.

Bountiful means "plentiful."

bewildered	cumbersome
brutal	dormant
blissful	ceaseless
valid	daunting
rhyme	simile
meter	couplet

Something that is **cumbersome** is heavy and difficult to move.

A person who is **bewildered** is very confused.

When an animal is **dormant**, it is sleeping.

Brutal means "cruel."

Something that is **ceaseless** is unending.

If you are very happy, you are **blissful**.

If a task is **daunting**, it is discouraging.

Something that is **valid** is true.

A **simile** uses the words *like* or *as* to compare two unlike things.

Words that **rhyme** have the same ending sound.

A **couplet** is two lines of poetry that usually rhyme.

Meter is the arrangement of beats in a line of poetry.

personification	alliteration
haiku	sonnet
metaphor	onomatopoeia
isthmus	oasis
peninsula	tributary
delta	valley

The repetition of the first sound of several words in a poem is **alliteration**.

In **personification**, a human characteristic is given to something that is not human.

A **sonnet** is a poem with 14 lines written in a certain meter and with a special rhyme scheme.

A **haiku** is a three-line poem in which the first and third lines have five syllables and the middle line has seven.

Onamatopoeia is a word that sounds like the thing it names; for example, *buzz* or *pop*.

A **metaphor** is a comparison of two unlike things.

An **oasis** is a fertile place in a desert where there is water, trees, and other plants.

An **isthmus** is a narrow strip of land that connects two large areas of land.

A branch of a river is called a **tributary**.

A **peninsula** is an area of land surrounded by water on three sides.

A **valley** is the land that lies between mountains or hills.

A **delta** is the dirt and sand that collect at the mouth of a river.

gorge	archipelago
plateau	strait
compliment	vigor
criticism	fatigue
unique	substantial
ordinary	flimsy

A chain of islands is called an **archipelago**.

A **gorge** is a deep, narrow valley that often has a stream running through it.

A **strait** is a narrow channel that connects two larger bodies of water.

A **plateau** is a large area of high, flat land.

Vigor is a feeling of great strength.

You give a **compliment** when you say something positive about someone or something.

Fatigue is a feeling of great tiredness.

When you say an unfavorable remark, you give a **criticism**.

Something that is **substantial** feels solid.

If something is **unique**, it is one of a kind.

If something is **flimsy**, it is weak or frail.

If something is **ordinary**, it is common.